HUNGER

Other Books in the Current Controversies Series:

HUNGER

David L. Bender, *Publisher*
Bruno Leone, *Executive Editor*

Katie de Koster, *Managing Editor*
Scott Barbour, *Senior Editor*

Scott Barbour, *Book Editor*
William Dudley, *Assistant Editor*

CURRENT CONTROVERSIES

Cover photo: SABA: Haviv

Library of Congress Cataloging-in-Publication Data

Hunger / Scott Barbour, book editor, William Dudley, assistant editor.
         p. cm. — (Current controversies)
      Includes bibliographical references and index.
      ISBN 1-56510-239-8 (lib. : alk. paper) — ISBN 1-56510-238-X
(pbk. : alk. paper).)
      1. Food supply. 2. Food relief. [1. Hunger. 2. Food supply. 3. Food
relief.] I. Barbour, Scott, 1963-   . II. Dudley, William, 1964-   .
III. Series.
HD9000.5.H814   1995
363.8—dc20

94-43376
CIP
AC

© 1995 by Greenhaven Press, Inc., PO Box 289009, San Diego, CA 92198-9009
Printed in the U.S.A.

Contents

Chapter 2: Is Hunger a Serious Problem in the United States?

Yes: Hunger Is a Serious Problem in the United States

No: Hunger Is Not a Serious Problem in the United States

Chapter 3: Can Technological Advances Increase Food Production?

Yes: Technological Advances Can Increase Food Production

No: Technological Advances May Not Increase Food Production

Chapter 4: How Can Hunger and Famine Be Reduced?

Foreword

By definition, controversies are "discussions of questions in which opposing opinions clash" (Webster's Twentieth Century Dictionary Unabridged). Few would deny that controversies are a pervasive part of the human condition and exist on virtually every level of human enterprise. Controversies transpire between individuals and among groups, within nations and between nations. Controversies supply the grist necessary for progress by providing challenges and challengers to the status quo. They also create atmospheres where strife and warfare can flourish. A world without controversies would be a peaceful world; but it also would be, by and large, static and prosaic.

The Series' Purpose

The purpose of the Current Controversies series is to explore many of the social, political, and economic controversies dominating the national and international scenes today. Titles selected for inclusion in the series are highly focused and specific. For example, from the larger category of criminal justice, Current Controversies deals with specific topics such as police brutality, gun control, white collar crime, and others. The debates in Current Controversies also are presented in a useful, timeless fashion. Articles and book excerpts included in each title are selected if they contribute valuable, long-range ideas to the overall debate. And wherever possible, current information is enhanced with historical documents and other relevant materials. Thus, while individual titles are current in focus, every effort is made to ensure that they will not become quickly outdated. Books in the Current Controversies series will remain important resources for librarians, teachers, and students for many years.

In addition to keeping the titles focused and specific, great care is taken in the editorial format of each book in the series. Book introductions and chapter prefaces are offered to provide background material for readers. Chapters are organized around several key questions that are answered with diverse opinions representing all points on the political spectrum. Materials in each chapter include opinions in which authors clearly disagree as well as alternative opinions in which authors may agree on a broader issue but disagree on the possible solutions. In this way, the content of each volume in Current Controversies mirrors the mosaic of opinions encountered in society. Readers will quickly realize that there are many viable answers to these complex issues. By questioning each author's conclusions, students and casual readers can begin to develop the critical thinking skills so important to evaluating opinionated material.

Current Controversies is also ideal for controlled research. Each anthology in the series is composed of primary sources taken from a wide gamut of informational categories including periodicals, newspapers, books, United States and foreign government documents, and the publications of private and public organizations. Readers will find factual support for reports, debates, and research papers covering all areas of important issues. In addition, an annotated table of contents, an index, a book and periodical bibliography, and a list of organizations to contact are included in each book to expedite further research.

Perhaps more than ever before in history, people are confronted with diverse and contradictory information. During the Persian Gulf War, for example, the public was not only treated to minute-to-minute coverage of the war, it was also inundated with critiques of the coverage and countless analyses of the factors motivating U.S. involvement. Being able to sort through the plethora of opinions accompanying today's major issues, and to draw one's own conclusions, can be a complicated and frustrating struggle. It is the editors' hope that Current Controversies will help readers with this struggle.

Introduction

On December 9, 1992, U.S. Marines began landing in Somalia to help provide food relief to a population in the throes of famine. While the Somalia mission—Operation Restore Hope—was criticized for a variety of reasons, few could object to its stated goal: to feed starving people. Indeed, in an era of advanced technology and communications, the fact that thousands of human beings faced death from lack of a need as basic as food seemed incredible and unconscionable to many. Over 300,000 people died in the famine, although the U.S. intervention is credited with preventing thousands of additional deaths.

The word *hunger* often evokes images of emaciated people, such as the victims of the Somalia famine. However, as *Los Angeles Times* writer Robin Wright notes, there are three degrees of hunger: acute, chronic, and hidden. Acute hunger (which applies to victims of famine) is a condition in which death is imminent due to an absolute shortage of food. Chronic hunger refers to a lack of food intake adequate for health, growth, and minimum energy needs. Hidden hunger describes those with a deficient diet for a prolonged period of time, which may result in a shortened life span.

It is widely agreed that hunger today is not caused by a global food shortage. Some commentators, such as Lester R. Brown, the president of Worldwatch Institute, predict that population growth, environmental degradation, and a shortage of new agricultural technologies will hinder the earth's capacity to produce enough food for its people in the future. Most experts contend, however, that current levels of food production are adequate to feed the world's population, which was 5.6 billion in 1994. And many agree with Stephen Budiansky of *U.S. News & World Report* that, with proper management, "the Earth's basic resources are vastly greater than what are needed to feed even the 10 billion people who are almost certain to inhabit the planet by the middle of the [twenty-first] century."

Rather than being a global problem, most analysts agree that hunger is a regional phenomenon with multiple causes, often compounded, that vary from place to place. As Scott Pendleton, a staff writer for the *Christian Science Monitor*, writes, "Despite the currency of phrases like 'world hunger' and 'global famine,' those conditions don't exist and probably never will. . . . Starvation is local." Inefficient use of resources, political instability, fluctuating economic conditions, and civil and ethnic conflict are some of the factors that contribute to hunger in different areas of the world.

Famine—the most severe and visible form of hunger—has historically been the result of natural phenomena such as droughts, floods, and crop failures. Today, however, advances in technology and transportation have made these natural factors less relevant. According to Kurt Jonassohn, a professor of sociology at Concordia University in Montreal, Canada, "Since the middle of the twentieth century the technology of storing, preserving and transporting food stuffs in large quantities over long distances has made it possible to deal with natural disasters so efficiently that famines should no longer be expected." Consequently, when famines do occur, they are increasingly viewed as "man-made" rather than natural disasters. For example, Jonassohn writes of Somalia that "in the fall of 1992 the evidence was quite clear that sufficient quantities of the essentials were in the pipeline. . . .The problem was not shortage but distribution."

The idea that famines are largely man-made suggests that they can be prevented by human action. This seems confirmed by the experience of India, which instituted a famine-prevention system in the 1880s designed to detect and intervene in conditions likely to culminate in famine. When famine appears likely, the government guarantees jobs for all workers and makes food available at reasonable prices. This system has largely been successful at heading off famine in India during the past century despite numerous food shortages. In addition, India's democratic political system (since its independence from Britain in 1947) is also credited with helping prevent famine. Under democracy, according to Alex de Waal, the associate director of Africa Watch, Indian government officials are motivated to stave off famine in order to remain on good terms with the electorate.

In politically unstable countries, on the other hand, famine often accompanies war. According to Robert W. Kates, director emeritus of the Alan Shawn Feinstein World Hunger Program at Brown University, "In all of the countries that have reported famine so far in the 1990s . . . armed conflict has been a major cause." Kates argues, moreover, that these famines have not all been inadvertent consequences of war: Warring parties have used food as a weapon, deliberately depriving people of sustenance by destroying and intercepting provisions and by impeding food production. According to Jonassohn, this use of starvation as a war tactic constitutes genocide.

To respond to this intentional starvation of populations, many support the use of humanitarian interventions, such as the one in Somalia, to alleviate hunger in zones of conflict. For example, Tony P. Hall, a Democratic congressman from Ohio, advocates the creation of a military "strike force," coordinated by the United Nations, to provide food relief in war-torn areas. While some oppose such interventions on the grounds that they violate the sovereignty of nations, others argue that sovereignty is forfeited by countries who use starvation as a weapon. According to Kates, "A new understanding of sovereignty rights must be developed that defers to urgent humanitarian needs. Stated simply, no nation has the right to starve its own or other people."

The persistence of hunger in the last decade of the twentieth century seems at odds with humankind's advances in science and technology. According to a report in the *New State of the World Atlas*, "The world is capable of feeding decently all its inhabitants. That it is conspicuously not doing so at present is the product not of necessity but of choice." The viewpoints in *Hunger: Current Controversies* explore the nature and extent of hunger worldwide and debate what measures should be taken to relieve and prevent its occurrence.

Chapter 1

What Are the
Causes of Hunger?

CURRENT CONTROVERSIES

Hunger in the World: An Overview

by Robin Wright

About the author: *Robin Wright is a staff writer for the* Los Angeles Times *daily newspaper.*

At the end of the 20th Century, an era marked by space exploration, computer wizardry and test-tube babies, the status of the human race may more accurately be reflected in a sobering statistic: 786 million people—almost one in every six on the globe—are suffering from acute or chronic hunger. More than a billion more face various forms of serious malnutrition.

"Somalia is a drop in the bucket," said Marc Cohen, one of the authors of "Hunger 1993," a publication of the Bread for the World Institute.

Despite mankind's advances, one of its biggest problems is primordial. And while the hardest-hit areas are in South and East Asia and sub-Saharan Africa, the trend is not limited to underdeveloped countries.

"Hunger and malnutrition remain as the most devastating problems facing the majority of the world's poor. Despite general improvements in food availability, health and social services, hunger and malnutrition exist in some form in almost every country," concluded a recent survey by the U.N. Food and Agriculture Organization.

Three Faces of Hunger

Experts refer to the three faces of hunger—acute, as in Somalia, where large numbers faced imminent starvation in 1992; chronic, as in poverty-stricken, overpopulated and resource-poor countries like Bangladesh, and the "hidden" hunger that is worldwide, plaguing even industrialized nations.

Even the United States has a growing problem. Between 1985 and 1992, the number of Americans suffering from hunger rose from 20 million to 30 million, the Tufts University School of Nutrition reported. It called the trend an epidemic.

Over the early 1990s, hunger has also become widespread in Eastern European countries, especially Russia, Bulgaria and Romania, while hunger in Albania has reached the level of sub-Saharan Africa, according to David Beckmann, president of Bread for the World, a grass-roots lobbying group on hunger issues in Washington.

But unlike previous periods, when famine fueled the cycles of starvation, the current crisis is all the more tragic because it is unnecessary.

"The world is capable of feeding decently all its inhabitants. That it is conspicuously not doing so at present is the product not of necessity but of choice," concludes a report in the "New State of the World Atlas," a survey of worldwide political and economic change.

Changes of the Past 40 Years

There have been major changes over the past 40 years in the problem of hunger—including advances and setbacks.

"Despite the enormous problem in Somalia and a number of other countries, the long-term trend since 1950—of the numbers suffering from hunger—is clearly downward," said Robert Kates, director of Brown University's World Hunger Program:

In 1969-71, more than 940 million people in the developing world—or 36% of its population at the time—were chronically undernourished, compared with 20% in 1990, according to the U.N. food agency.

> *"There have been major changes over the past 40 years in the problem of hunger—including advances and setbacks."*

The good news can be traced to breakthroughs in the 1970s and early 1980s. "Over the course of the 1970s, new governments did something about food security. Places like Niger and Indonesia invested real resources in producing food and becoming more self-reliant," Cohen said.

Major Strides

China and India, the world's most populous countries, which also had the largest numbers suffering from hunger, also made major strides through better food production and distribution and by introducing work-for-food programs.

As a result, economists and relief agencies doubt China will again experience the kind of major starvation witnessed in 1958-62, when 15 million to 30 million people are estimated to have died.

"It was a real turning point when one of the two most populous countries in the world, which had been famine-prone, learned to successfully deal with famine and prevent famine-related deaths," Kates said.

The United States also made striking gains in reversing hunger and malnutrition in the 1970s, largely through federal food programs.

The second breakthrough evolved during the last cycle of African drought in the early 1980s, particularly in Ethiopia, when the international community learned how to provide and distribute mass aid. Early warning systems were also developed to detect weather patterns, so relief organizations and donor nations could remain one step ahead of new famines.

The improvements in dealing with food production, aid logistics and weather mean that epidemics of hunger are now mostly "man-made. Starvation is now often a political problem," said James T. Hill, economist with the U.N. food agency.

"The world now has systems in place that mean the only times people starve is when someone wants them to starve," Beckmann said.

Setbacks

But there were also setbacks in the 1980s, as the hunger crisis became more complex, weaving together such disparate factors as birthrates, debt crises, ancient ethnic or clan rivalries, misuse of land and water resources, and even political change.

"The 1980s were tough times, particularly in Africa and Latin America. In 1983, we had the longest recession since the Great Depression, which provoked the debt crisis from which many have still not recovered," Beckmann said.

To deal with their financial crises, many countries in the mid- and late 1980s either opted or were forced to cut the very programs—notably in nutrition and health—developed in the 1970s to counter hunger. Third World governments were often more willing to cut welfare services than defense expenditures, just as many donor nations favored military aid over social programs.

Growing Population

That shift coincided with a period when the global population neared 5 billion—compared with 2 billion in 1930—and began to threaten the "caring" capacity of the land, said J. Joseph Speidel, president of the Population Crisis Committee.

By the end of the decade, political and economic frustrations were also spawning unprecedented global change. But as whole political systems—from apartheid to Marxism—collapsed, the new openings also freed up old animosities among religious, tribal, national and clan groupings.

In 1990, all of those factors exploded in Somalia—as per capita annual income sunk to $150, as a soaring birthrate (the average family exceeded six children) meant a doubling of the population within 24 years, and finally as the political system dissolved into the anarchy of clan warfare.

> *"The hunger crisis became more complex [in the 1980s], weaving together such disparate factors as birthrates, debt crises, . . . and even political change."*

All of those factors also do not bode well for the three faces of hunger in the early 1990s.

The worst crises of acute hunger in southern Africa have been eased somewhat by recent rains and decent harvests. . . .

But many acute cases—the vast majority in strife-torn areas—have almost no imminent prospects of relief. "The only places on Earth where people are dying of famine is where there is a simultaneous famine and war, like in Mozambique, Sudan and potentially Liberia and Afghanistan," Kates said.

Hurdles to Progress

Economists and relief agencies say that the major remaining hurdle in dealing with acute hunger is finding a mechanism, forum or force to deal with the strife that prevents aid distribution.

"The bottom line is that many developing nations have no prospects of restoring programs to deal with . . . hunger . . . any time soon."

Various attempts to create humanitarian space within the context of armed conflicts, such as "corridors of tranquillity," have been successful in Sudan and Angola but haven't worked in Yugoslavia. "We're making hesitating and slow progress," Kates said, "to what would be a major human achievement."

The overall forecast for chronic and hidden hunger and malnutrition may be bleaker, largely because poverty, high birthrates and poor use of resources have created a vicious cycle.

"People are getting poorer, and the rate of development growth, food production and wealth are not keeping up with the population," said Bronek Szynalski, director of emergency relief for the U.N. World Food Program in Rome.

Rich and Poor Nations

Indeed, the gap between rich and poor nations grew to new extremes over the past decade. In 1981, the GNP per capita in the developed world was $8,600, compared with $700 in poor countries. By 1990, per capita income in the developed world more than doubled to $17,900, while in poor countries income rose by only $110, reports the Population Crisis Committee.

And lowering birthrates would take time to make a difference. "Even if we immediately went to a two-child family around the world, the population would still grow by 3 billion people until it stabilized," Speidel said.

Population growth strains already limited land available for agriculture.

The bottom line is that many developing nations have no prospects of restoring programs to deal with chronic or hidden hunger and malnutrition any time soon. Meanwhile, "the international community is not able to cope with all the crises. Everybody wants the United Nations to do something, but it has limited resources," Szynalski said.

But developing countries are not alone. For similar reasons, Eastern Europe has become one of the fastest-growing regions of hidden and potentially chronic hunger and malnutrition.

Albania, a largely agricultural country, now depends on foreign aid for 75% of its food, while 30% of children outside the capital suffer from malnutrition. Families unable to feed their children are now surrendering them to orphanages, according to Bread for the World.

In Bulgaria, 60% of the average household's expenditures went for food in 1991, while food prices in Czechoslovakia went up 70% between 1989 and 1991. And even in areas of Eastern Europe and the former Soviet Union where there is more food, free markets have often made it too expensive.

Hunger in the United States

Neither is the United States exempt. "1992 has been a bad year for hungry people in this country," Beckmann said.

"The U.S. recession and structural changes in the economy led to a 26% increase in requests for emergency food assistance in major cities in 1991. And as of April, 1992, a record number of Americans—23 million, or 10%—were dependent on food stamps."

In response to the soaring need in the United States, more than 55,000 private agencies now sponsor food programs, compared with only a few in the early 1980s, according to Bread for the World.

"Yet," Beckmann noted, "they can't keep up."

Overpopulation Causes Hunger

by Robert S. McNamara

About the author: *Robert S. McNamara was president of the World Bank from 1968 to 1981. In previous years he was United States secretary of defense and president of the Ford Motor Company.*

For thousands of years, the world's human population grew at a snail's pace. It took over a million years to reach 1 billion people at the beginning of the last century. But then the pace quickened. The second billion was added in 130 years, the third in 30, and the fourth in 15. The current total is some 5.4 billion people.

Although population growth rates are declining, they are still extraordinarily high. During this decade, about 100 million people per year will be added to the planet. Over 90% of this growth is taking place in the developing world. Where will it end?

The World Bank's latest projection indicates that the plateau level will not be less than 12.4 billion. And Nafis Sadik, director of the United Nations Population Fund, has stated that "the world could be headed toward an eventual total of 14 billion."

What would such population levels mean in terms of alleviating poverty, improving the status of women and children, and attaining sustainable economic development? To what degree are we consuming today the very capital required to achieve decent standards of living for future generations?

Three Factors of Environmental Stress

To determine whether the world—or a particular country—is on a path of sustainable development, one must relate future population levels and future consumption patterns to their impact on the environment.

Put very simply, environmental stress is a function of three factors: increases in population, increases in consumption per capita, and changes in technology that may tend to reduce environmental stress per unit of consumption.

Robert S. McNamara, "The Population Explosion," *The Futurist*, November/December 1992. Reproduced with permission from *The Futurist*, published by the World Future Society, 7910 Woodmont Ave., Suite 450, Bethesda, MD 20814.

Were population to rise to the figure referred to by Sadik—14 billion—there would be a 2.6-fold increase in world population. If consumption per capita were to increase at 2% per annum—about two-thirds the rate realized during the past 25 years—it would double in 35 years and quadruple in 70 years. By the end of the next century, consumption per capita would be eight times greater than it is today.

Some may say it is unreasonable to consider such a large increase in the per capita incomes of the peoples in the developing countries. But per

> *"Since the mid-1980s, increases in worldwide food production have lagged behind population growth."*

capita income in the United States rose at least that much in this century, starting from a much higher base. And today, billions of human beings across the globe are now living in intolerable conditions that can only be relieved by increases in consumption.

A 2.6-fold increase in world population and an eightfold increase in consumption per capita by 2100 would cause the globe's production output to be 20 times greater than today. Likewise, the impact on nonrenewable and renewable resources would be 20 times greater, assuming no change in environmental stress per unit of production.

On the assumptions I have made, the question becomes: Can a 20-fold increase in the consumption of physical resources be sustained? The answer is almost certainly "No." If not, can substantial reductions in environmental stress—environmental damage—per unit of production be achieved? Here, the answer is clearly "Yes."

Reducing Environmental Damage

Environmental damage per unit of production can—and will—be cut drastically. There is much evidence that the environment is being stressed today. But there are equally strong indications that we can drastically reduce the resources consumed and waste generated per unit of "human advance."

With each passing year, we are learning more about the environmental damage that is caused by present population levels and present consumption patterns. The superficial signs are clearly visible. Our water and air are being polluted, whether we live in Los Angeles, Mexico City, or Lagos. Disposal of both toxic and nontoxic wastes is a worldwide problem. And the ozone layer, which protects us all against skin cancer, is being destroyed by the concentration of chlorofluorocarbons in the upper atmosphere.

But for each of these problems, there are known remedies—at least for today's population levels and current consumption patterns. The remedies are costly, politically difficult to implement, and require years to become effective, but they can be put in place.

The impact, however, of huge increases in population and consumption on such basic resources and ecosystems as land and water, forests, photosynthesis, and climate is far more difficult to appraise. Changes in complex systems such as these are what the scientists describe as nonlinear and subject to discontinuities. Therefore, they are very difficult to predict.

Let's examine the effect of population growth on natural resources in terms of agriculture. Can the world's land and water resources produce the food required to feed 14 billion people at acceptable nutritional levels? To do so would require a fourfold increase in food output.

Modern agricultural techniques have greatly increased crop yields per unit of land and have kept food production ahead of population growth for several decades. But the costs are proving to be high: widespread acceleration of erosion and nutrient depletion of soils, pollution of surface waters, overuse and contamination of groundwater resources, and desertification of overcultivated or overgrazed lands.

The early gains of the Green Revolution have nearly run their course. Since the mid-1980s, increases in worldwide food production have lagged behind population growth. In sub-Saharan Africa and Latin America, per capita food production has been declining for a decade or more.

What, then, of the future? Some authorities are pessimistic, arguing that maximum global food output will support no more than 7.5 billion people. Others are somewhat more optimistic. They conclude that if a variety of actions were taken, beginning with a substantial increase in agricultural research, the world's agricultural system could meet food requirements for at least the next 40–50 years.

> *"As world population continues to increase, the likelihood of meeting global food requirements will become ever more doubtful."*

However, it seems clear that the actions required to realize that capacity are not now being taken. As a result, there will be severe regional shortfalls (e.g., in sub-Saharan Africa), and as world population continues to increase, the likelihood of meeting global food requirements will become ever more doubtful.

Similar comments could be made in regard to other natural resources and ecosystems. More and more biologists are warning that there are indeed biological limits to the number of people that the globe can support at acceptable standards of living. They say, in effect, "We don't know where those limits are, but they clearly exist."

Sustainability Limits

How much might population grow and production increase without going beyond sustainable levels—levels that are compatible with the globe's capacity for waste disposal and that do not deplete essential resources?

Jim MacNeil, Peter Winsemaus, and Taizo Yakushiji have tried to answer that question in *Beyond Interdependence*, a study prepared recently for the Trilateral Commission. They begin by stating: "Even at present levels of economic activity, there is growing evidence that certain critical global thresholds are being approached, perhaps even passed."

They then estimate that, if "human numbers double, a five- to ten-fold increase in economic activity would be required to enable them to meet [even] their basic needs and minimal aspirations." They ask, "Is there, in fact, any way to multiply economic activity a further five to ten times, without it undermining itself and compromising the future completely?" They clearly believe that the answer is "No."

Similar questions and doubts exist in the minds of many other experts in the field. In July 1991, Nobel laureate and Cal Tech physicist Murray Gell-Mann and his associates initiated a multiyear project to try to understand how "humanity can make the shift to sustainability." They point out that "such a change, if it could be achieved, would require a series of transitions in fields ranging from technology to social and economic organization and ideology."

The implication of their statement is not that we should assume the outlook for sustainable development is hopeless, but rather that each nation individually, and all nations collectively, should begin now to identify and introduce the changes necessary to achieve it if we are to avoid costly—and possibly coercive—action in the future.

One change that would enhance the prospects for sustainable development across the globe would be a reduction in population growth rates.

Population and Poverty

The developing world has made enormous economic progress over the past three decades. But at the same time, the number of human beings living in "absolute poverty" has risen sharply.

When I coined the term "absolute poverty" in the late 1960s, I did so to distinguish a particular segment of the poor in the developing world from the billions of others who would be classified as poor in Western terms. The "absolute poor" are those living, literally, on the margin of life. Their lives are so characterized by malnutrition, illiteracy, and disease as to be beneath any reasonable definition of human dignity.

"Millions of children in low-income families receive insufficient protein and calories to permit optimal development of their brains."

Today, their number approaches 1 billion. And the World Bank estimates that it is likely to increase further—by nearly 100 million—in this decade.

A major concern raised by poverty of this magnitude lies in the possibility of so many children's physical and intellectual impairment. Surveys have shown that millions of children in low-income families receive insufficient protein and calories to permit optimal development of their brains, thereby limiting their capacity to learn and to lead fully productive lives. Additional millions die each year, before the age of five, from debilitating disease caused by nutritional deficiencies.

High population growth is not the only factor contributing to these problems; political organization, macroeconomic policies, institutional structures, and economic growth in the industrial nations all affect economic and social advance in developing countries. But intuitively we recognize that the immediate effects of high population growth are adverse.

> *"The developed nations should also initiate a discussion of how their citizens . . . may . . . adjust their consumption patterns."*

Our intuition is supported by facts: In Latin America during the 1970s, when the school-age population expanded dramatically, public spending per primary-school student fell by 45% in real terms. In Mexico, life expectancy for the poorest 10% of the population is 20 years less than for the richest 10%.

Based on such analyses, the World Bank has stated: "The evidence points overwhelmingly to the conclusion that population growth at the rates common in most of the developing world slows development. . . . Policies to reduce population growth can make an important contribution to [social advance]."

Reducing Population Growth

Any one of the adverse consequences of the high population growth rates—environmentally unsustainable development, the worsening of poverty, and the negative impact on the status and welfare of women and children—would be reason enough for developing nations across the globe to move more quickly to reduce fertility rates. Taken together, they make an overwhelming case.

Should not every developing country, therefore, formulate long-term population objectives—objectives that will maximize the welfare of both present and future generations? They should be constrained only by the maximum feasible rate at which the use of contraception could be increased in the particular nation.

If this were done, I estimate that country family-planning goals might lead to national population-stabilization levels that would total 9.7 billion people for the globe. That is an 80% increase over today's population, but it's also 4.3 billion fewer people than the 14 billion toward which we may be heading. At the consumption levels I have assumed, those additional 4.3 billion people could require a production output several times greater than the world's total output today.

Assuming that nations wish to reduce fertility rates to replacement levels at the fastest possible pace, what should be done?

The Bucharest Population Conference in 1974 emphasized that high fertility is in part a function of slow economic and social development. Experience has indeed shown that as economic growth occurs, particularly when it is accompanied by broadly based social advance, birth rates do tend to decline. But it is also generally recognized today that not all economic growth leads to immediate fertility reductions, and in any event, fertility reduction can be accelerated by direct action to increase the use of contraceptives.

It follows, therefore, that any campaign to accelerate reductions in fertility should focus on two components: (1) increasing the pace of economic and social advance, with particular emphasis on enhancing the status of women and on reducing infant mortality, and (2) introducing or expanding comprehensive family-planning programs.

Much has been learned in recent years about how to raise rates of economic and social advance in developing countries. I won't try to summarize those lessons here. I do wish to emphasize, however, the magnitude of the increases required in family planning if individual countries are to hold population growth rates to levels that maximize economic and social advance.

The number of women of child-bearing age in developing countries is projected to increase by about 22% from 1990 to 2000. If contraception use were to increase from 50% in 1990 to 65% in 2000, the number of women using contraception must rise by over 200 million.

That appears to be an unattainable objective, considering that the number of women using contraception rose by only 175 million in the past *two* decades, but it is not. The task for certain countries and regions—for example, India, Pakistan, and almost all sub-Saharan Africa—will indeed be difficult, but other nations have done as much or more. Thailand, Indonesia, Bangladesh, and Mexico all increased use of contraceptives at least as rapidly. The actions they took are known, and their experience can be exported. It is available to all who ask.

A global family-planning program of the size I am proposing for 2000 would cost approximately $8 billion, with $3.5 billion coming from the developed nations (up from $800 million spent in 1990). While the additional funding appears large, it is very, very small in relation to the gross national products and overseas development assistance projected for the industrialized countries.

Clearly, it is within the capabilities of the industrialized nations and the multilateral financial institutions to help developing countries finance expanded family-planning programs. The World Bank has already started on such a path, doubling its financing of population projects in the current year. Others should follow its lead. The funds required are so small, and the benefits to both families and nations so large, that money should not be allowed to stand in the way of reducing fertility rates as rapidly as is desired by the developing countries.

The developed nations should also initiate a discussion of how their citizens, who consume seven times as much per capita as do those of the developing countries, may both adjust their consumption patterns and reduce the environmental impact of each unit of consumption. They can thereby help ensure a sustainable path of economic advance for all the inhabitants of our planet.

Overpopulation Has Caused Hunger in Africa

by Fred Sai

About the author: *Fred Sai is president of the International Planned Parenthood Federation.*

At the very heart of the African continent, there is a dreadful warning of what can happen when population pressures become too intense. Overcrowding and land shortages are important factors (among such others as poverty and poor governance) in the tragic inter-ethnic conflicts in Rwanda [resulting in 500,000 deaths and 2 million refugees].

Overcrowding

Overcrowding reaches terrible proportions: in the country as a whole there are 405 people for every square kilometre—and this rises to as many as 560 in Ruhengeri Prefecture. These are densities more usually seen in urban areas, imposed on a rural country.

Crowding on the country's limited agricultural land is already almost unthinkably high—and before the 1994 civil war the population was set to double in just two decades. In 1990 there were 6.2 Rwandans for every cultivatable hectare; this will almost certainly rise to 9.1 by the end of this decade, and to 12.6 by 2010.

Landholdings have fragmented. Even 10 years ago, families of up to eight people were living off plots as small as 0.13 hectare (approximately 30 by 40 metres) in Gisenyi and Cyangugu Prefectures. And these tiny plots will inevitably shrink further as population densities increase.

Land Under Pressure

In Rwanda—as wherever fertilizers and the other high-technology inputs needed to increase yields are scarce—population pressure causes more marginal land to be brought under the plough. Pastureland and forests are turned into cropland. Fallow periods are reduced, giving the soil less time to recover. All of this leads to soil erosion and, in the long run, to reduced soil fertil-

Fred Sai, "Hope, and a Warning, in Africa," *Our Planet*, vol. 6, no. 3, 1994. Courtesy of Banson, London.

ity. Between 1970 and 1986, the amount of cultivated land in Rwanda increased by more than 50 per cent, from 528,000 to 826,500 hectares. As a result, the amount of fallow land was cut almost in half and 60 per cent of the pastureland disappeared, as it shrank from 488,000 to 199,000 hectares. This has particularly affected the minority Tutsi people, traditional pastoralists.

People do modify their social behaviour under such pressures, and Rwandans have been marrying later and having smaller families. Young

> *"It is the rapidity of population growth which causes so much stress and suffering."*

men have to wait longer to acquire the *rugo*—the small plot of land necessary for raising a family; and when they do, they know they will have difficulty supporting the same number of children as their parents had.

Family Planning

Knowledge and use of family planning have risen rapidly in the last decade, if from a very low base. In 1983 only 1 per cent of people used modern methods of contraception; by 1992 this had risen to around 13 per cent. Over the same period the average age of marriage for women rose to 23—the highest in Africa—and the total fertility rate fell, from 8.5 to 6.2 children per woman. But the relentless increase in population continues to outpace the ability of the land to sustain its people.

The evidence is all too clear: nearly half of all Rwandan children under five suffer from chronic malnutrition, stunting their growth. Despite better antenatal care and increased vaccination, the child mortality rate remains high: 150 of every 1,000 children die before their fifth birthday.

All beings react to overcrowding, and there is no doubt that it has played its part in, quite literally, preparing the ground for the tragedy of Rwanda. It serves as a warning for the rest of the continent.

A Rapid Rate of Growth

It has often been said that land is the one thing Africa has in plenty. So, the argument goes, population growth is no problem. This is simplistic. It fails to take into account both the low natural carrying capacity of much of the continent's land and the capriciousness of its climate. It also conveniently ignores the fact that it is the rapidity of population growth which causes so much stress and suffering. Africa's average growth rate of 3 per cent per year is far higher than those in most other developing regions, and much greater than those experienced in the past by the now developed world.

Twenty-nine of the 36 poorest countries in the world are in Africa. Inevitably, illiteracy rates are high, infrastructure is inadequate, and health services are rudimentary—all making it especially difficult to introduce family planning programmes.

In recent decades, urbanization and the breakdown of traditional values have led to more childbearing than used to be socially acceptable. Every day, some 10,000 African women resort to unsafe abortion—evidence of their frustrated desire to control their fertility.

Over half the population of most African countries is under the age of 15, providing a vast pent-up demographic momentum throughout the continent. Even if Kenya, for example, were to attain the two-child family overnight, its population would continue to grow for another two generations, eventually doubling.

There are encouraging signs of the beginnings of change—but they are only sporadic and the tempo is still slow. In recent years, most African governments—nudged by global advocacy efforts and their own family planning associations—have come to accept that fewer, better spaced births produce healthier children and mothers. All but a fanatical few have dropped their earlier opposition to family planning on the grounds that it is imposed by the West, or a neocolonialist plot designed to decimate African populations. Many have simply found themselves unable to cope with the development demands of their rapidly growing populations. . . .

> *"Urbanization and the breakdown of traditional values have led to more childbearing than used to be socially acceptable."*

In sub-Saharan Africa as a whole, only 9 per cent of married women are using contraceptives, as against 36 per cent in North Africa and the Middle East, 40 per cent in South and Southeast Asia and 60 per cent in Latin America. Only a few countries—such as South Africa, Zimbabwe, Botswana and Kenya—have family planning programmes successful enough to increase contraceptive use to around 50, 45, 35 and 33 per cent respectively.

The Kenyan Example

Kenya provides the most dramatic example. Contraceptive use rose threefold in the 1980s in Kenya. Fertility fell 22 per cent from 8.3 to 6.5 children per woman, and the average desired family size fell 35 per cent from 7.2 to 4.7 children.

Traditional Kenyan values favour many children. But rapid population growth has put farmland under pressure in many areas, making big families less advantageous. Higher female literacy has helped promote new attitudes to family size. Increasingly, parents want to send their children to school, and rising school costs have made it much more expensive to educate large families.

These trends have fuelled the demand for family planning. The government is strongly committed to providing diversified and accessible family planning services—an essential feature for the success of any population programme—so there has been a strong uptake and birth rates have fallen. There is still a high unmet need for family planning in Kenya, and birth rates will surely fall further as this demand is gradually satisfied. Botswana, too, has made notable strides through a combination of better development and strong family planning programmes.

Twenty-four African governments, ruling three-quarters of the continent's people, now view their population growth rates as too high. Their concerns are social, economic and environmental.

Facing the Facts

Many of them wonder how they will provide the schools, hospitals and jobs for the next generation. Many are concerned about food supplies: only a few countries, such as Zimbabwe, have carried out agricultural policies that have enabled them to become self-sufficient in food. Some are deeply worried about the growing incapacity of the environmental resource base to sustain still more people.

In many regions, particularly the Sahel, population growth has already exceeded the carrying capacity of the land. Some 200 million people, out of the present African population of 550 million, receive less than 90 per cent of the minimum of 2,200 calories a day needed to maintain an active working life; another 150 million are subject to acute food deficits, and 30–50 million are actually starving.

African countries face many other desperate situations which are precipitated or made worse by high birth rates. But governments do seem to have faced up to the fact that high population growth rates are among the factors preventing them from satisfying their peoples' development aspirations. And this offers hope that the Rwandan warning will be heard.

Environmental Limits on World Food Production Can Lead to Hunger

by Lester R. Brown

About the author: *Lester R. Brown is president of the Worldwatch Institute, an environmental research group.*

As the nineties unfold, the world is facing a day of reckoning. Many knew that this time would eventually come, that at some point the cumulative effects of environmental degradation and the limits of the earth's natural systems would start to restrict economic expansion. But no one knew exactly when or how these effects would show up. Now we can see that they are slowing growth in food production—the most basic of economic activities and the one on which all others depend.

A Loss of Momentum

After nearly four decades of unprecedented expansion in both land-based and oceanic food supplies, the world is experiencing a massive loss of momentum. Between 1950 and 1984, world grain production expanded 2.6-fold, outstripping population growth by a wide margin and raising the grain harvested per person by 40 percent. Growth in the world fish catch was even more spectacular—a 4.6-fold increase between 1950 and 1989, which doubled the seafood catch per person. Together, these developments reduced hunger and malnutrition throughout the world, offering hope that they would one day be eliminated.

But in recent years these trends in food output per person have been reversed with unanticipated abruptness. By 1993, the fish catch per person had declined some 7 percent from its historical high in 1989. And after 1984, the growth in grain production slowed abruptly, falling behind that of population. From 1984 until 1993, grain output per person fell 11 percent. Historians may well see 1984 as a watershed year, one marking the transition from an era of rapid

Abridged from Lester R. Brown, "Facing Food Insecurity," in *State of the World 1994.* Reprinted by permission of Worldwatch Institute, Washington, D.C.

growth in food production to one of much slower growth.

In a world of growing food insecurity, grain output per person becomes a proxy for progress, a basic indicator measuring success in accelerating food output and slowing population growth. It readily measures the effect on demand of both population growth and rising affluence, as the latter boosts the amount of grain used to produce livestock products.

> *"Soil erosion, air pollution, soil compaction, aquifer depletion, . . . and the waterlogging and salting of irrigated land are all slowing the rise in food output."*

Human demands are approaching the limits of oceanic fisheries to supply fish, of rangelands to support livestock, and, in many countries, of the hydrological cycle to produce fresh water. Even as these constraints become more visible, the backlog of unused agricultural technology is shrinking in industrial and developing countries alike, slowing the rise in cropland productivity. At the same time, soil erosion, air pollution, soil compaction, aquifer depletion, the loss of soil organic matter, and the waterlogging and salting of irrigated land are all slowing the rise in food output. At present, there is nothing in sight to reverse the worldwide decline in grain output per person.

Declining Food Production

The bottom line is that the world's farmers can no longer be counted on to feed the projected additions to our numbers. Achieving a humane balance between food and people now depends more on family planners than on farmers. . . .

Between 1950 and 1990, the world added 2.8 billion people, an average of 70 million a year. But between 1990 and 2030, the world is projected to add 3.6 billion, an annual average of 90 million. Such growth in a finite environment raises questions about the earth's carrying capacity. Will the earth's natural support systems sustain such growth indefinitely? How many people can the earth support at a given level of consumption?

As food production per person falls, the nature of famine itself is changing. Traditionally it was geographically defined, concentrated where there were crop failures. With today's worldwide food distribution system, malnutrition so severe that it is life-threatening is found mainly among the Third World's landless rural laborers and urban poor. Although the hungry are more dispersed and less visible, they are no less numerous. The latest U.N. assessment puts the number of malnourished at close to 1 billion, nearly one in five persons.

The ideological conflict that dominated the four decades from 1950 to 1990 is being replaced by the conflict between our steadily growing demand for food and the earth's physical capacity to satisfy those demands. In a world of spreading hunger, desperate people may cross national borders in unprecedented numbers in their search for food. The deteriorating balance between food and people in one way or another will increasingly preoccupy national political leaders, re-order national priorities, and dominate international affairs. . . .

Environmental Limits

During the last four decades, economic policies dominated the evolution of the global economy. During the next four, environmental limits interacting with population growth will have far more influence. Fully 96 percent of the projected addition of 3.6 billion people between 1990 and 2030 will occur in the Third World. In countries where demands already exceed local carrying capacity, the resulting deforestation, overgrazing, soil erosion, and aquifer depletion will accelerate and spread—creating a highly unstable relationship between people and their natural support systems. The changing relationship is clearly visible at the global level, where population growth is outrunning production of oceanic fisheries, rangelands, and croplands.

Between 1950 and 1989, the world fish harvest—a major source of animal protein—increased from 22 million to 100 million tons, lifting the supply per person from an average of 9 kilograms to 19. This phenomenal growth may have ended, however. Marine biologists from the U.N. Food and Agriculture Organization estimate that oceanic fisheries may not be able to sustain a harvest higher than that of recent years. If they are right, then the rise in the seafood catch per person of the past four decades has come to an end, to be replaced by a steady decline for as long as population grows.

> *"As food production per person falls, the nature of famine itself is changing."*

The world's rangelands, another major source of animal protein, are also under growing pressure. Between 1950 and 1990, world output of beef and mutton increased 2.6-fold, raising the per capita supply some 26 percent. With extensive overgrazing on every continent, however, rangelands—like oceanic fisheries—may be at their maximum carrying capacity. If so, rangeland production of beef and mutton may not increase much, if at all, in the future. Here, too, availability per person will decline indefinitely as population grows.

If the supply of fish, beef, and mutton is to expand in the future, it will have to come from feeding fish in ponds or livestock in feedlots. And this in turn will depend on producing more grain. Yet production of grain—the mainstay of the human diet, accounting for half of human caloric intake consumed directly and part of the remainder consumed indirectly as livestock products—has also slowed. Between 1950 and 1984, the world grain harvest grew at a record 3 percent a year, boosting per capita grain availability by some 40 percent. But from 1984 to 1993, annual growth slowed to less than 1 percent, dropping per capita availability by 11 percent. . . .

New information on the sustainable-yield potential of the three food production systems—fisheries, rangelands, and croplands—makes it easier to project future output. The experience of recent decades with overfishing and overgrazing gives a sense of the limits to the carrying capacity of fisheries and rangelands. And with grain yield per hectare in countries now growing much more slowly and the cropland area essentially fixed, trends can now be predicted with some confidence, assuming no dramatic new breakthroughs.

If oceanic and inland fisheries cannot sustain a catch any greater than the record catch of 1989, and if—for purposes of calculation—it is assumed that additional grain will not be available to sustain future growth in aquaculture, seafood supply per person will decline steadily from now until 2030, reversing the trend of the last 40 years. By then, the per capita seafood supply, which peaked at 19 kilograms in 1989, will be back down to 11 kilograms—only slightly above the level in 1950.

Pressures on rangelands are similar to those on fisheries. With extensive overgrazing on every continent, the rangeland production of beef and mutton is unlikely to increase much if at all, leading to a steady decline in per capita supply. This affects most directly the pastoral economies of Africa, the Middle East, and Central Asia.

The Importance of Grain

Trying to maintain the historical growth in seafood supplies of 2 million tons a year would require an enormous increase in fish farming, which would use vast amounts of land, water, and feed. Even though fish are among the more efficient converters of grain into meat, needing only 2 pounds of feed per pound of weight gain, this would still require 4 million tons of additional grain per year. And if the million-ton-per-year historical growth in beef and mutton output from rangelands is to rest on expanded feeding in feedlots, it will take an additional 7 million tons of grain each year, since steers in a feedlot typically require 7 pounds of grain for each pound of additional live weight gain. Thus maintaining the historical growth in both fish and beef supply would take 11 million tons of additional grain each year, an amount roughly equal to the annual increase in the world grain harvest in recent years.

This raises the question of how rapidly grain production can be expanded, either by increasing planted area or by raising land productivity. Prospects for a major expansion of cropland that is economically profitable and environmentally sustainable are not good, since there is little fertile land waiting to be plowed. . . .

> *"Prospects for a major expansion of cropland that is economically profitable and environmentally sustainable are not good."*

Grain production per hectare is a natural process, one that relies on photosynthesis to convert solar energy into biochemical energy. Albeit modified by human intervention, it is—like all natural processes—subject to the biological limits of nature. These boundaries have been pushed back with great success during the last several decades, but that does not mean this can go on forever.

The engine driving the rise in grain yields from mid-century onward was the expanding use of fertilizer—specifically the synergistic interactions of rising fertilizer use with expanding irrigation and the spread of grain varieties that were responsive to ever heavier applications of fertilizer. This formula was phenomenally successful from 1950 to 1984, when fertilizer use climbed from 14 million to 126 million tons. Moving to a new high nearly every year, it was one of the most predictable trends in the world economy. During this time, each additional ton of fertilizer applied boosted grain output 9 tons.

> *"Slowly rising grain yields per hectare are a matter of particular concern for countries where massive population gains are projected."*

Fertilizer and Yield

But 1984 was the last year in which a large increase in fertilizer use led to a comparable gain in world grain output. During the next five years farmers continued to use more fertilizer, but their crops did not respond much. Each additional ton of fertilizer used raised grain output by less than 2 tons. Given such a weak response, applying more fertilizer was clearly not a money-making proposition. Farmers' reaction, both predictable and rational, was to use less. Between 1989 and 1993, they cut fertilizer use some 12 percent. Even excluding the precipitous drop in the former Soviet Union following economic reforms, usage elsewhere dropped by 3 percent.

The phenomenal growth in fertilizer use from 1950 to 1984 was due in part to the record growth in irrigation from 1950 to 1978. Since then, however, irrigation has expanded at scarcely 1 percent a year. And new varieties that would respond strongly to still heavier applications of fertilizer have not been developed. Restoring rapid, sustained growth in fertilizer use and, hence, in the world grain harvest is not likely unless someone can develop varieties of wheat, corn, and rice that are far more responsive to fertilizer than those now available.

Failure to recognize this recent slowdown in yield gains and the reasons for it can generate overly optimistic projections. In a study entitled *The World Food Outlook: Malthus Must Wait*, World Bank economists Donald O. Mitchell and Merlinda D. Ingco project world food supply and demand to 2010, assuming that the rate of growth in grain yield per hectare between 1960 and 1990 will simply continue until 2010. This makes for a rather hopeful set of projections. Unfortunately, there is no scientific foundation for this assumption, given the dramatic slowdown in the rise of grain yield per hectare during the late eighties and early nineties. Indeed, from 1990 to 1993, the first three years in the 20 years projected, worldwide grain yield per hectare actually declined. . . .

Environmental degradation is also slowing the rise in yields. The earlier rapid rise in fertilizer use may have obscured the negative effects on yields of soil erosion, air pollution, waterlogging and salting, and other forms of degradation. But where fertilizer use is no longer rising, these effects may become more visible.

Few countries that have doubled or tripled grain yields during the last several decades can expect to match that record during the next few with existing technologies. Most have either already achieved the easy dramatic rises or lack the natural conditions needed to do so. . . .

Not surprisingly, slowly rising grain yields per hectare are a matter of particular concern for countries where massive population gains are projected. These new yield trends help explain why annual growth in the world harvest dropped from an average of 30 million tons from 1950 to 1984 to 12 million tons from 1984 to 1992. If population grows as projected and farmers cannot increase grain output by more than 12 million tons per year, per capita supplies will continue to diminish, dropping from the historical high of 346 kilograms in 1984 to 248 kilograms in 2030. In effect, the next four decades could be a mirror image of the last four, with grain availability levels in 2030 returning to those of 1950.

A Shortage of New Technologies

The contrast between mid-century and today in terms of the backlog of agricultural technology could not be more striking. When the fifties began, there was a great deal of technology waiting to be used. Justus von Liebig had discovered in 1847 that all the nutrients extracted from the soil by crops could be replaced in mineral form. Gregor Mendel's work establishing the basic principles of heredity, which laid the groundwork for future crop breeding advances, was done in the 1860s. Basic irrigation technologies had been around for several thousand years. Hybrid corn varieties were commercialized well before mid-century. And the dwarfing of wheat and rice plants in Japan to boost fertilizer responsiveness dates back a century.

As these long-standing technologies have been exploited during the last four decades, no new technologies that could lead to quantum leaps in world food output have taken their place. As a result, the nineties begin with the more progressive farmers looking over the shoulders of agricultural scientists seeking new yield-raising technologies only to discover that they have little to offer. The pipeline of new yield-raising agricultural technologies has not run dry, but the flow has slowed to a trickle.

"The pipeline of new yield-raising agricultural technologies has not run dry, but the flow has slowed to a trickle."

Most future growth in grain output must therefore come from exploiting technologies not yet fully used. Technological advances that could dramatically expand food output include a wholesale reduction in the cost of desalting seawater or the redesign of the photosynthetic process to enable it to convert solar energy into biochemical energy more efficiently. Unfortunately, leading scientific bodies, such as the National Academy of Sciences and the Royal Society of the United Kingdom, do not hold out much hope for such far-reaching breakthroughs in the foreseeable future. . . .

Examining Different Countries

With grain yields now plateauing in some countries, with national fish catches unlikely to increase much, if at all, and with rangelands widely overgrazed in most countries, there is an urgent need for national assessments of carrying capacity. Otherwise, there is a real risk that countries will blindly overrun their food carrying capacity, developing massive deficits that will collectively exceed the world's exportable supplies. Recent data showing the level at which the rise in grain yield per hectare is slowing or levelling off in countries with a wide range of growing conditions provide all governments with the reference points needed to estimate the population carrying capacity of their croplands.

China, which already has one of the slowest population growth rates in the developing world, is projected to add 490 million people over the next four decades, increasing to 1.6 billion in 2030. Currently it is adding 14 million people per year. Meanwhile, its economy is expanding at 10 percent or more annually, fueling steady rises in consumption of pork, poultry, eggs, and fish—all produced with grain.

> *"There is a real risk that countries will blindly overrun their food carrying capacity."*

On the supply side, rapid industrialization in China, including the construction of thousands of factories during this decade, is consuming vast amounts of cropland even as the rise in per hectare yield of rice and wheat is slowing. The result, according to a detailed study commissioned by the Australian government, is that China's grain imports could go from 12 million tons in 1993 up to 50–100 million tons by the end of this decade, with the latter amount being above current U.S. exports. If China's economy expands as planned and its population grows as projected, its grain import needs are likely to continue to soar, exceeding by 2015 the world's current exportable grain supplies.

India—already faced with extensive soil erosion and falling water tables—will be adding 590 million people by 2030, even more than China, as its population increases to 1.44 billion. With wheat yields that have already tripled and rice yields that are rising more slowly than in the past, India will find it difficult to support these growing numbers.

The United States, though it is the world's third most populous country, has kept demand for grain well below the sustainable yield of its land, maintaining a large exportable surplus. However, with population projected to expand by 95 million as a result of natural increase and immigration during the next four decades, pushing the total to 345 million in 2030, large areas of farmland will be claimed for housing, schools, and shopping centers. Unless some way can be found to reestablish the rapid rise in yields that prevailed from 1950 to 1984, the exportable grain surplus—which dropped from 100 million tons in the early eighties to 70 million tons in the early nineties as consumption climbed and as highly erodible cropland was converted to grassland— may well continue to fall.

> *"The food needs of the 90 million added each year can be satisfied only by reducing consumption among those already here."*

Ethiopia was unable to expand grain production fast enough to keep pace with the 30 million people added between 1950 and 1990. Now it is projected to add, in the next four decades, 106 million people—which would triple its 1990 population. Few believe this will happen. The only question is whether the projected growth will not materialize because the transition to smaller families accelerates or because starvation checks the growth. . . .

Exporters and Importers

Aside from the obvious value to governments of doing such assessments, these studies collectively give a sense of the future relationship between import needs and exportable supplies. During the past decade, world grain exports totalled roughly 200 million tons annually, with close to half coming from the United States. The other half came from Argentina, Australia, Canada, France, South Africa, and Thailand. With world grain exports even more concentrated than those of oil, the risk that a U.S. crop shortfall presents to the more than 100 grain-importing countries is clear. . . .

Even while national carrying capacity assessments are under way, a global set of projections is needed, one that draws on them and analyzes the human carrying capacity of the planet. Without this global effort, countries with soaring import needs will have no way of knowing whether exportable supplies will be available. This assessment could be used as a basis for international discussion. And, like national studies, it should be updated every two years or so, taking into account the availability of new farming technologies, fresh evidence of the effects of environmental degradation on food production, and the most recent data on population growth.

Carrying capacity projections at the global level give a sense of global options as well. For example, the world grain output projections discussed earlier assumed annual growth of 12 million tons, yielding a harvest in 2030 of 2.2 billion tons. This could satisfy populations of varying sizes, depending on consumption levels. At the U.S. consumption level of 800 kilograms per person a year, such a harvest would sustain 2.75 billion people—half as many as are alive today. At the Italian consumption level of 400 kilograms, it would support

5.5 billion people, the 1993 world population. And at the Indian level of 200 kilograms, it would support 11 billion people. Although much of humanity aspires to the U.S. diet, population growth has foreclosed that option.

At its peak of 346 kilograms in 1984, world grain output per person was well above the 300 kilograms of China and climbing toward the 400 kilograms of Italy. But that trend has been reversed. The harvest for 2030 of 2.2 billion tons would provide an average of 248 kilograms for each of the 8.9 billion people projected for that year—28 percent below the historical high. Stated otherwise, average grain consumption per person in 2030 would be well below that of China today, and falling toward that of India. Coming at a time when U.N. estimates show nearly 1 billion people in developing countries already failing to get enough calories to maintain normal levels of physical activity and when 36 percent of all preschool children in developing countries are below weight for their age, this prospective decline is not a pleasant one. . . .

Stabilizing Our Numbers

New information on the carrying capacity of both land and oceanic food systems argues for a basic rethinking of national population policies, for an accelerated international response to unmet family planning needs, and for the recasting of development strategies to address the underlying causes of high fertility. As national demands cross the sustainable-yield thresholds of biological support systems, the resource base itself is being consumed. In this situation, the question may not be what rate of population growth is sustainable but whether growth can continue without reducing living standards. Even now, the food needs of the 90 million added each year can be satisfied only by reducing consumption among those already here.

In a world where the cropland area is not expanding, grain yield per hectare has to rise as fast as population growth merely to maintain the existing inadequate supply of food. But with the rise in yields slowing so dramatically, reversing the decline in per capita grain production under way since 1984 may now depend on quickly slowing population growth. Otherwise, hunger may continue to spread, claiming more and more lives. . . .

The question at this hinge point in history is a simple one. Can we mobilize to reverse the continuing decline in food production per person that now clouds the future of civilization? If we start thinking seriously about what it will take to do this, then we may also begin to understand how different the future will be from the recent past.

What will future historians write of us? Will they say that we were the generation whose selfish pursuit of materialism and inability to limit family size put civilization at risk? Or will they say that the initiatives that we took in the nineties put the world on an environmentally sustainable path? Only we can provide the answer.

Desertification Contributes to World Hunger

by Michael Glantz

About the author: *Michael Glantz is a senior scientist for the National Center for Atmospheric Research and directs the center's Environmental and Societal Impacts Group.*

Desertification can be defined as the creation of desert-like conditions where none had existed in the recent past. Although the concept has become most closely associated with arid areas along desert fringes, it is now applied to high rainfall areas like the Amazon rainforest. Desertification is a mega-concept. It encompasses many processes such as wind and water erosion, soil salinization, overgrazing, waterlogging and deforestation. It also has competing definitions, of which there are more than a hundred. This perspective sees desertification as a process of change, rather than just the end result of that change.

The Human Factor

Desertification has a natural as well as a human component. In the ancient past its occurrence was dependent on land-climate interactions. In the past several thousand years the equation has been expanded to include humans. Today, desertification is dependent on land-climate-human interactions. Desertification in specific regions is occurring over decades and years instead of centuries and millennia. The difference is the human factor. We have not learned to live in harmony with our natural environment.

Many Americans believe desertification is a third world problem and not one we need be concerned about in North America. Yet aspects of desertification are under way in our country: degraded rangelands, major dust storms, decreasing soil fertility. Do we have a federal office of desertification control? No. Do we have a Bureau that deals with soil erosion? Yes. With grazing practices? Yes. While it appears that we are not doing much in North America to combat desertification (the mega-concept), we are quite active in combating those land-

Michael Glantz, "Desertification," *Buzzworm*, January/February 1991. Reprinted by permission of the author.

use problems that degrade our soil's productivity.

In North America desertification is an economic problem. It is a different situation, however, in the third world where the inability to cope with aspects of desertification that encroach on agricultural fields, rangelands and on human settlements can mean the difference between life and death. Many people in sub-Saharan Africa live from one season to the next. They are on their own when it comes to survival, as their governments are either unwilling or unable to assist them. When the fertility of their soils declines, bringing down food production with

> *"The inability to cope with aspects of desertification . . . can mean the difference between life and death."*

it, they become malnourished, finding it even more difficult to work their fields. Ultimately they must abandon their land in search of land not yet degraded by human activities.

Decades ago when population densities were lower, farmers could migrate to new areas, leaving their farmland fallow. Over time, the fields would recover and in a decade or two the farmers would rotate their farming back to the original site. With most of the arable land already in production, there is no possibility of letting the land lie fallow. Making a bad situation worse, animal manure is often collected in the fields to be used as fuel, eliminating a sorely needed source of fertilizer.

Poor countries do not have the funds to combat desertification. Industrialized countries apparently do not have the desire to address the sources of desertification in the third world in a major way. Lip service to combating desertification will not do the job. Training programs and technique transfer (as opposed to technology transfer) are necessary aspects of arresting desertification processes. It is far cheaper to train people to avert desertification than to reclaim land that has already been desertified.

A Long-Term Problem

Desertification is a long-term, low-grade, but cumulative environmental problem that, like air pollution, acid rain and global warming, keeps getting put on the back burner while governments address seemingly more pressing issues. Solutions, however, are often known but not applied for lack of appropriate funding. It will take lots of money to combat it. But those funds will have to be used more wisely in the future than they have been in the past. Education and training at the local level should be the highest priorities for agencies seeking to bring an end to desertification in those countries whose inhabitants are most threatened by the process.

Desertification deserves at least equal attention as other environmental changes that threaten "our plundered planet." Only time will tell if humans are smart enough to give it that attention.

Hunger Is Not Caused by Overpopulation

by Sheldon Richman

About the author: *Sheldon Richman is a senior editor at the Cato Institute, a libertarian think tank in Washington, D.C. He has written frequently on population and economic issues.*

A central tenet of the pop creed is that there are too many people in the world. One cannot go through a week of watching television, listening to radio talk shows or reading newspapers and magazines without seeing mournful references to overpopulation.

Overpopulation is never far from the minds of our leaders. State Department Counselor Tim Wirth told the United Nations in 1993 that President Bill Clinton "understands the cost of excessive population growth to the health of women, to the natural environment and to our hopes for alleviating poverty." In his best-selling book, *Earth in the Balance*, Vice President (then-Sen.) Al Gore wrote, "No goal is more crucial to healing the global environment than stabilizing human population." During the presidential campaign, Clinton said that global population growth poses the "single greatest threat to ecosystems and the quality of life on Earth."

Everyone knows that the world has too many people. But as American humorist Henry Wheeler Shaw wrote in *Josh Billings' Encyclopedia of Wit and Wisdom* in 1874, "The trouble with people is not that they don't know but that they know so much that ain't so." Overpopulation ain't so, and the measures designed to address it will hurt.

Too Many People?

How many people are too many? We know that 5.5 billion people walk the Earth today. But that number by itself says nothing. Maybe it is too few. How can we tell?

The prefix "over" implies a standard. For example, "overweight" implies a standard linked to height. By what standard is the Earth overpopulated? Certainly not living space. The world's entire population could fit into Jacksonville, Fla., with everyone having standing room. Dense cities often are surrounded by nearly empty countryside. For overpopulation to be real, there must be conditions that are undesirable and unmistakably caused by the presence of a certain number of people. If such indications cannot be found, we are entitled to dismiss the claim of overpopulation.

> *"The television pictures of starving, emaciated Africans are heartbreaking, but they are not evidence of overpopulation."*

In arguing their case, believers in overpopulation make vague, tautological references to a standard known as "carrying capacity," colorfully illustrated with stories about gazelle herds and bacteria (anything but human beings). When the verbiage is cleared away, what are adduced as the symptoms of overpopulation? Famine, deepening poverty, disease, environmental degradation and resource depletion. Yet on no count does the evidence support the anti-population lobby's case.

The television pictures of starving, emaciated Africans are heartbreaking, but they are not evidence of overpopulation. Since 1985, we have witnessed famine in Ethiopia, Sudan and Somalia. Those nations have one thing in common: They are among the least populated areas on Earth. Although their populations are growing, the people there are not hungry because the world can't produce enough food; they are hungry because civil war keeps food from getting to them. Moreover, the very sparseness of their populations makes them vulnerable to famine because there aren't enough people to support sophisticated roads and transportation systems that would facilitate the movement of food.

No Food Shortage

In the 20th century there has been no famine that has not been caused by civil war, irrational economic policies, deliberate retribution or natural disaster. In addition, the number of people affected by famine has fallen compared with the late 19th century—not just as a percentage of the world's population but in absolute numbers.

Food is abundant. Since 1948, according to the U.N. Food and Agriculture Organization and the U.S. Department of Agriculture, annual world food production has outpaced the increase in population by about 1 percent. Today, per capita production and per-acre yields are at all-time highs. Prices of agricultural products have been falling for more than 100 years. The average inflation-adjusted price of those products, indexed to wages, fell by more than 74 percent between 1950 and 1990. While Lester Brown of the Worldwatch Institute and noted butterfly expert Paul Ehrlich predict higher food prices and increasing scarcity, food is becoming cheaper and more plentiful.

That good news is due largely to technological advances (the "green revolution") that have provided better seeds, fertilizers, pesticides and methods of farming. The only obstacles to agricultural progress are the impediments created by governments. Imagine what the world would be like today if the fertile farmland of the former Soviet Union, China or India had been in productive private hands operating in free markets for the past several decades. Since permitting market incentives in agriculture, India has become a net food exporter, and agricultural production in China has boomed.

The Earth Can Feed 40 Billion People

Catastrophists argue that the bright past does not imply a bright future; they assert that mankind has crossed some fateful threshold. But the Earth is capable of feeding many more people than are now alive. The late Roger Revelle of Harvard University (whom Gore claims as a mentor) estimated that Africa, Asia and Latin America alone, simply by using water more efficiently, could feed 35 billion to 40 billion people—seven to eight times the current world population—and that assumes no change in technology.

Those who annually predict imminent famine seize on any change as evidence that man's alleged strain on the biosphere is finally beginning to show. Thus, if the price of seafood rises, they announce that the seas are nearing exhaustion. They never consider the myriad other possibilities, such as the shift in diet from meat to fish, the decline of the Russian fishing industry during the dissolution of the Soviet Union or the lack of property rights in the oceans and lakes.

> *"Africa, Asia and Latin America alone, simply by using water more efficiently, could feed 35 billion to 40 billion people."*

The most telling indication of the trend in food production is the presence of a farm lobby in every industrial capital. Those lobbies spend millions of dollars a year to persuade their governments to hold food prices up and food supplies down. They apparently don't expect help from nature.

The catastrophists' claim that the population explosion causes famine, poverty, disease and environmental degradation founders on a single undeniable fact: the global plunge in the death rate. All over the world, people are living longer. More babies survive infancy than ever before, and more people are reaching old age, a development that economist Julian Simon calls "man's triumph over death." It should be the occasion for celebration, but the catastrophists prefer sackcloth.

Let's see what has been happening. In the period from 1950 to 1955, there were 159 infant deaths per 1,000 live births in the developing world. By the first half of the 1980s, the number had plunged by more than 42 percent—to 92. In East Asia, infant mortality dropped 71 percent. In South America, the drop averaged 52 percent. In Africa, infant mortality dropped 38 percent. In the industrialized world, the rate fell more than 69 percent.

The increase in life expectancy at birth has been equally dramatic. Between 1950 to 1955 and 1980 to 1985, the average increase worldwide was 13 years, up 29 percent. In the industrialized world, life expectancy went from 65 years to 73 years. But the biggest news was in the developing world, where life expectancy went from 41 years to more than 56—a 38 percent increase.

> *"The catastrophists' cliche that a growing population is an obstacle to development is especially barren."*

"The increase in average life expectancy during the twentieth century," wrote the late David Osterfeld in *Progress Versus Planning: How Government Stifles Economic Growth*, "equals or exceeds the gains made in all the preceding centuries combined."

During that same period, the total fertility rate (the average number of children born per woman) fell everywhere. Worldwide, the rate fell from 5 to 3.6. (The rate that produces population stability, or replacement, is 2.1.) The developing world's rate dropped from 6.2 to 4.1—more than halfway to the replacement rate. East Asia went from 5.5 to 2.3, South America from 4.9 to 3.6. Bringing up the rear, again, was Africa, where the rate fell only from 6.5 to 6.4.

Thus the world's population has been heading toward stabilization for at least 30 years. The population controllers will credit that to their efforts. But there is a simpler explanation: As economies develop and people become better off materially, they have fewer children. That phenomenon is well established in demography. It explains what happened in the West, where today the fertility rate is 2.0 or lower—below replacement rate.

In preindustrial, agricultural economies, children provide farm labor and social security; children are wealth. In a developed economy, parents invest resources (for education and the like) in their children; they are an expense. Moreover, as societies become industrialized and modern consumer goods and services become available, people find sources of satisfaction other than children. So they have fewer kids. A low fertility rate, writes British economist Peter Bauer, is an effect, not a cause, of development.

So the screeching about the need for population control programs in the developing world, which shift childbearing decisions from couples to the state, is ill-conceived. Besides, such programs are an affront to human dignity, privacy and liberty, whether they compel women to have abortions and to be sterilized (as China does) or "merely" deprive people of their income and vital services because they want more children than the government desires for them.

Population and Development

The catastrophists' cliche that a growing population is an obstacle to development is especially barren. Studies show a strong correlation between affluence and longevity; as the late Aaron Wildavsky, a political scientist at the University of California at Berkeley, liked to say, wealthier is healthier. The lengthening life expectancy in the developing world is evidence that population growth cannot be increasing poverty.

Similarly, the West grew rich precisely when its population was increasing at an unprecedented rate. The world's population was relatively stable from before 8000 B.C. until the late 18th century, a period of miserable poverty for mankind. "In preindustrial Europe," writes historian Carlo Cipolla, "the purchase of a garment, or the cloth for a garment, remained a luxury the common people could only afford a few times in their lives." At the dawn of industrialization, the world's population was about 750 million. After that, it skyrocketed. The time it took for the population to double fell from 35,000 years before 1650 to 243 by 1750, then to 116 during the second half of the 19th century. By 1970 the doubling time reached a low of 35 years. Yet all that time (with the exception of wartime), the industrialized societies grew richer. Between 1776 and 1975, while the world's population increased sixfold, real gross world product rose about eightyfold.

In our own century we have seen a replay of the Industrial Revolution. After World War II the population of Hong Kong grew more quickly than that of 19th century England or 20th century India—at the same time that the resource-poor island colony was growing rich. The experiences of Japan, South Korea, Taiwan and Singapore reinforce the point.

The Source of Ideas

The increases occurring in population and in wealth have not been merely coincidental. They are causes and effects of each other. Today, with few exceptions, the most densely populated countries are the richest. Any mystery in that is dispelled by the realization that people are the source of ideas. The addition of people geometrically increases the potential for combining ideas into newer, better ideas. Those who wish to stifle population growth would condemn hundreds of millions of people in the developing world to the abject deprivation that characterized the West before the Industrial Revolution.

The initially plausible claim that more people deplete resources faster has no more foundation than the catastrophists' other arguments. Price is the best indication of relative scarcity. For centuries, resources of every kind, including energy, have been getting cheaper. In 1990 energy on average was 46 percent cheaper than it was in 1950; minerals were 48 percent cheaper, lumber 41 percent cheaper, food 74 percent cheaper. (The only thing getting more expensive is labor, an indication of the scarcity of people.) Technology enables us to find more resources and to use them more efficiently. Doubling the efficiency of our use of oil would be

> *"People don't deplete resources. They create them."*

equivalent to doubling the available supply of oil. Natural resources, in other words, do not exist in fixed supplies.

Natural Resources

Actually, natural resources do not exist at all. All resources are manmade. Something is not a resource until it can accomplish a human purpose. Before Benjamin Silliman, a Yale University chemist, discovered in 1855 that kerosene (a better illuminant than whale oil) could be distilled from crude oil, oil was not a resource. It was black gunk that ruined farmland and had to be removed at great expense. Silliman turned oil into a resource not by changing its chemical composition but by making a discovery. Nature does not provide resources, only materials.

The latest evidence of that truth is the information revolution that swirls around us. It is made possible by silicon computer chips and threads of glass (fiber-optic cables). Both are made from sand—one of the world's most abundant substances. Thanks to human ingenuity, a common substance that was merely part of the landscape has become a tool of revolutionary human advancement. People don't deplete resources. They create them.

Nothing written here implies that population growth does not bring problems. Quite the contrary; but as economist Simon says, it also brings problem solvers who apply their intelligence, discover and invent solutions, and—here is the key—leave human society better off than it was before the problems arose. Doubters need only study the quality of life on the pre-Columbian North American continent, when several million Indians barely scratched out their subsistence amid the same "natural resources" that today enrich the lives of billions of people worldwide.

An Important Precondition

A caveat: Human advancement is not automatic and cannot withstand complacency. It has a precondition without which all that is written here may be ignored.

That precondition is liberty—specifically, the individual's right to think, produce, trade and profit from his achievements. In institutional terms, liberty consists of free markets, the rule of law protecting property and contracts, and strict limits on government power. Civilization's successes have another thing in common in addition to growing populations: capitalism.

The Policies of Northern Nations Contribute to Famine in Africa

by John Prendergast and Terence Miller

About the author: *John Prendergast directs the Horn of Africa Project for the Center for Concern, a Catholic research and advocacy organization located in Washington, D.C. He has written extensively on development and social justice issues. Terence Miller worked for the Maryknoll Office of Peace and Justice.*

One statistic really says it all. During the 1980s, of the seven million children who died each year of malnutrition-related causes throughout the world, five million of those children were African.

Seventy-five percent of the world's hungriest nations are in Africa, according to the U.S. Agency for International Development. Mozambique, Somalia, Ethiopia, Sierra Leone, and Chad lead the way. African countries account for 18 of the top 20 nations in the "low human development" category used by the United Nations Development Program, which factors in life expectancy, literacy, and economic progress. The World Bank finds that African nations comprise more than 90% of the world's most indebted countries and 60% of those with the lowest incomes.

Decline in Food Production

There has been a steady decline in food production per person during the last two decades in Africa. People's access to food (their 'entitlement') has eroded further because of a number of shocks to the African food system. War, drought, unfavorable terms of trade, misguided economic policies, mounting debts, ecological deterioration, political upheaval, and further marginalization of women in the economy have all reduced Africa's ability to feed itself. The resulting economic insecurity has helped sustain extremely high population growth rates, since children are perceived as a form of insurance for parents as they grow

"Roots of the Food Crisis," chapter 1 of *A Guide for Activists: Handbook on African Hunger* by John Prendergast and Terence Miller. Washington: Maryknoll Justice and Peace Office, 1992. Reprinted with permission.

older. Another part of the problem, the Structural Adjustment Programs of the World Bank and the International Monetary Fund, will also be examined.

A. Colonial Legacy

As early as the sixteenth century, European traders began a process of looting and pillaging Africa that continues in a much subtler guise to this day. For four centuries, Europe's colonial empires extracted *raw materials* (cotton, coffee, livestock feed, groundnuts, and an assortment of minerals, most important of which was gold, which helped underpin Europe's growing money economy) and *human beings* (nearly 23 million able-bodied farmers exported as slave labor). The only real change in Africa's external relationship with big corporations and banks is that dollars (in the form of debt payments and capital flight) have replaced slaves as the most valued export, although slave trading is still alleged to exist in Mauritania and Sudan.

Economic Changes

The colonists geared African economies to produce for external demands rather than internal needs, and this was sustained by most of the post-Independence governments. Capital intensive, high technology farming systems rapidly emerged via Northern aid. Small farmers and herders increasingly have lost control of their land and labor. This has led to a reduction of self-sufficient farming, which alternative sources of income and employment have not been able to replace quickly enough in many places. Economic processes which took centuries in Europe are taking only generations in Africa. Growing hunger, social disruption, and conflict inevitably result.

At the local level, families who earn money rather than produce for themselves often have access to a much wider variety of goods, often leading to improved nutrition. But in the event of a physical or economic shock such as drought or conflict, families become unable to afford rising food prices and often are forced to sell livestock or other assets, or borrow money from local lenders at exorbitant rates of interest. Either way, the result is increasing impoverishment and inequality.

"Development" projects initiated by Northern donors and African governments have often contributed to this growing poverty and inequality. Until quite recently, very little effort was put into studying or respecting the local approaches of African farmers and pastoralists. Assuming that African solutions were primitive, Northern governments and aid organizations favored approaches developed in Europe and North America, and their heavy machinery and chemical fertilizers often destroyed fragile African soils. Natural ecosystems have been degraded through the exploitation of forest, soil and water resources in pursuit of short-term economic gain, threatening the sustain-

> *"Seventy-five percent of the world's hungriest nations are in Africa."*

ability of food systems. Local decision-making processes were also under-mined, as most projects lacked popular participation in their formulation and implementation.

B. Agricultural Trade, Food Aid, and the Debt Trap

Initiated during the colonial period, the strategy of exporting raw materials and importing finished products was destined to produce an economic crisis. World market prices for raw materials and cash crops have fluctuated wildly on a downward trend during the post–World War II period, while prices of manufactured imports increased five to ten percent annually. Also, cotton has been replaced by synthetic fibers, copper by glass fiber optics, and sugar by cyclamates and Nutrasweet. Africa has lost $50 billion as a result of falling commodity prices and substitution since 1986.

> *"As early as the sixteenth century, European traders began a process of looting and pillaging Africa that continues in a much subtler guise to this day."*

No matter how efficiently or by how much African countries increase their traditional exports, it would be impossible to turn the situation around. For example, when the Ivory Coast increased cocoa exports, lower world prices resulted, thus reducing instead of increasing earnings. And when African countries have tried to export finished products, they have met trade barriers in the North. Even the World Bank has criticized the U.S., Japan and many European countries for "[erecting] high barriers to imports . . . from developing countries and then [subsidizing] their own exports," all the while telling African countries to tear down their trade barriers.

Food Aid

In non-emergency situations, the dumping of subsidized grain or the delivery of food aid often benefits the donor more than the recipient. There are Northern financial interests in the production of surplus grain, the sale of machinery, fertilizer, and chemicals, the processing of food, the storage and shipment of grain, and the actual delivery of food by an assortment of aid agencies. Food aid is also used by some Northern countries to promote long-term dependence on their food exports.

Since the late 1960s, Africa has withstood droughts which forced unplanned food imports, wars which necessitated weapons purchases, huge oil price increases, global recession, and declining prices for their own exports. Much of this was paid for by accumulating mountains of debt. By 1990, Africa's debt stood at $272 billion, double its 1980 level and equal to ninety percent of the region's Gross Domestic Product.

Despite unprecedented amounts of aid, between 1982 and 1990 Africa was a net supplier of capital to the North, transferring a net $4 billion. In sum, writes

P. Spitz, the "forces of extraction" out-balance the "forces of retention."

C. Lack of Democratic Participation

An important reason for the decline of food security in Africa has been political exclusion, resulting from single-party, state dominated, authoritarian rule. In recent years, food riots and other forms of instability in many countries have led to the expansion of repressive security systems. But in other countries, demands for more democratic societies have finally borne fruit. Elections have been held for the first time in an unprecedented number of countries, although the influence of the military remains strong in many newly democratic governments.

In most places, though, women continue to be excluded from decision-making processes. "Development" programs often assign land and give credit and extension services only to men, and stress export crops that compete with women's efforts at producing food crops. According to Pat Kutzner, "All such male-biased, gender-blind forms of 'agricultural progress' have eroded the productivity of Africa's women farmers."

D. War

War erodes people's entitlement to food in a number of different ways: it destroys crops, land and the environment; reorients resources from development to the military; disrupts trade and economic activity; blocks access to emergency aid; displaces populations; and suppresses press freedoms, and civil rights. War is the most frequent reason for famine.

War and Outside Intervention

Liberia, Mozambique, Angola, Uganda, Ethiopia, Sudan, Somalia, and Chad are just a few of the countries which have experienced famine-causing wars. Many of Africa's wars had been fueled by superpower politics. For example, the former Soviet Union transferred $1 billion per year to Ethiopia to fund a government which helped cause over a million deaths in the latter half of the 1980s. The United States sent tens of millions of covert military aid to UNITA, a rebel group in Angola. The lethal aid was halted in 1990, but not before 331,000 children were killed as a result of war tactics, including the use of land mines manufactured in Louisiana.

Africa spends $14 billion a year on ammunition and weapons. For the cost of one tank, an African government could build 1,000 classrooms. One helicopter is worth the salaries of 2,000 school teachers. Perhaps most insidious of all, the presence of large supplies of arms and armies facilitates military solutions to problems, both domestic and international. Strong militias are as useful for quelling rebellions and dissent as they are for waging war against neighboring countries.

> *"The delivery of food aid often benefits the donor more than the recipient."*

Local disputes have traditionally been a means of resolving disputes over access to resources. With the advent of extremely destructive modern weapons and their easy accessibility, local disputes easily escalate into civil wars, which are easily exploited by outside interests. As analyst Nick Cater notes, "Conflict in Africa has become synonymous with gross violations of human rights and deliberate attempts to destroy the assets and way of life of local groups. And when food aid is available to assist affected populations, it too is used as a weapon of war. Rebel movements are equally prone to exploit humanitarian assistance in this way."

> *"Somalia, and Chad are just a few of the countries which have experienced famine-causing wars. Many of Africa's wars had been fueled by superpower politics."*

E. World Bank and IMF Structural Adjustment

The International Monetary Fund (IMF) and the World Bank have responded to the crisis with what are called Structural Adjustment Programs, or SAPs. African governments must adopt SAPs in order to have their debt rescheduled and to get aid from Northern donors. SAPs have become the most debated aspect of development policy of the last decade.

Gift-wrapped in free market ideals, SAPs are primarily geared toward getting African governments to repay loans and to keep them exporting raw materials as efficiently as possible. SAPs require governments to adhere to stringent economic policies which reduce spending and consumption, promote exports, remove trade barriers to imports, devalue African currencies, and privatize government-controlled industries and markets.

Assumptions Behind SAPs

The basic assumptions behind SAPs are that increased trade will lead to economic growth, and economic growth by itself will significantly reduce hunger and poverty. In practice, though, these policies have led to a severe contraction of African economies at the expense of the poor and the environment. Some analysts have demonstrated how similar policies by the international financial community in the 1920s contributed to the Great Depression, the rise of fascism, and global conflict.

Three key components of SAPs will be examined below.

• *Promoting Exports:* The only way African countries will repay their debts and earn dollars to buy Northern products is to produce for export. World Bank and IMF economists say that exports stimulate economic growth as well as alleviate trade imbalances. But a heavy emphasis on exports results in less emphasis on production of goods for internal needs, so it's no surprise that there are nearly always shortages of basic goods. Export promotion fails to address the development of internal markets, which are crucial for real economic development.

Another problem is that most African nations tend to produce a narrow range of commodities, leaving their economies extremely vulnerable to crop failures or the declining prices of African commodities in the world market. Lower prices for their goods force African countries to produce even more just to keep their earnings constant. With help from African governments and donors such as the World Bank, larger farmers and agribusinesses have increased their land-holdings in order to maintain profits, often at the expense of small farmers and the environment.

• *Reducing the Role of Government:* In response to SAPs, African govern-ments have slashed budgets, reduced public payrolls, sold government agencies, and begun to charge for certain social services such as health and education. User fees have made health care and education unaffordable for millions in many African countries. Payroll reductions have left hundreds of thousands of former government workers unemployed.

The most direct impact, though, may be the demand of most SAP agreements to eliminate subsidies on food consumption. Although these subsidies were cer-tainly inefficient and untargeted, their across-the-board removal (along with currency devaluations) has led to sudden decreases in food security, as the price of grain skyrockets beyond the reach of many vulnerable African consumers.

These price increases have often led to food riots in various African countries. This has given some gov-ernments another excuse to increase security spending, which has so far remained untouched by SAP agree-ments, although lip service is increas-ingly being given to this important discrepancy.

> *"A heavy emphasis on exports results in less emphasis on production of goods for internal needs."*

• *Increasing Farm Prices:* Increasing prices paid to farmers is a policy de-signed to increase incomes and production. This policy has resulted in some production increases, but in many countries the increase was far less than pre-dicted. Farmers in Africa have often been constrained by a lack of labor and in-puts (seeds, tools, fertilizer, oxen), or by merchant middlemen who benefit most from the increases in some places.

A more negative finding has been that increases in producer prices have made some farmers more food insecure, because many small farmers are net pur-chasers of food. Higher prices paid for food production have often resulted in higher prices for food in local markets. Producers need to be fairly compen-sated, but not at the expense of consumers.

Wars Are the Primary Cause of Famine

by Robert W. Kates

About the author: *Robert W. Kates is director emeritus of the Alan Shawn Feinstein World Hunger Program, a research and educational organization based at Brown University, Providence, Rhode Island.*

As we witnessed the starvation, disease, and dying in Somalia in the early 1990s, it was surely difficult to remember that Somalia was the site of the greatest triumph of 20th-century international public health. There, in October 1977, Ali Maow Maalin, a 23-year-old cook in the town of Merca, was identified in the *Bulletin of the World Health Organization* as having "the world's last endemic case of smallpox." Now, more than 15 years later, Somalia may again prove to be a turning point in the much longer and larger human struggle to end deaths from famine. To understand that opportunity amid all the pain and suffering requires a sense of that long struggle, an assessment of the trends in cause, prevalence, and prevention of modern famines, and the specific challenges of undertaking humanitarian action in the midst of armed conflict.

Famines in Human History

Food shortage and subsequent starvation are what is popularly conceived of as famine: an absolute shortage of food within a bounded area, usually caused by the failure or destruction of crops or by wartime sieges or blockades. But studies of major modern famines—in the Soviet Union in 1932 through 1934, Bengal, India, in 1943, China in 1958 through 1961, and Ethiopia in 1972 through 1973 and 1984 through 1986—indicate that widespread hunger and starvation can occur even when food is available if large numbers of people lose their capacity to produce, purchase, exchange, or receive food. Thus, a sudden increase in food prices, a drop in laborers' incomes, or a change in government policy can create hunger for millions even in the absence of the more familiar causes of food shortage: droughts, floods, pests, or armed conflict.

Robert W. Kates, "Ending Deaths from Famine," *The New England Journal of Medicine* 328:1055-57, 1993. Copyright 1993, Massachusetts Medical Society. All rights reserved. Reprinted with permission.

Famine is as old as humanity. Its occurrence is inferred from paleoforensic data in the Harris lines of long bones and in the Wilson bands of teeth. . . . And it is carefully documented in what historian J.D. Post calls the "last great subsistence crisis in the Western world," which hit Europe and North America in 1816.

The 1816 crisis was also a turning point in the struggle to end deaths due to famine. The year was known in New England as "the year without summer," when wet, cold weather throughout North America and Western Europe was triggered by the dust veil that followed the eruption of Mount Tambora in Indonesia. Crop

> *"Over time, the natural causes of famine—drought, flood, pests, and disease that lead to crop failure and animal death—have become relatively less important."*

and harvest failures combined with the unsettled economic conditions in post-Napoleonic Europe led to widespread food crises. But in this case, unlike the frequent famines of the previous century, European states and cities organized to prevent famine deaths by raising funds and importing food from Russia and the Baltic states. The new commitment not to accept deaths due to famine as inevitable was seen everywhere in Europe except two areas, Ireland and Transylvania, each still beyond the pale of the dominant empires of Great Britain and Austro-Hungary. This commitment would again fail the Irish in 1847 and particular populations in the two world wars of this century, but overall it would hold in Europe and then be gradually extended to other parts of the world. To this day, the 19th-century famine codes serve as a basic framework for the highly successful programs of famine prevention and relief in India.

Multiple Stresses

Famine, while frequent in history, is never ordinary. Food is the most basic of human needs, and mechanisms to cope with periodic food shortage are features of the earliest social systems. For the mechanisms of famine prevention to fail, multiple stresses, such as the "year without summer" coinciding with an economic depression, are almost always required. Over time, the natural causes of famine—drought, flood, pests, and disease that lead to crop failure and animal death—have become relatively less important. Social causes of famine have become correspondingly more important as the nature of food procurement has changed from simple access to natural resources and the help of kinfolk to a complex set of productive resources, exchanges, and gifts. And throughout time, famine created in the course of war has persisted, even as the scale and technology of warfare have changed.

Food sources now include the entire globe instead of the area bounded by the earlier limits of a day's walk, a hunting trip, or a seasonal migration. This enlargement of scale, however, so important to the reduction of scarcity, renders some areas marginal and courts catastrophe when errors in food-system management occur. Big food systems can make big mistakes. Thus, the worst famine of the 20th century, the Chinese famine of 1959 through 1961, in which between 15 million and 30 million people died, was rooted primarily in state policies connected with the ill-fated "great leap forward" that devastated the Chinese food-producing system while ignoring the warning signs of increasing stress.

Famine is the only form of hunger that one is likely to see on television. The power and immediacy of the medium creates a sense of widespread and increasing vulnerability. Yet the numbers affected by famine—now 15 million to 35 million at risk—are relatively small. Other less acute forms of hunger, however, are much more common. The recent International Conference on Nutrition estimated that 780 million people in developing countries lack access to enough food to meet their basic daily needs for health, growth, and light activity (an average daily caloric requirement of 1.54 times the basal metabolic rate). In addition, one child in six in the world is born underweight, and almost two in five children are underweight by the age of five. Some 2 billion people, mostly women and children, are deficient in one or more of the three major micronutrients: iron, iodine, and vitamin A.

A Downward Trend

The total population residing in countries where episodes of famine have been reported in the *New York Times* can serve to indicate the population at risk. . . . By this measure, the trend in famines since the end of World War II is clearly downward, reflecting a lessening of the prevalence of famine and a major shift in the incidence of famine from populous Asia to less-populated Africa. The total population in countries with reported famine peaked in the period from 1957 through 1963 at a yearly average of almost 788 million, then declined to a yearly average of 264 million in 1978 through 1984. This decline continued over the next seven years (from 1985 through 1991), when the combined population of famine-plagued countries averaged 141 million. And it declined further in 1992, when famine was reported only in Somalia and Sudan, which have a combined population of 35 million.

In 1989, an ad hoc international group meeting in Bellagio, Italy, found that it was theoretically possible to halve hunger in this decade by building on the successful efforts that were currently under way. Four specific goals were adopted: to eliminate deaths from famine; to end hunger in half the poorest households; to cut malnu-

> *"In all of the countries that have reported famine so far in the 1990s . . . armed conflict has been a major cause."*

trition in half among mothers and children; and to eradicate iodine and vitamin A deficiencies. The optimism that underlay these commitments, even in the midst of disaster, was based on the long-term downward trend in the size of the populations affected by famine and the knowledge that most of the elements required to prevent famine were already in place.

The effort to cope with drought, flood, war, and famine in the 1980s led to major improvements in the global emergency-food-aid system. Early-warning systems, dispersed emergency stocks, continuing commitment on the part of donors, and improved logistical and distributional capability either now exist or can readily be brought into being. An important international early-warning system coordinated by the United Nations Food and Agriculture Organization was established in 1975, and several regional systems are in operation as well. Some 2 to 4 million metric tons of emergency food aid have been distributed annually in recent years. With the continuing commitment of donors, it should be possible to place emergency stocks near where they may be most useful and to deliver them when and where needed.

> *"The key obstacle to eliminating deaths due to famine remains the destruction or interdiction of civilian food supplies in zones of armed conflict."*

Famine and War

In all of the countries that have reported famine so far in the 1990s—Angola, Ethiopia, Liberia, Mozambique, Somalia, and Sudan—armed conflict has been a major cause. Indeed, "food wars"—conflicts in which a principal feature has been the destruction or interdiction of civilian food supplies or of resources to produce food—became a consistent feature of the Cold War years. For example, in 1989, there were 19 such food wars. In the 1990s, armed conflict became the dominant cause of famine worldwide.

Thus, the key obstacle to eliminating deaths due to famine remains the destruction or interdiction of civilian food supplies in zones of armed conflict. The rudiments of the international protection of civilians' right to food exist in the form of the Universal Declaration of Human Rights, the International Covenant on Economic, Social, and Cultural Rights, and most specifically, the 1977 protocols to the Geneva Conventions of 1949 that prohibit starvation of civilians as a means of combat. Ad hoc humanitarian efforts to deliver food to civilian populations in conflict-torn Mozambique and southern Sudan had some success in staving off mass starvation. But the efforts broke down with the eruption into armed conflict after the Cold War of political, ethnic, religious, and even clan-based rivalries. Old and new conflicts threaten civilian food supplies in Afghanistan, Angola, Azerbaijan, Bosnia-Hercegovina, Croatia, the Kurdish regions of Turkey, Iran and Iraq, Liberia, Mozambique, Somalia, and Sudan.

The current efforts in Somalia follow in the path of the "corridors of tranquillity" established in southern Sudan (routes successfully negotiated with the help of strong international pressure to provide cross-border relief within that zone of conflict) and the opening of the port of Massawa in the Eritrean-Ethiopian conflict. Another precedent was the direct use of force by the Allied Coalition to ensure a protected Kurdish enclave in Iraq. These efforts paved the way for the military force led by the United States that has provided the necessary space for humanitarian relief operations in Somalia.

If the operations in Somalia are to be a turning point in the long struggle against famine, they must lead to the development of rules of humanitarian intervention. The reluctance of some to intervene in Somalia and of many to undertake similar operations in Bosnia arises partly from the sense that the United States and the world are now on a slippery slope. Many Americans are concerned that intervention will bring, at worst, other Lebanons and Vietnams or, at best, continued tasks and moral fatigue for the United States in its role as the would-be world policeman. For the world, intervention conjures up fears that the now lone superpower will interfere in the affairs of other nations wherever its imperial designs or concerns raised by CNN's television coverage take it. Thus, while there is a pressing need to move along the process of humanitarian intervention if we are to realize the promise of ending deaths from famine, there is also a need to take the process beyond the media-mediated moral claims that require both public exposure and enormous death tolls to bring forth action. (A beginning can be found in the Providence Principles on Humanitarian Action in Armed Conflict, which identify the primacy of life-threatening suffering wherever it may occur and assert that assistance should be appropriate to local needs and given

> *"No nation has the right to starve its own or other people."*

in a nonpartisan and open manner.) Most important, and most controversially, when humanitarianism and sovereignty clash, a new understanding of sovereign rights must be developed that defers to urgent humanitarian needs. Stated simply, no nation has the right to starve its own or other people.

Beyond such emerging principles, there is a need for a new system of humanitarian assistance, a graduated response that uses armed intervention only as a last resort. Such a system would require the various United Nations agencies, the International Committee of the Red Cross, the regional intergovernmental groups, and the international and national nongovernmental organizations to be prepared for a range of appropriate responses to the humanitarian needs of civilian populations in conflict, including protection by armed forces and preventive enforcement of the peace.

Into the Unknown

Our intervention in Somalia takes us into the truly unknown territory of world order and disorder, of conflicts of principles and claims of compassion, and the reach and overreach of power. If we are not to be overwhelmed by the difficulty of traveling into the unknown, it is useful to recall the true length and nature of the journey.

Genocidal Governments Create Famine

by Kurt Jonassohn

About the author: *Kurt Jonassohn is a professor of sociology and the director of the Montreal Institute for Genocide and Human Rights Studies at Concordia University, Montreal, Canada.*

Scholarly attempts to understand the causes of genocide, the appearance of famines, and the generating of flows of refugees have been seriously hampered by overspecialization. Each of these areas has given rise to a considerable body of literature, which, however, rarely shows signs of familiarity with that of the others.

Genocides, Famine, and Refugees

Genocides, including the Nazi Holocaust, have been written about very widely. Most scholars deal with only one genocide as either of the Armenians or of the Jews. Only recently has a small, but growing, group of scholars begun to apply a comparative approach to the study of genocides. Yet, not enough attention has been paid by either of these groups to the deliberate use of hunger and starvation on the part of the genocidal power. Nor has there been much scholarly concern with refugees, the survivors who have managed to escape the killings.

Famine is an age-old phenomenon that has periodically ravaged mankind. Episodes of famine have been studied and written about at great length. Most of the literature attributes the outbreak of famine to natural events, as was appropriate throughout much of history. But since the middle of the twentieth century the technology of storing, preserving and transporting food stuffs in large quantities over long distances has made it possible to deal with natural disasters so efficiently that famines should no longer be expected. But famines do persist and continue to be blamed on natural events. Only a very small portion of the huge famine literature deals with so-called man-made famines. Authors using this term deal with cases of famine that were the unanticipated consequence of

Kurt Jonassohn, "Famine, Genocide, and Refugees," *Society*, September/October 1993. Copyright 1993, Transaction Publishers. Reprinted with permission.

misguided policies.

The Chinese government for example, as Roderick MacFarquhar and John Fairbank write in *The Cambridge History of China*, "insisted that the peasants leave the land fallow in 1959 to avoid losses from not having enough storage facilities to handle the anticipated surplus." The anticipated surplus naturally never materialized and the land that remained fallow contributed to the famine. Hardly anyone deals with the deliberate and intentional use of famine as a method of persecution or as a weapon in conflicts. This seems all the more surprising since hunger, starvation, and famine have been used in this manner throughout history as in the many cases when a city was besieged until it either ran out of food and water or short of both.

> *"Refugees fleeing from famines are not fleeing from natural event, but are victims of persecution and even genocide."*

Refugees, too, have become an increasingly serious problem due to their dramatically rising numbers. The demands on the resources of international and humanitarian organizations are escalating. Although a variety of policies that might help cope with the growing numbers of refugees are being examined and explored, until recently, there has been little awareness of the fact that refugees fleeing from famines are not fleeing from natural event, but are victims of persecution and even genocide.

Two related questions must be raised here. First, how would our understanding and explanations be affected if we were to study genocide, famine, and refugees not in isolation, but as different aspects of the same phenomenon? Second, how would our understanding be changed if the flow of refugees were regarded as an early warning sign of a catastrophe in the making?

These two questions are, of course, intimately related: were we to accept the information carried by refugees as factual, and were we to develop a more complex understanding of the genocidal process, then the international community would at least have the opportunity to intervene. Whether anyone will take advantage of this opportunity will depend more on political and economic considerations than on humanitarian concerns.

Definitions

Starvation and famine are generally defined as lack of food and water in sufficient quantities to sustain life. But even this simple definition has become problematic. As Robert Kates and Sara Millman have pointed out in the chapter "On Ending Hunger: The Lessons of History" in *Hunger in History:*

> . . . for the first time in human history it is possible to contemplate the end of food scarcity, famine, and mass starvation. With the exception of its intentional creation or perpetration as a weapon of war or genocide, a combination of effective early-warning systems, national, and global emergency food re-

serves, and improved experience with distribution and food-for-work programs has brought the end of famine well within sight.

This raises the question of whether an up-to-date definition of famine and starvation should not include a reference to the intent of the perpetrator?

Genocide and refugees have been defined by the United Nations on separate occasions with quite conflicting results. The United Nations Convention on the Prevention and Punishment of the Crime of Genocide restricts the victims of genocide to members of "a national, ethnical, racial or religious group as such."

The Convention Relating to the Status of Refugees states, "The term 'refugee' shall apply to any person who . . . owing to well-founded fear of being persecuted for reasons of race, religion, nationality, membership of a particular social group or political opinion, is outside the country of his nationality. . . ."

These definitions of genocides and refugees, unsatisfactory for many reasons, have given rise to much critical examination. When taken in context, two contradictions become apparent. The two definitions define different groups and the second one defines a geographical area, which the first one does not. The difficulty becomes clearer when we think of a group of refugees fleeing from genocide. They will be recognized as refugees only if they are outside the country of their nationality, and they will be recognized as victims of genocide only if they belong to one of the four specified groups.

> *"Most contemporary famines are the result of planned campaigns against victim groups and not the result of natural catastrophes."*

Most observers agree, however, that victims of genocide may belong to groups other than those mentioned, and that refugees may be found inside the country of their nationality. Victims of genocide are members of any group that a perpetrator tries to eliminate. A refugee is any person fleeing from life threatening violence.

Deliberate Actions

The major activity of the United Nations High Commission for Refugees and of most NGOs (non-governmental organizations) that deal with famines is to provide the victims with food, shelter, and medical supplies. There is no question that these supplies are needed, but the need is often not the result of shortages, but of the deliberate withholding of available staples. For instance, in the fall of 1992 the evidence was quite clear that sufficient quantities of the essentials were in the pipeline in Somalia. The problem was not shortage but distribution. Supplies go to those with the guns, not to those with the empty stomachs.

In Bosnia the victims of "ethnic cleansing" are starving while Serbia is exporting food to Russia in exchange for technology and weapons. This tragedy is reaching comic proportions when it is announced that warships will enforce the embargo against Serbia by patrolling the Adriatic coast while it is generally known that violations of the embargo are taking place primarily via the Danube.

Most contemporary famines are the result of planned campaigns against victim groups and not the result of natural catastrophes. In fact, premeditated use of starvation has been a central part of many genocides. The attraction of this method for perpetrators is manifold. It conserves food resources that may already be in short supply. It allows the perpetrators to hide their real motives behind an apparent natural disaster. Because it requires neither advanced technology nor a highly developed bureaucracy, this method can be applied by even the poorest country. It weakens the victims physically and lowers their resistance to epidemics, while undermining their morale and their ability to resist. And eventually it kills.

Understanding the deliberate use of starvation as a form of persecution should and can have wide-ranging consequences for action. It forcefully brings out the fact that humanitarian supplies reach the victims only rarely. In the majority of cases such supplies enrich the perpetrators who will sell them on black markets and use them in bartering for arms and ammunition. The alternative requires the international community to establish enforcement mechanisms for the various United Nations conventions designed to deal with such human rights violations.

Evidence of Genocide

Famines are evidence of genocide, not of food shortages. It is, of course, quite possible to carry out genocide without first starving the victims, but such cases have become rare in the late-twentieth century. If there is an advantage to the victims, it is in favor of starvation because of the slowness with which it escalates to famine. That extra time creates at least the possibility of resistance, of outside help arriving in time, or of escaping. It is the information carried by such early escapees that ought to alert the world to the need for action.

We know very little about the onset of genocides, and obtaining accurate information in moments of crisis is often very difficult. This particular quest for knowledge is not only inspired by scholarly curiosity, but by desire to help the victims of persecution, and by the possibility, in theory at least, of interfering in the evil designs of the perpetrators. However, either possibility requires a base of accurate information on which to develop appropriate policies and actions. But such accurate information is remarkably difficult to obtain by conventional means.

In cases of incipient genocides, the usual channels of information are almost always blocked or distorted. The perpetrator country usually denies annihilating a group as well as any intention of doing so. Visas to enter such countries are often impossible to obtain, access to the relevant areas is predictably blocked, or only brief, stage-managed visits are arranged to convince outside observers that nothing out of the ordinary

> *"Famines are evidence of genocide, not of food shortages."*

is taking place. Information from the perpetrator governments, if available at all, is full of distorted facts and/or denials.

Other obvious sources of information are foreign diplomats, journalists, Red Cross workers, and representatives of other humanitarian aid organizations as well as academic specialists. Unfortunately, evidence thus obtained is also suspect because the observers are likely to omit or distort information that might get them evicted from the perpetrator country, or denied entry in the future. Finally, there are those emigrés and refugees who have managed to escape in time. Their testimony is almost always considered equally suspect because of obvious personal bias.

> *"The lack of accurate information played a decisive role in the case of the Ethiopian famine."*

None of this information reaches the outside directly. It is always predigested for us by the media and by academic and diplomatic experts who add their own biases and ideological interpretations. The results thus distorted are often responsible for much suffering and large numbers of deaths. Why should this be so? Because reality gets lost in the process of transmission. Evidence presented by the perpetrator governments and their sympathizers receives credibility. Ideological interpretations are accorded more attention than simple facts. Evidence from refugees is totally discredited. Thus, any conceivable policy or action is very likely to fail because it is based on deceptions, misinterpretations, lack of accurate information, or downright lies.

An early assessment of the accuracy of victims' testimonies was done by Marie Syrkin. In the fall of 1945, in the wake of the Second World War, she took the first passenger ship that left New York for the Middle East. Her purpose was to interview survivors of Hitler's death camps and participants in Jewish resistance, the majority of whom then were to be found in what was then Palestine. The results of her investigation were published in 1947 and were subsequently reissued thirty years later.

In that interval a great deal of documentary evidence has become available, as well as much more testimony, and has been carefully analyzed and verified by many professionals. However, Syrkin notes in her introduction to the new edition that these materials support the evidence of the witnesses she had interviewed as essentially accurate. She adds that there was little she would omit now, though, of course, there is much that she could now add. The important point is that these early interviews, with victims soon after their escape, yielded essentially accurate data.

Famine in Ethiopia

Jason Clay and Bonnie Holcomb illustrated dramatically how the lack of accurate information played a decisive role in the case of the Ethiopian famine. While the world was shocked into action by the news of mass starvation, nobody seemed willing to inquire into the causes of the famine. Humanitarian organizations poured in substantial quantities of money and materials without a sound base of information. Most of them accepted whatever the Ethiopian government said and restricted their activities to the places to which they were given access. At the same time, they refused to contribute any money at all to research designed to elicit accurate information for fear of possible adverse reaction by the Ethiopian government.

Although their humanitarian motives were admirable, their actions were to a very great extent misguided in that they perpetuated the situation that had produced the famine in the first place. Even their food distribution program was of limited assistance because only a little food reached those in need and then only in certain areas, specified by the government.

One of the important indicators that most helping organizations seem to ignore consistently is the meaning of the famine they seek to alleviate. At the present stage of the world's development serious starvation among a group is one of the first sure signs that this group has been singled out for victimization. Starvation due to natural causes can now be dealt with by appropriate governmental action. Man-made starvation that is the unintended consequence of dysfunctional social organization or misguided social policies can equally be avoided if appropriate actions are taken as soon as it is recognized.

Government Action

Ethiopia and Kenya in the 1980s provide a most instructive demonstration of government action in a crisis brought about by crop failures due to lack of rain. No serious famine conditions arose anywhere in Kenya because the government reacted to this emergency by importing food stuffs and distributing them through the established wholesale and retail channels. The media did not even pay attention to the crop failures in Kenya.

The Ethiopian famine, on the other hand, received world-wide attention without a discussion of its man-made origin and without appropriate action that such a discussion might have prompted. Neither governments nor NGOs seem to have drawn the obvious conclusions from the example set by Kenya.

"Starvation due to natural causes can now be dealt with by appropriate governmental action."

The significance of Clay's and Holcomb's contribution lies in the fact that they showed that a great deal of information can be collected in a short time and at very modest cost. They were never granted a visa for Ethiopia and therefore were limited to interviewing those refugees who had reached the Sudan. They were fully aware of the problems of interviews with refugees and the use of the information thus obtained. Being denied access to Ethiopia forced them to be very careful with their research design and to pay particular attention to validity and reliability. The results demonstrate, as did earlier research, that refugees are excellent sources of information provided the information is collected and analyzed by competent researchers.

These results, as well as subsequent information, confirm that the famine in Ethiopia was man-made, that starvation was deliberately used by the government of Haile-Mariam Mengistu against groups opposed to it, and that the Western assistance programs did very little to change that scenario. Unfortunately it takes more than accurate information to stop or prevent a genocide. But without information any action is likely to be misguided and ineffectual.

Clay and Holcomb demonstrated conclusively that it is possible to obtain reliable information from refugees in spite of the trauma they have suffered from their experiences. Whether governments and NGOs are prepared to accept such information and act on it is quite another matter. But in the future they will not be able to discount the information obtained from refugees quite so cavalierly.

World Refugees

More recently, Bill Frelick took up this issue in the *World Refugee Survey* (1988) because genocides have become more frequent and are responsible for increasing refugee flows. He addresses several significant issues that will have to be addressed if there is going to be international intervention. Even when news leaks out, barriers of disbelief remain and need to be overcome. In order to do so it is important to produce evidence of intent, which is an essential part of the

"Studying refugee flows, genocides, and famines as isolated, independent phenomena can only lead to erroneous interpretations of results."

definition of genocide. Perpetrators of genocide only rarely declare their intent as openly as did Hitler in *Mein Kampf* or Hujjatu'l-Islam Qazai, president of the revolutionary court in Shiraz, justifying the destruction of Iran's Baha'i community. The credibility the world accorded the news of the persecution of the Baha'is contributed greatly to generating support and helped to interrupt the killings.

Therefore, other kinds of evidence of intent need to be examined. Here both the number of refugees and their testimony play a crucial role. Frelick suggests a variety of methods for obtaining this evidence and for establishing its credibility. Though most of these methods are the stock-in-trade of anthropologists and sociologists who engage in field research, they are frequently ignored by journalists, diplomats, and the representatives of the various aid organizations. These methods include such elementary measures as establishing the credibility of the interviewer, finding a private setting that excludes peer group pressures, establishing trust, using reliable translators, verifying the accuracy of the translation, and matching the sex of the interviewer with that of the interviewee.

While such methods may appear elementary to the social scientist, they are often very difficult to implement in the field. However, they are absolutely crucial if the evidence collected from refugees is going to be accorded credibility by the world.

A Willingness to Act

Studying refugee flows, genocides, and famines as isolated, independent phenomena can only lead to erroneous interpretations of results. Treating them as components of a larger process is an essential part of their problematic. It is only a part because it is the essential basis for intervention, but it does not insure that such interventions will in fact take place. For that to happen, international meetings and organizations need to acquire the willingness to act on their various pronouncements on human rights, instead of merely passing resolutions.

World Bank Policies Contribute to World Hunger

by Atherton Martin

About the author: *Atherton Martin, an official of the Development Institute, works with grassroots groups in the Caribbean. The following is taken from his keynote address to a 1993 World Bank Conference, entitled "Overcoming Global Hunger."*

In the last 500 years, there have been four major threats to the survival of humanity—(1) slavery, (2) fascism, (3) hunger and (4) environmental degradation. One of these has been overcome—slavery! To a greater or lesser extent, fascism, hunger and environmental degradation persist. Slavery was overcome by the action of people in the South and the North who were outraged by the very thought of one human being owning another human being!

The other threats to our humanity . . . await the action of people who are similarly outraged at the thought [of] the pain and indignity of hunger and [who declare that] the horror of starvation of even one human being will not be tolerated.

We Refuse to Accept Hunger

As the representatives of NGOs (non-governmental organizations), many of us from the countries of the world normally associated with the phenomenon of hunger, we simply refuse to accept hunger as a feature of life on earth. As NGOs we are convinced that an end to hunger is not only possible but imperative. We believe that for every person going hungry anywhere in this world, there should be a Tony Hall willing to go to extraordinary lengths to draw attention to the shameless fact that we have the capacity to prevent that indignity. [Hall went on a twenty-two-day fast in April 1993 to protest congressional inaction on hunger issues and draw attention to the plight of hungry people.]

We salute the courage and persistence of that US Congressman, who when all else failed, was prepared to resort to embarrassing the US Congress, the US public, and the world into paying attention to the tragedy of hunger.

We also salute the courageous persons throughout the world and inside the World Bank, who have received that message from Rep. Tony Hall and decided to act on it.

NGOs Have a Special Role

As NGOs we believe that we have a special role in this and other efforts aimed at drawing attention to the problem of global hunger. Simply put, we are prepared to be the conscience of many people in rich and poor countries who see hunger, reject it and have decided to end it!

We are prepared to be the conscience of those who understand the cause of the deepening crisis of global hunger as it relates to development policies and strategies, many of which have been advocated and financed by the World Bank and other international financial institutions over the past 50 years.

We are prepared to be the eyes and ears of the millions who are unable to be here, who are unable to read your documents, who are unable to see the opulence of your work stations, who are unable to be here to tell you themselves what it means to go hungry! We are your conscience saying, "No! Enough! Let us put a stop to this!"

To put a stop to this means that we must change the way we do business! For the Bank, probably the single most critical institution relating to the issues of global economic activity in recent decades, this means changing the way that things are done inside the Bank, between the Bank and other financial institutions, as well as between the Bank and its client governments and the people who are governed.

Needed World Bank Changes

Instead of administering structural adjustment programs to our countries, the Bank needs to focus on making adjustments to its own operations that would allow it, for example:

- To establish procedures and mechanisms that allow the experiences and the expertise of poor women, workers, farmers, youth and others to inform and shape policies and programs of the Bank.
- To subject itself and its work to the scrutiny of those same groups who are most affected by its actions, and to be responsive and accountable to the poor in whose name it addresses these issues of hunger.
- To make the links between its policies and programs in such areas as trade, education, health, housing, nutrition and other important spheres of human life, and the phenomenon of global hunger, and to insist on an integrated approach to the design and implementation of Bank policies and programs.

> *"The medicine of structural adjustment has not helped stop global hunger."*

68

- To admit that the medicine of structural adjustment has not helped stop global hunger, which means that the Bank should stop trying to administer that potion to our countries.
- To agree to regular interaction with those who work with and represent the poor so that NGOs from the countries of the South, together with our partner NGOs from the North, would make year-round input into the process of transforming the Bank into an instrument for development that is responsive to the needs of the poor and hungry among us.

People at the Center

It is already clear from this that our perception of economics places people at the center and is substantially different from the notion of economics that is espoused by the Bank.

Lest we be misunderstood, however, we wish to make it clear that NGOs recognize the need for international trade as one means of stimulating economic activity. However, we in turn ask that the Bank recognize the need for trade arrangements that not only earn foreign exchange but meet the needs of the people for jobs, housing, health care, food and other life essentials.

In the same vein, if the Bank accepts the need for large developed economies to protect their microchip industries and the intellectual property rights that go with it, we insist that it recognize the need for countries such as ours to protect national and regional markets for our products.

> *"One more decade of . . . 'business as usual' and there will be so many hungry people . . . that even the actions of a transformed World Bank would be to no avail."*

We note that such measures on the part of poor countries attract the label "protectionist" and "unfair trading practice," and often result in economic retaliation. We also note that the Bank is often in the role of prodding the compliance of poor countries with trade liberalization as a conditionality for financing.

We note, however, that even when large countries resort to direct cash subsidies to protect their own producers, as in the case with rice, wheat, corn and many other commodities in the United States, for example, these measures are not considered protectionist, they do not attract retaliatory measures, and the Bank, among others, remains silent on these blatant violations of the principles of "free trade."

Poor Countries Cannot Afford Free Trade

A case in point: The United States has only this year [1993] used its PL 480 food aid program in Jamaica to force Guyana's rice out of that Caribbean market. Rice is a commodity which attracts some of the highest subsidies in the United States, and we have calculated that whereas Caribbean rice producers in

Guyana receive no subsidies, just one of the five rice support programs in place in the United States pays an average of US $50,000 per year to each rice farmer. If this is the free trade that we are being told about, it is no wonder that poor countries cannot engage in free trade! We simply cannot afford it.

What does all this business of trade have to do with hunger? Well, the Bank insists that we produce more crops for export since that is the way we will earn foreign exchange which can then be used to buy cheap, subsi-

> *"The standard prescriptions for growth have not ended poverty or hunger."*

dized food from the rice countries. But by insisting on this dependence on a narrow range of commodities for export, it is destroying one of the only safety nets that poor countries can afford—the diversity of mixed farming which addresses some of our food needs.

How many of you would invest all the money that you have saved up for your daughter's college education in the option on the stock market? That is exactly what you are asking us to do.

Does the Bank have any alternative? Certainly!

The conditions attached to lending the Bank's resources can be tied increasingly to rewards for efficient management of scarce resources; food security based on local production; the effective involvement of women in the production, preparation, distribution and trading of goods and services; the processing and manufacture of goods that make use of local raw materials and foster linkages between sectors of the economy; the creation of jobs for the armies of young people that populate our rural and urban areas; and other such indicators of a development that is sustainable, equitable, participatory and self-reliant.

The practice of providing loans for development projects, yet insisting that most of the money be spent to purchase high-priced equipment and personnel from the rich countries of the North, defeats the purpose of national self-sufficiency and regional integration and undermines any chance we might have to develop South-South trade or the capacity to become globally competitive. This can be stopped.

Of course the Bank can change! The problem is that a Bank run by people whose life experience is light-years removed from that of those whom it purports to serve may not be able to understand that its policies and programs in support of cash crop production, export-led growth, large-scale dams and mega-hydro-electric plants often destroy the capacity for food production of previously self-provisioning communities, exposing people to food shortages and eventually hunger.

Let us not forget that Congressman Hall's fast was about hunger. Hunger here, hunger there, hunger everywhere—even in this richest country of the world. Let us [also] not forget, however, that it has taken a 21-day fast by one US Congressman to bring the World Bank to the table to eat of the food of reality. The suffering and death of thousands, hundreds of thousands, even millions of African and other children, women and men from lack of food was not enough to do that.

The Bank can let it be known that from today the knowledge, skills and expertise of people from the South and the North will be mobilized and focused on diagnosing, treating and curing the global malady of hunger. One more decade of structural adjustment and "business as usual" and there will be so many hungry people all over the world, so much degradation of our soils, so much pollution of our waters and our air, such complete destruction of our forests, so much debt, so much inequitable trade, such widespread disease, such a breakdown in family and community cohesion, such civil conflict, that even the actions of a transformed World Bank would be to no avail.

Now is the time to change the partners, to change the process, to change the tools of diagnosis and analysis, to prescribe and administer a different treatment to an earth and its people that are urgently in need of intensive care.

. . . This will be so only if the Bank and others, including the US Congress, are big enough to admit that change is needed, big enough to admit that the Bank's staff, as talented as many of them are, do not have a patent on the skills of economic analysis, planning and management for growth and development.

The Bank must also be big enough to admit that there are people, even in the countries where hunger and starvation are endemic, who have the skills, the experience and the commitment to play a critical role in the campaign to end hunger.

Center on Hungry People's Needs

. . . The only chance that the Bank has to be a part of this campaign to end hunger, once and for all, is to ensure that the needs of those with the greatest stake in ending hunger—the hungry—become the centerpiece of the Bank's imperative for action.

NGOs, by virtue of our evolution into institutions that know and understand these needs intimately, have the unique capacity to facilitate this new partnership, this new contract for survival, this new grand alliance for a world free from the horror of hunger. The Bank for its part is challenged to be a sensible, flexible and reliable partner with the people, especially those in greatest need.

If the horror of global hunger forces the Bank to do one thing, it should be to change the terms of engagement and to do all that is necessary to make it possible for local people, poor people, hungry people, to accept the Bank as a partner in this quest to end hunger. Our message to the Bank, therefore, is simple, "Come to terms with the fact that the standard prescriptions for growth have not ended poverty or hunger. The chance for a change begins and ends with the people on the ground because, very simply, nothing grows from the top down—not trees, not economies, and certainly not people."

Desertification Is Not a Serious Threat

by William K. Stevens

About the author: *William K. Stevens is a contributor to the* New York Times.

Common wisdom has it that the deserts of the world are on the march, steadily expanding, permanently converting pastures and croplands to sand dunes, and that human mistreatment of the drylands that flank the deserts is responsible.

But scientists using the most up-to-date investigative techniques have found no evidence that this is true, at least in the case of the Sahara and its immediate environs, everyone's favorite and most serious example of what is called "desertification." In view of the lack of evidence, many experts suspect that the threatening image of encroaching deserts may be more myth than fact.

The findings, based largely on satellite measurements, are forcing a reassessment of just what is happening in the arid and semi-arid drylands along the desert's perimeter, which have turned out to be more resilient than once thought. . . . Some leaders of the international effort to halt drylands degradation have backed away from the idea that deserts are expanding. In fact, they and others say, the very term desertification confuses the issue and obscures what is really going on in the drylands.

Emerging Evidence

No one denies that what is taking place in the drylands is serious. As in much of the rest of the world, growing population and economic pressures are depleting the soil, damaging vegetation and natural ecosystems, depressing agricultural yields and threatening the future survival of those who live in the regions between deserts and more humid grasslands. Drylands' sparse rainfall and inevitable droughts make them more vulnerable than more humid regions.

The degradation is serious enough to the 900 million people who live in these regions, which cover a quarter of the earth's land mass. But are the drylands turning into permanent deserts? Not likely, according to the emerging scientific evidence.

Images obtained by the National Aeronautics and Space Administration from meteorological satellites show that from 1980 through 1990, the boundary between the Sahara and the Sahel drylands region on its southern border—actually a vegetative transition zone rather than a sharp line—did not move steadily south, as conventional wisdom would have it.

The Shifting Boundary of the Desert

The maximum, minimum and average latitude of the vegetation boundary where the Sahara meets the Sahel (to the south), based on information from weather satellites from 1980 to 1990.

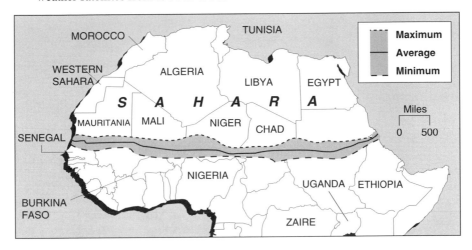

Source: Dr. Compton J. Tucker and *The New York Times*

Rather, the vegetation line moved back and forth in conjunction with rainfall patterns, creeping northward in wetter years and southward in drier ones. The shifts from one year to the next ranged from 30 to 150 miles along the border, but no overall trend could be discerned one way or the other.

Swedish scientists at the University of Lund, combining a variety of data collected by satellites and aircraft with ground observations, examined the Sahara-Sahel border in the Sudan for the period 1962 to 1984, when the border was thought to be moving southward. The studies found that this was not happening. The Swedish scientists also found, contrary to what some had argued, no evidence that patches of

> *"Are the drylands turning into permanent deserts? Not likely."*

desert were spreading outward from villages and water holes within the drylands area of the Sahel. And they found no changes in vegetation cover and crop productivity that could not be explained by variations in rainfall.

Major oscillations between extended dry and wet climate patterns are a normal and governing fact of life in the drylands, said Dr. James E. Ellis, an ecologist who heads the Center for Environment and Sustainable Agriculture, a research group in Morrillton, Arkansas, run by the Winrock Corporation, a private voluntary organization.

Long-term rainfall records show that the climate in Africa's drylands has shifted back and forth between periods of extended drought and higher rainfall for at least the last 10,000 years. On the basis of long-term studies in Kenya, Dr. Ellis believes that climate keeps the drylands in a continual state of disequilibrium, and is a bigger influence on the dynamics of drylands ecology than people are.

The Role of Climate

While the evidence taken together suggests that climate is the major influence on crops and natural ecosystems in the Sahel, it does not yet prove the case. The scientific record is too sparse and short at this point, says Dr. Compton J. Tucker of the space agency's Goddard Space Flight Center, who conducted the 1980–1990 satellite studies. Forty to 50 years of observations may be necessary to determine for sure whether the desert is spreading and, if so, whether climate or human activity is most responsible.

The evidence does not mean that deserts are not spreading, but simply that "we can't find it," says Dr. Ulf Hellden, the leader of the Swedish team. Nevertheless, he said, "our hypothesis is that climate is responsible

> *"We can explain 70, perhaps 80 percent of the food productivity variability with rainfall statistics."*

for whatever land degradation is taking place" in the Sahel. "We know we can explain 70, perhaps 80 percent of the food productivity variability with rainfall statistics, which leaves another 20 to 30 percent we cannot explain," he said.

The prime candidate for explaining that 20 to 30 percent is human activity, argues W. Franklin G. Cardy, a Canadian who directs the Nairobi-based desertification control program of the United Nations Environment Program, or UNEP, which has led the struggle to halt drylands degradation. Scientists have identified a number of factors contributing to land degradation in the Sahel and other arid regions. Cattle, camels and goats overgraze the land. Excessive grazing and cultivation by fast-growing populations reduce vegetation and encourage soil erosion by wind and water. In wet years in some localities, herders move farther north in search of new stretches of greener grass. Farmers move in behind them and plow up the land. When dry years return, the herders return to find the land plowed up, while the farmers cannot get a crop and the soil blows away, just as it did in the American dust bowl of the 1930's.

"There is no doubt in my mind" that excessive grazing and cultivation are causing serious land degradation in drylands, said Dr. David Hillel, an environmental scientist, hydrologist and soil expert at the University of Massachusetts at Amherst.

Not least of the problems is that when precipitation does return to degraded land, it takes only a little rainfall to cause much erosion. One problem, Mr. Cardy said, is that it is "extremely difficult" to measure land degradation scientifically.

"It's invisible, essentially," he said. "The farmer knows he or she has less and less crop, knows that it's not going to be sustainable. The farmer will tell you, but not quantifiably."

> *"Scientific evidence did not confirm any human-made trend toward desert-like conditions."*

In the Sahel, the problem has been exacerbated in the last 25 years by below-average rainfall, according to the conclusions of international experts who met in Sweden to examine the situation in 1990. This has led some experts to wonder whether any concern over desertification would have emerged had the last quarter-century been a wet cycle rather than a dry one.

The group that met in Sweden also concluded that scientific evidence did not confirm any human-made trend toward desert-like conditions. Rather, it supported the view that dryland ecosystems are resilient and bounce back after a drought. The scientists noted that population growth could reduce this resilience, but they added that outward migrations when conditions got bad enough could allow the land to recover. The scientists did not rule out the possibility of a future trend toward desert conditions as a result of human activity.

The proposition that deserts are expanding dates to the early years of this century. The idea that regenerating drylands on the edge of the deserts would stop the spread emerged at about the same time. Over the years, anecdotal evidence convinced many scientists, development experts and much of the public that deserts were indeed advancing. By the 1970's, this view had long since moved into the mainstream; in 1972, the United States Agency for International Development asserted that the Sahara was moving southward at 30 miles a year. But many scientists in time came to see the anecdotal evidence as unconvincing. Go to the drylands in the dry season of a drought year, they pointed out, and the land will certainly look like a desert. But in many cases, they added, the same land would look different in a wet year.

As the new evidence has emerged in the last decade, UNEP, for one, has modified its view considerably. Mr. Cardy calls the concept of expanding deserts and advancing sand dunes "largely invalid." And he believes, along with Dr. Hillel and others, that the term "desertification" should be jettisoned.

A Political Artifact

It persists, Mr. Cardy and others say, mainly as a political artifact, a way to call attention to one regional expression of the global problem of land degradation, and thereby attract financial assistance. African countries, in fact, extracted the promise of a desertification treaty at the 1992 Earth Summit in Rio de Janeiro as the price of their support of other countries on other issues.

And so the term desertification hangs on, though its definition was enlarged in Rio to encompass more than human activity as a cause of deterioration of drylands. The definition adopted by the Rio delegates reads: "Desertification is land degradation in arid, semi-arid and dry sub-humid areas resulting from various factors, including climatic variations and human activities." No mention of desert encroachment. . . .

Unless the characteristics of the drylands are documented according to scientific standards, said the scientists who met in Sweden in 1990, "there is a risk that the desertification issues will become a political and development fiction rather than a scientific fact."

Chapter 2

Is Hunger a
Serious Problem
in the United States?

CURRENT CONTROVERSIES

Chapter Preface

The measurement of hunger depends in part on its definition. To most people in the developed countries, hunger is a relatively mild, temporary discomfort that might result from missing a meal. Few U.S. citizens will ever experience the severity of hunger endured by victims of famine such as occurred in Somalia in 1992, claiming over 300,000 lives. Hunger of that magnitude seems remote to Americans, existing only as media images of a distant nightmare.

Many commentators insist, however, that hunger of a less dramatic nature is pervasive in American society. In the early 1990s, various organizations published studies purporting that hunger was a serious problem among the nation's children. In 1991, the Food Research and Action Center (FRAC) concluded that one in eight children under the age of twelve had been hungry at some time during the previous year. The Tufts University Center on Hunger, Poverty, and Nutrition Policy stated in 1993 that 18 percent of the nation's children periodically do not have enough to eat. And in 1994, David Beckmann, president of Bread for the World, wrote that "in the United States, every fifth child lives below the poverty line and faces hunger. As a result, many of these children suffer permanent learning and health losses."

Critics reject the idea that large numbers of American children are starving. They contend that hunger-prevention organizations, in an attempt to attract media attention and garner popular support for their cause, exaggerate the problem by redefining "poverty" as "hunger." While many children may indeed live in poverty, critics argue, few suffer from acute hunger or malnutrition. For example, Robert Rector, a policy analyst at the Heritage Foundation, reviewed government surveys of food and nutrient intake and concluded that poor and nonpoor children of all races receive above-adequate amounts of protein and most vitamins and minerals. He concludes that "the current generation of American children—even poor children—is undoubtedly among the best nourished in human history."

Whether—and to what extent—hunger is a serious problem in the United States is the subject of the following chapter.

Hunger Is a Serious Problem in the United States

by Laura Shapiro

About the author: *Laura Shapiro is a senior writer for* Newsweek, *a weekly newsmagazine.*

Eileen is nervous, but she's hungry, too. She downs a plateful of American chop suey and two dishes of red gelatin. This isn't what she's used to—eating dinner at a soup kitchen in Lynn, Massachusetts—but neither is much else in her current life. Eileen, 34, grew up in the comfortable Boston suburb of Belmont—"with a silver spoon in my mouth," she says. In 1993 she had a $42,000-a-year job as a hospital lab technician. Since then she has lost job, apartment and boyfriend. She and her 13-year-old daughter went on welfare and moved into public housing. In January 1994, Eileen signed up for food stamps. "It's very humiliating," she says. Each month she gets $130 in food coupons, but now there are two weeks to go until the next allotment, and no food in the house. Already this month she has picked up groceries from a Salem food pantry—soup, hot dogs, noodles, crackers, beans and peanut butter. But it's hard to stretch the food when her daughter's friends visit constantly, and constantly eat. So here they are. Her daughter was reluctant to eat at a soup kitchen because she was afraid it would be full of bums. Now she pushes away her tray after eating half her dinner and says she's not very hungry. Eileen is frantic. If the girl gets hungry at home later, there won't be anything to give her. "Next time you have to make sure you eat every drop," she says angrily.

A Startling Statistic

And that's the end of the story—except for all the other people in it. In March 1994 Second Harvest, a nationwide network of food banks, released a major new study on hunger in America. The results show that more than 25 million Americans, nearly half of them under 17, now make use of food pantries, soup kitchens and other food-distribution programs. That's 1 out of 10 Americans forced to eat at least occasionally on the dole—a startling statistic for one of the world's richest countries. Some poverty experts are skeptical. "I don't believe that many people are hungry," says Robert Haveman, an economist at the University of Wisconsin's poverty-research institute. "People living in poverty are getting food stamps. Maybe they visit a food bank once a year, but that doesn't mean food banks are meeting a nutritional need in the population."

> *"People don't have the money to pay the rent and the heating bills and buy food."*

But people at the front lines of hunger relief say that the study confirms what they see daily: the effects of widespread unemployment and underemployment. According to the survey, nearly a third of the households making use of emergency food programs have someone working full or part time. "People don't have the money to pay the rent and the heating bills *and* buy food," says Shoshana Pakciarz, executive director of Project Bread, which funds emergency feeding programs in Massachusetts. Second Harvest's results jibe with previous hunger surveys by organizations like the Urban Institute and the Food Research and Action Center (FRAC), as well as poverty statistics.

Christine Vladimiroff, executive director of Second Harvest, says it's time for Americans to put aside their assumptions about hunger. "The face of hunger has changed," she says. "It's no longer just the single man on the street. It's children, mothers, the newly unemployed, the working poor."

And it's families like the Williamses—all 12 of them. Easter and Nathaniel Williams of Chicago, both 41, and their children, ages 1 to 19, could teach a thing or two about managing hunger to the newcomers in the ranks. Around the third week of the month, for instance, when food stamps run out, you start letting everyone sleep late. "Then you can combine breakfast and lunch," says Easter. Brunch is rice or maybe oatmeal; dinner is rice or beans. "The trick is to feed them late with a lot of water and then put them to bed," she says. When supplies dwindle, she and Nathaniel skip meals; occasionally the older children do, too.

No Poster Children

American hunger has no poster children, no skeletal famine victims clutching tin plates. Certainly the children in the waiting room of Dr. Deborah Frank's clinic at Boston City Hospital look healthy and cheerful, if a bit skinny, as they munch on peanut butter and graham crackers. But the giggly toddler isn't a toddler at all, she is 6 years old. And the 9-month-old baby weighs as much as an infant of 12 weeks. Frank's clinic, which treats severely malnourished children, is one of eight in Massachusetts, set up in 1984 after a state survey found that 10 percent of low-income children under 5 showed signs of malnutrition. "The kid's whole future is at stake here," says Frank, who runs her own food pantry so that families can take home the high-calorie foods their children need to catch up. Similar clinics are opening across the country.

But most hungry children don't show it. "It's a silent problem," says Christin Driscoll of FRAC, which surveyed children nationally and found 5.5 million underfed. "Maybe they're just a few pounds underweight, or a little shorter. It won't show up in physical exams, but even short-term undernutrition can cause concentration problems. These kids are going to school. But they're falling behind."

At Lyndhurst Elementary School in Baltimore, where more than half of the children are eligible for a free school breakfast, hunger is visible chiefly when school has been closed for a while. "With all the snow days this year, we're sure the children aren't eating well," says Lula Sessoms, a regional cafeteria manager. "The day the children came back to school, breakfast was like, 'Give me something to eat!'" Stephanie Lambert, 10, says she always gets up in time for school breakfast: on a recent morning it was juice, Frosted Flakes, milk, toast and a fried "breakfast bar" of potatoes, ham and egg. If she doesn't eat, she says, "I don't feel like doing my work. I get a headache and my stomach starts hurting."

> *"[The Food Research and Action Center] surveyed children nationally and found 5.5 million underfed."*

Theresa never gets a headache from hunger. At 30, she's been on welfare much of her life and feeds her four kids by faking residence in several Massachusetts towns, so that she can use their emergency food programs. "I'm street smart," she says. She knows that the Salvation Army in Salem is generous, and that St. Mary's Church in Lynn gives out fresh bread on Mondays, but the food pantry is stingy. Often Theresa and her children take home so much food they end up feeding leftovers to the birds. Even the family's pet iguana is provided for: it gets shredded carrots and escarole.

Debate Over Programs

People like Theresa make it tough for hunger activists to argue for increased federal funds. "You could never spend your way out of this problem," says Robert Rector, a policy analyst for family and welfare issues at the Heritage Foundation, a conservative think tank, who is a strong critic of federal anti-hunger programs. He maintains there is no evidence for widespread hunger or undernutrition in America, and dismisses the results of the Second Harvest study as a "pseudodefinition" of hunger. "The more programs you have that hand out food for free, the more people will use them," he says.

"There is some welfare fraud," agrees J. Larry Brown, director of the Center on Hunger, Poverty and Nutrition Policy at Tufts University in Medford, Massachusetts. But he believes it's the economy that prompts most people's visits to food programs, not their desire for free red gelatin. "We could end hunger in a matter of six or eight months," he says, by expanding the food-stamp program and increasing funding for such targeted programs as WIC (Special Supplemental Food Program for Women, Infants and Children). Research backs up Brown's view. WIC, for instance, has successfully reduced the incidence of iron deficiency among low-income children—a deficiency that can lead to cognitive disabilities.

But everyone who knows the faces of American hunger knows that food alone isn't enough. Georgette Lacy, a Chicago welfare mother, remembers seeing two boys, 3 and 5, scavenging for something to eat in her building's garbage incinerator. "Their mother was strung out on rock cocaine," she says. Vladimiroff of Second Harvest acknowledges that supplying dinner is only a temporary solution to a problem rooted in poverty and often entangled in social chaos. "Feeding people is one thing, and ending hunger is another," she says. Her real goal is the latter.

Hunger Is a Serious Problem Among Minorities

by Victor Perlo

About the author: *Victor Perlo is a member of the National Board of the Communist Party, USA.*

In 1991 there were 259 million people in the United States. Of these, 69 million, or 26.6 percent of the total, were racial minorities. These figures, although linked to the 1991 reports of the U.S. Census Bureau, are more accurate than the official underestimation of the official census count, which significantly understated the actual population. It excluded the million-plus people in prisons and jails and other institutions, a sizable proportion of the homeless, and the half-million servicemen stationed overseas. Thus the estimate of 259 million people is 7.8 million more than the official census report.

Nearly half the additional 7.8 million are African Americans: about half the prison population, at least half the homeless, and a significant proportion of the overseas armed forces are Black. Latinos are also disproportionately represented in some of these uncounted categories, although not as much as African Americans. There are also unknown numbers of Latinos in this country without documents and they, of necessity, avoid all contact with authorities. In addition, accounts vary greatly regarding the number of American Indians.

The undercounting of minorities is not an accident. It is a result and an expression of deliberate racist discrimination, especially against African Americans. . . .

Unified Struggle

The racist discrimination and oppression against African Americans is very severe in almost every respect. Segregation, discrimination in access to capital and the extra prices Black people have to pay for insurance, credit, commodities and services are generally most extreme against African Americans.

The racist prejudices and practices of the ruling class against Black people are most overt, consistent and cruel. The increase of police arrests, beatings,

Abridged from Victor Perlo, "Racism and Poverty," *Political Affairs*, February 1993. Reprinted with permission.

murders of [Black people] is alarming.

The struggles of African Americans for equality have had a direct bearing on and objectively aid the struggles of all oppressed peoples.

The similarities and extent of oppression of Blacks, Latinos, Native Americans and Asians are stronger than the differences. Thus the interest of all oppressed peoples is decisive in their united struggles alongside the working class against the racist capitalist class. It is important to understand, at the same time, that the propaganda that white working people, on the whole, are gainers from the oppression of minority peoples is a harmful illusion.

The intensification of racism during the past 20 years coincides with, and is connected to, the all-around offensive against the entire working class in the economic and political arenas. White workers have lost heavily from declining real wages, escalating unemployment, loss of trade union rights. True, their losses have not been as extensive as the losses of the oppressed minority peoples. But that is not a consolation to the hungry white families and workers permanently thrown out of jobs after decades of work.

The losses of the working class cannot be reversed without unity of Black, Brown and white workers, unity that is based on active struggle to bring about a satisfying way of life for workers of all races.

Poverty

Poverty is recognized as an evil in any society. Poverty has been a conspicuous factor throughout the existence of the capitalist system of production. Poverty in the United States today is not merely having a lower-than-average income and not being able to afford luxuries. Poverty, which afflicts many millions of U.S. residents, means suffering. It means hunger. It means evictions and, more and more, homelessness. It means humiliating appeals—sometimes successful and sometimes not— for reluctant official or private handouts in order to survive. It means illness, lack of adequate medical care and for millions it means death.

The scourge of poverty is magnified by racism, an ugly fact of life that constantly permeates the segregated communities of African American, Latino and Native American peoples. And racism has become an increasingly important factor, in some respects decisive, in causing and maintaining large-scale poverty.

"Poverty, which afflicts many millions of U.S. residents, means suffering. It means hunger."

In 1973 there were "only" 23 million people living in poverty, according to official counts. That was a "low" point, having fallen from the 40 million in 1960 before escalating again to 36 million in 1991.

These 36 million—and by more realistic measure, 70 million people—lack nourishing food, decent housing, access to health care and the other components of a standard of living needed for survival and good health. This is a far cry from a state regarded as adequate according to the socially accepted norms in the United States at the end of the 20th century—and still further removed from the "middle class" standard touted by the media as "typical" of the average American family.

> *"The majority of the hungry and homeless are African Americans and Latinos."*

Not only are these millions of Americans without adequate income, but the meager government support measures—won during the periods of the New Deal and the civil rights militancy of the 1960s, the "Great Society"—have been radically curtailed. More and more the approach of government bigwigs, wealthy families, churches and foundations is to depend on "private charity."

From Dickens to Reagan-Bush

From the time of Charles Dickens in England, this device has been used by those responsible for poverty and hunger to bring credit to themselves for good deeds by yielding, with much publicity, a minuscule part of the profits they derived from exploiting the many for minimal alleviation of the privations of a few selected sufferers.

Of course, the number of poor increases when there is a downturn in the business cycle, just as an upturn results in less poverty. And economic conditions were on an upturn in the period 1960–1973; it was a time of rising real wages and higher median family income. It was also the time of reform legislation fostered by the civil rights and labor struggles of the 1960s against discrimination and segregation, against the Vietnam War, for better working conditions.

But the period since 1973 has been characterized by declining real wages, stagnant or declining median family income, a capitalist offensive against labor and its unions and, during the 1980s, increasingly brazen racism spearheaded by the Reagan-Bush Administrations. In this period of reactionary political power there was a sharp curtailment and, in some instances, elimination of previously hard-won programs to reduce and relieve poverty, even as the need for such measures has risen. The increase of 13 million—55 percent—in the number of people living in poverty since 1973 is stark proof of the decay and cruelty of U.S. capitalist society.

Hunger

New York State's Westchester County is one of the country's "wealthiest" in terms of per capita income. Many rich people live there. But according to a report of Reverend John Duffell, a food bank administrator:

> Westchester County must address a growing problem that is forcing thousands of county children to go to bed hungry. . . . Together, the county's pantries and kitchens served 2.5 million meals in 1990—up from 1.5 million in 1988.

It is the human face of hunger in Westchester that we need to see. . . . The face of children who line up with their parents at 5 a.m., even in the rain, to ensure that they will receive a bag of groceries before they run out.

According to a survey in Long Island's Suffolk County [New York]—by no means a poverty area:

One-quarter of low-income families experienced hunger. Hunger keeps children from paying attention in class, leaves them three times more likely to suffer . . . illnesses, and forces them to miss more school days than children who eat enough.

Almost half of those families said they ran out of money for food an average of five days a month. In half the households, adults did without food or skimped on portions when money was low. In 22 percent of the households, adults said they cut back on their children's meals by eliminating food or cutting portions.

The economy of New York City declined sharply during the late 1980s and early 1990s. With that decline came mass homelessness and hunger.

A *New York Times* editorial headed "Hunger, a Growth Industry," tells of one non-profit outfit, City Harvest, which expanded by 30 percent in 1992. With eight vehicles operating around the clock seven days a week, it distributed 6 million pounds of food to soup kitchens, food pantries, etc., in New York—up from 4.6 million pounds in 1991. Even so, it covers only 130 of the 750 distribution points in the city.

> *"More and more children are going hungry, subsisting on one nutritionally deficient handout-meal a day."*

City Harvest collects the leftovers from banquets, weddings, bar mitzvahs, holiday parties, corporate feasts, movie shoots and charity balls. Comments the *New York Times*, "There's no shortfall in supply or, unfortunately, in demand." The article calls for a $2 million federal grant so that the company can double its provision of garbage to the hungry. There are 120 similar operations existing in 38 states. And this is at a time when the U.S. government subsidizes the destruction of billions of dollars' worth of oranges, grains and other farm products so that monopoly cartels can raise prices!

Far out of proportion to their numbers, it is the African Americans, Latinos and Native Americans who are the victims of this dehumanizing "charity" which substitutes for the most elementary public social program.

Homelessness

Homelessness, along with hunger, has become a major cause of suffering for the first time since the 1930s. Estimates of those without any home—sleeping in the streets and in alleys, in cardboard shacks, in subways, in bus and railroad stations, or in public shelters—run into the millions. Many more are forced to live "doubled-up"; the official figure is about 7 million, but the actuality is certainly much more as families hide their predicament to avoid eviction. With rents high and rising and rental housing in short supply, with banks quick to foreclose on mortgage delinquencies, the unemployed and those working at poverty wages are all too often forced to choose between food and shelter—a choice no one should ever have to make.

The United States Conference of Mayors, at a meeting in 1988, issued a report on a survey of changes in hunger and homelessness in 27 major cities. Almost everywhere conditions had deteriorated tragically during 1988, and nowhere had they improved:

> Requests for emergency food assistance increased in 88 percent of the responding cities, by an average of 19 percent. The requests for assistance did not decrease in any of the cities. . . . In 62 percent of the cities, emergency food assistance facilities had to turn people away because of lack of resources. . . .

> During the past year requests for emergency shelter increased by an average of 13 percent across the survey cities. All but two cities registered an increase.

In urban centers, smaller cities as well as metropolitan spreads, the majority of the hungry and homeless are African Americans and Latinos. In many of the rural poverty areas, whites are often in the majority. But overall, racism has intensified the poverty, the inhumane and unnecessary suffering of the oppressed peoples of the United States. . . .

Children in Poverty

What is especially alarming is the fact that children, of all ages, suffer most acutely from poverty. And it is the African American children who are affected more than others.

A Washington research group [the Joint Center for Political and Economic Studies] found:

> Among Blacks in poverty, no group more fully dramatizes the depth of the problem before us than their children. They are not only the most vulnerable victims of poverty; they are also, literally, the future. If current trends hold, these children will be increasingly hard-pressed to overcome the burdens imposed by poverty. Growing numbers of them will not succeed.

An important and well-documented conclusion of the study is that the rise in female-headed families is

> not enough to account for the growing numbers of Black children living in poverty. In fact, declining economic opportunity had played at least as great a part in increasing the prevalence of childhood poverty. . . .

> Of particular importance are findings regarding the deepening of poverty, with the slide of many Black families from the working poor category to the ranks of the dependent poor. Families caught in this downward shift are not only subject to greater economic deprivation; but without employment they also

have less opportunity to enter the economic mainstream. Since 1973, and especially during the 1980s, there has been a continuous whittling away at the government relief programs, so that more and more children are going hungry, subsisting on one nutritionally deficient handout-meal a day.

The suffering of the millions of white impoverished children is cause of deep concern, of course. But the actuality is that no relief for children, of any race, including white, can be achieved without implementation of measures to reduce and reverse the extreme racism of American society, notably in its economic relations.

Hunger Is a Serious Problem Among the Elderly

by Michael J. McCarthy

About the author: *Michael J. McCarthy is a staff reporter for the* Wall Street Journal.

For four months, John Fisher has waited in nutritional limbo.

The 86-year-old retired Michigan truck driver has been on a waiting list, along with a thousand other elderly Detroit residents, for free hot meals delivered weekdays. Widowed, Mr. Fisher can't cook because arthritis makes it difficult for him to stand long, even to boil soup.

His monthly $541 Social Security check barely covers rent, utilities and other basics. With the nearest grocery store more than a mile away from his tidy downtown apartment, Mr. Fisher, who suffers also from diabetes and glaucoma, treks three blocks with his cane to Theodore's Family Dining and buys the cheapest entree: the $3.50 fish and chips. He eats half, and carries the rest home. "It's a long, painful walk," he says.

Carlos Castillo, 71, applied for the meals in February, writing on his application: "Please help me. I just got out of the hospital. Please, I need the meals now and every day. Thank you. I will appreciate it." He died in September before his turn came up on the waiting list. Over his handwriting, the application now has two words: "Cancel. Deceased."

Growing Problem

More than two decades after the creation of a federal law aimed at providing free meals to anyone over 60, several million older Americans are going hungry—and their numbers are growing steadily. Federal food programs can't keep up with the nation's rapidly graying population. "For the first time, we have growing waiting lists," says Fernando Torres-Gil, assistant secretary for aging at the U.S. Department of Health and Human Services (HHS). "The level of malnutrition and real hunger is only increasing."

This wasn't always the case. In the 1970s, public concern about the plight of the elderly poor mobilized what until then had been only a pilot program: The federal Meals on Wheels movement, in which local communities began providing government-subsidized, home-delivered meals. Demand surged. By 1993, 827,000 elderly had such meals delivered, and another 2.5 million received subsidized lunches at senior centers.

"Federal food programs can't keep up with the nation's rapidly graying population."

But interest in the issue has slipped over the past decade as the national spotlight shifted to the expanding ranks of affluent retirees, a silver-haired generation healthier and more prosperous than their earlier counterparts. As a result, elderly-nutrition programs have been eclipsed by broader issues like health-care reform and preserving Social Security amid federal deficit slashing.

The Urban Institute, sensing the emergence of a huge but hidden problem, conducted a nationwide study in 1993 of elderly hunger. The institute, a private, nonprofit social and economics policy-research group based in Washington, D.C., estimated after the study that as many as 4.9 million elderly people—about 16% of the population aged 60 and older—are either hungry or malnourished to some degree, often because they are poor or too infirm to shop or cook. Further, it found that at least two-thirds of needy older people aren't being reached by federal food-assistance projects, including food stamps. The institute partly faulted systemic flaws: Aging groups hadn't traditionally focused on hunger, while hunger advocates hadn't targeted the elderly.

Meanwhile, funds for federal nutrition programs haven't kept pace with either the rising cost of food or the surging tide of older people. Increases in funding trailed the inflation rate throughout the 1980s, and in the 1990s program budgets have risen only marginally.

In contrast, the elderly population swelled by more than 20% in the 1980s alone.

A Dismal View

Concerned, HHS began in the fall of 1993 a two-year, $2.4 million study to evaluate the federal meals program, to quantify such things as how many people are on waiting lists nationwide. Awaiting results, Mr. Torres-Gil says his agency has enlisted the Agriculture Department to help craft plans to feed more older people, adding, "The problem has gotten bigger than the both of us."

And it is certain to worsen. Some 9 million people 65 or older live alone, putting them at increased risk for poor nutrition, and their numbers are expected to grow to 11 million within a decade, according to HHS figures.

Given current funding levels and an aging population, David Turner, a social worker in Salt Lake City, Utah, echoes a sentiment heard at many nutrition sites: "We don't have a prayer."

Already, the view from the trenches is dismal. The people on lengthy waiting lists in many cities usually represent only a fraction of those who really need meals. In Detroit, for example, 2,200 elderly people get home-delivered meals. But for Thanksgiving and Christmas 1993, when seasonal sentiments sparked private donations, Detroit was able to deliver holiday meals to 4,500 elderly shut-ins.

Unable to feed that total daily, Paul Bridgewater, Detroit's aging-department director, says, "We're nowhere near meeting demand."

The meals programs in Detroit, like those in other cities, are funded substantially by federal funds, which HHS splits up among the states based on the relative size of their population 60 or older. Each state then subdivides the pot according to its needs, with preference given to the poor.

Each local aging agency can determine how it can best stretch its money: Some prepare meals in-house, some pay a caterer; a few hire drivers, although most use volunteers. Some hire and some contract out social workers who can screen and assess the needs of older people. Some deliver two meals a day, many only one.

The Detroit aging agency, for example, contracts out meal preparation and relies almost exclusively on 300 volunteers, who use their own cars for deliveries. Most take meals to 25 people on weekdays, driving 20 miles a day on average.

> "As many as 4.9 million elderly people . . . are either hungry or malnourished to some degree."

In Michigan, federals funds for meal projects, $13.8 million in 1993, were down 3% from 1988 levels. During the same period, with the aid of special allocations, state funding increased 19%. The net result for Detroit is that it had a 1993 elderly-nutrition budget of $3.3 million—13% less than in 1983. Back then, Detroit served 6,000 older people. Today it can feed only 4,800 a day, primarily because of the higher cost of food.

In New York state, 2,500 older people are on waiting lists for home-delivered meals. About 62,000 people are on the program, but state surveys suggest as many as 10,000 more actually need them. Says Ed Kramer, an aging-department official for the state: "There are a lot of hidden elderly, particularly in urban areas and high-rises, who are literally starving to death."

Aging and Nutrition

The mismatch of funds and need comes amid trailblazing research on growing old. Conditions once considered the unavoidable ravages of aging—from cataracts to mental lethargy to slow-healing wounds—may really stem from poor diets, deficits of vitamins and other nutrients, researchers say.

Geriatric specialists recently coined the term "anorexia of aging." It isn't like anorexia nervosa, in which people develop an aversion to food or an obsession with weight. The poor appetite and debilitating weight loss of the elderly have a range of causes: depression, dementia, denture problems and eating alone. Poverty is often a factor, but one national survey found that more than one in five older Americans, regardless of income, routinely skips at least one meal a day. And poor nutrition raises the risk of a fall, which is for many a prelude to costly medical care.

That something as basic as nutrition could be a problem in a country of vast resources illustrates how older individuals, their families and government agencies have been caught unprepared by the combination of increased life expectancy and frailty. Some advocates of the elderly say long-term solutions will have to be more creative, perhaps offering tax incentives so more family members can buy and prepare meals for older relatives.

Federal Programs

But for now the main weapon against hunger remains the federal nutrition programs. Funded under the Older Americans Act, passed in 1965 when Lyndon Johnson was president, the congregate-dining and home-delivery projects allow anyone over age 60 to apply for free meals, regardless of income. Many of those who use the program donate something, but more than half of the participants nationally are poor.

Because the elderly-nutrition program is not an entitlement—as opposed to, say, Social Security—Congress has discretion to approve whatever funds it decides will meet the need. "This is one of the places Congress can fine-tune funding when they must pay for entitlement programs," says Jean L. Lloyd, nutrition officer at the HHS's administration on aging.

Nineteen ninety-three saw a small funding increase for the meal projects, but Congress in September 1994 left the budget flat, at nearly $470 million. Along with another $150 million from the Agriculture Department, which reimburses states for some food costs, the financing has to stretch far and wide.

Even if the 3.2 million people who receive meals in congregate dining rooms or through home delivery got only one meal per day, the government funding works out to about 53 cents a day per person. Concluded a 1992 Government Accounting Office report on the elderly poor: "Funding for nutrition services cannot possibly provide comprehensive food assistance to the entire eligible population."

> *"Conditions once considered the unavoidable ravages of aging . . . may really stem from poor diets, deficits of vitamins and other nutrients."*

For many years, the meals projects could count on potent advocates such as Rep. Claude Pepper, the legislative champion of the elderly who died in 1989. Even a lobbying group as powerful as the American Association of Retired Persons, based in Washington, says that in recent years the best it has been able to do is stave off "devastating cutbacks," says Jo Reed, senior coordinator for consumer issues.

The National Association of Meal Programs, an Alexandria, Virginia, trade group composed of providers of congregate and home-delivered meals, lobbies for increased funding, but says it has not been very successful either. Noting that her group's constituents are often frail or isolated, Margaret Ingraham, legislative representative, says, "We just don't have the political clout."

Strapped Projects

The result is that the meals projects, much like the elderly they serve, have become severely strapped. In Chicago, the city had to pump $700,000 in community-development block grants early in 1994 to eliminate a waiting list of 650 people for delivered meals. In Baton Rouge, Louisiana, the aging office, citing budget problems, began soliciting donations from meal recipients in 1993, prompting some poor people to drop from the program. In Salt Lake City, channeling money to the meals program has meant taking it away from another service—creating yet another waiting list—in which workers help frail elderly people with grooming, laundry and cooking in their homes.

Sometimes the people reached by the overwhelmed food programs still must battle hunger. The Friendly Neighborhood Center, a congregate dining room in Salt Lake City, serves only one meal a day. Among the dozens who file in for the weekday lunch are the sickly thin women some call the "stick ladies." Seated at folding tables around a big bingo board, the women

"Government funding works out to about 53 cents a day per person."

sometimes secretly slip lunch portions into their purses. "They're trying to stretch one meal into two or three," says one program manager.

Central Florida's Osceola County, where nearly a quarter of the population is 60 or older, offers a glimpse of what the rest of the country faces. In 1994, the Osceola County aging department had to jump hurdle after hurdle just to keep from axing any of the 400 people, averaging 87 years of age, who rely on it for cooked and delivered meals.

With federal funds flat in 1993 at $76,763, the agency persuaded several area restaurants to donate $50,000 in food. That helped, but the department still couldn't meet its goal of eliminating its waiting list of about 50 people. So, the agency found a dirt-cheap caterer to take over meal-preparation: the Osceola County Jail.

Using prisoners to fill food boxes for the elderly, and with the warden not charging for labor, the county cut expenses by more than half, to 58 cents a meal from $1.78. It wasn't a smooth transition, though. One of the first days, the meals rolled outside the barbed-wire fences two hours late because an inmate, threatening suicide, had grabbed a knife in the jail's kitchen.

Hoping to wipe out the waiting list soon, Beverly Houghland, the aging-council's executive director, says, "The hardest thing you'll ever have to do is tell someone that you can't give them meals."

Yet it happens daily all over the country. In Detroit, when meal recipients go into the hospital and have deliveries stopped, they sometimes can't get them restarted once they return home. Someone on a waiting list has been given their spot in the program. Says one frustrated case manager, Frances Taylor, "It's like deciding who is going to get in the lifeboat and who has to stay in the water."

Detroit's aging department does set some priorities. In October 1994, for instance, the agency rushed meals out to one couple after discovering how the 87-year-old husband and his wife, 83, were getting to the grocery store. The husband, who was nearly blind, steered their car—instructed by his wife, who was too frail to drive but could watch the road from the passenger side.

Higher food costs in 1993 forced Orlando, Florida, to abandon a two-decade-old practice of serving hot dinners. Now the city offers cold breakfasts, with cheaper fare like sweet rolls or cereal, to the roughly 600 older people it serves, for a saving of about 40 cents a meal, or $50,000 annually. (By law, each meal, breakfast or otherwise, must have at least one-third of a day's recommended dietary allowances.)

Even with the cheaper menu, Orlando still must depend on an all-volunteer force, which can make deliveries chaotic. One day in summer 1994, Danette Klemens, Orlando's Meals on Wheels director, had to deliver food to 10 older people left waiting after a volunteer's car broke down. Some days, as many as 30 routes go unserved, because volunteers are sick, late or no-shows. Volunteers must use their own cars and absorb gasoline costs—even though some cruise the city's poorest streets and are sometimes approached for drugs. Occasionally a route is missed altogether.

The Lifeline

But for many elderly recipients in Orlando, the daily food package is a delicate lifeline. One particular stop is so disturbing that the aging office tries to forewarn new volunteers. A meal deliverer's knock at the screen door one day is answered by a slight-framed woman creeping on her knees. She reaches up, clutches her two meal cartons, and crawls back inside the apartment.

A stroke years ago left Marjorie Norris, 84, unable to stand, and moving in and out of her wheelchair is painful, so she doesn't use it. Hobbling about on her knees, she can't stretch up to the range of her white stove, neglected so long that cobwebs cover the burners. Asked if she can cook, she quickly replies, "Oh, yes. I make my own coffee."

Orlando estimates that it only reaches about 25% of the elderly who need meals delivered. Says Donna Stiteler, former president of Orlando's elderly agency, "How the rest are making it, we have no idea."

Hunger Is Not a Problem in the United States

by Robert Rector

About the author: *Robert Rector is a policy analyst for family and social welfare issues at the Heritage Foundation, a conservative public policy research institute in Washington, D.C.*

"A startling number of American children are in danger of starving . . . one out of eight American children is going hungry tonight." So began a CBS Evening News broadcast in March 1991. This headline-grabbing charge came from a survey conducted by the Food Research Action Center (FRAC), a liberal food advocacy group, sponsored by the Kraft Corporation, one of America's largest food-processing companies.

CBS got it wrong. FRAC actually reported that one out of eight children in the United States had been "hungry" at some time during the prior year, not each night as the network reported. This shocking statistic has since passed into media and political folklore. . . . The *New York Times*, the *Boston Globe*, the *Washington Post*, the *Chicago Tribune*, the *Christian Science Monitor*, and *USA Today* all gave the FRAC report saturation coverage.

No Scientific Basis

All of these media accounts ignored the FRAC study's lack of scientific basis. In contrast to numerous other studies of nutrition in America, FRAC did not measure actual food or nutrient consumption. Instead, FRAC asked American families subjective questions about whether they would like to have more or a wider variety of foods. The FRAC survey was deliberately so vague that it actually "discovered" that large numbers of middle-class children were hungry as well.

FRAC's startling assertions of widespread hunger in America are flatly contradicted by scientific surveys conducted by the Food and Nutrition Service of the Department of Agriculture and the Centers for Disease Control of the Department of Health and Human Services. These surveys, which measure actual

Abridged from Robert Rector, "Food Fight," *Policy Review*, Fall 1991. Reprinted by permission of The Heritage Foundation, Washington, D.C.

food consumption and physiological status in the U.S. population, show little evidence of hunger or insufficient calorie and protein intake among poor children or poor adults. Vitamin and mineral consumption are in most cases well above recommended norms and little difference is found between the level of nutrients consumed by poor and affluent children. Overall, government research finds no significant health problems among the poor caused by general food shortages.

> *"The top nutrition-related health problem among poor Americans is not hunger and undernutrition—but obesity."*

Rather, the top nutrition-related health problem among poor Americans is not hunger and undernutrition—but obesity. . . .

The FRAC study claimed that 40 percent of poor children suffer hunger, which it defined as "a physical condition that comes from not eating enough food due to insufficient economic . . . resources," and as a state of "chronic mild undernutrition." This is a reasonable definition of hunger; but what are the actual facts about undernutrition and malnutrition in the United States?

Government Surveys

For over 50 years the federal government has painstakingly surveyed food and nutrient consumption within the United States. In each decade since the 1930s the U.S. Department of Agriculture (USDA) has conducted at least one "food consumption survey," using extensive interviews with representative samples of households to determine the actual amount of food consumed by each household on various days throughout the year. These surveys permit comparisons of average food and nutrient consumption in households from different socioeconomic strata.

The USDA food consumption surveys provide the government with preliminary data to identify potential nutritional problems within the general population and various socioeconomic sub-groups. The government then follows this preliminary data with periodic targeted physiological and anthropometric (body structure) surveys that provide a far more precise assessment of nutritional status within the population. Past surveys include the Health Examination Surveys of the early 1960s (HES I and HES II) and the National Health and Nutrition Examination Survey (NHANES) of the early 1970s. Between 1976 and 1980, the Centers for Disease Control (CDC) conducted NHANES II, collecting hematological [blood], biochemical, anthropometric, and other medical data from a representative sample of tens of thousands of Americans. The NHANES II data are critical to an accurate assessment of protein, vitamin, mineral, and caloric deficiencies.

Neither the USDA food consumption surveys nor the NHANES II study found evidence of malnutrition among poor children. In fact, they show very little difference in the nutritional content of food consumed by low-income children compared with those in affluent American families.

Overabundant Protein

One of the most serious forms of malnutrition is protein deficiency. Proteins are amino acids that act as the fundamental building blocks of life. Without a sufficient intake of protein, humans suffer growth retardation, impaired mental functioning, and fatigue; a very severe deficiency can lead to death. Fortunately, protein is abundant in many food sources including meat, milk, poultry, fish, soy, nuts, corn, and beans. Although protein deficiency still plagues developing nations, it is essentially non-existent in the United States.

As part of the NHANES II survey, CDC offices analyzed serum albumin levels among Americans. Low levels of serum albumin, the most common protein in the blood, are the clearest indicator of protein-caloric malnutrition. Of a total representative sample of 15,457 persons, however, only 19 individuals, or less than one-tenth of 1 percent, showed signs of protein deficiency. Moreover, there were no differences between races or between poor and non-poor persons.

A 1985–1986 USDA food consumption survey likewise found no signs of protein deficiency among young children. Preschool children from families with incomes below 75 percent of the poverty level ($8,242 for a family of four in 1985) consumed 54.4 grams of protein per day, compared with 53.6 grams for children in families with incomes above 300 percent of poverty (roughly $33,000 for a family of four in 1985). Black preschool children consumed 56.9 grams of protein, compared with 52.4 grams for white children. Surprisingly, protein and calorie consumption was slightly higher among children in the central cities than in the suburbs. On average, protein intake of both poor and upper-middle-income children exceeded 200 percent of U.S. recommended standards.

> *"Of a total representative sample of 15,457 persons, . . . only 19 individuals . . . showed signs of protein deficiency."*

Thus, as the *Nutrition Monitoring Update*, a summary report prepared jointly by the Department of Health and Human Services and the USDA, concluded in 1989: "Protein is not considered to be a current public health issue . . . there is no evidence of health problems associated with deficiency or excess." Where protein deficiency does occur, it is not linked to poverty. Indeed, poor as well as affluent Americans of all ages have diets rich in meat and protein in comparison with the rest of the world, and greatly exceed recommended daily requirements.

Vitamins and Minerals

As Table 1 shows, consumption of essential vitamins and minerals among both high- and low-income preschool children also generally exceed USDA standards, often by more than 50 percent. In only a few instances does nutrient consumption fall below recommended levels. The few shortfalls that occur among poor children appear among higher-income children as well. The USDA data show not only that the average nutrient consumption of poor and higher-income children was very similar, but that the variation (or statistical spread around the average) was quite similar in both groups as well. Moreover, since the recommended USDA standards for consumption of vitamins and minerals are conservatively set above the levels needed for good health for most persons and USDA underestimates the nutrients in some foods due to lack of information—an average deficiency of a nutrient does not necessarily indicate a significant nutritional problem.

Table 1

Average Per-Capita Consumption of Nutriments as a Percentage of Recommended Daily Allowances, Children Under Age 6 in 1985

	Family Income Below 75% of Poverty Threshhold	Family Income Above 300% of Poverty Threshhold
Protein	211	213
Vitamin B-12	211	164
Thiamin	192	152
Vitamin A	186	230
Vitamin C	179	164
Riboflavin	181	182
Folacin	149	158
Niacin	138	145
Phosphorous	120	127
Vitamin B-6	113	133
Vitamin E	113	102
Magnesium	105	126
Calcium	94	99
Zinc	76	73

Source: USDA, Low Income Women 19–50 Years and Their Children 1–5 Years, 4 Days, pp. 64–65, 72–73.

For example, the 1985 USDA study of preschoolers showed that average zinc consumption fell below recommended standards for both poor and higher-income children by some 25 percent. But the NHANES II hematological study found only 2 to 3 percent of all children had low serum zinc levels. Low serum zinc was only slightly more common among poor children. Zinc aids in the metabolism of protein. Severe deficiencies can lead to stunted growth, increased susceptibility to infection, and mental lethargy, and may even contribute to sickle cell anemia. Peanut butter, meat, poultry, seafood, cheese, milk, and whole-grain cereals are all good sources of this trace mineral.

Similarly, while USDA surveys found that higher-income school-aged children consume much higher levels of fruit and fruit juice, the lower consumption of fruit among poor children did not result in vitamin C deficiency. The NHANES II hematological survey found no evidence of low levels of serum vitamin C among children under age 11. Between 1 and 2 percent of American teen-agers were found to have low serum vitamin C levels, but this was more common among non-poor than poor teen-agers. Although vitamin C is abundant in fruits, especially oranges, lemons, and strawberries, it can be found in a number of other foods as well, including green peppers, brussels sprouts, tomatoes, and potatoes. Scientists are still not sure exactly how vitamin C is utilized by the body, but it does play a role in metabolizing protein. It also works to strengthen the immune system. A serious vitamin C deficiency can cause bleeding gums and reduce the body's natural ability to heal wounds. A complete lack of vitamin C in the diet is potentially fatal; it is also almost unheard of in modern times.

Calcium, which makes up 2 percent of the body weight of an adult, is another vital mineral. Not only does it build up teeth and bones, calcium also aids in proper nerve function, blood clotting, and muscle contraction, among other functions. Calcium deficiencies can lead to osteomalacia, a softening of the bones, or osteoporosis, a brittling of the bones. Fortunately, it is fairly easy to get through food sources an adequate amount of calcium. Two cups of milk a day for adults fulfills RDA requirements; three cups of milk takes care of the greater needs of adolescents. Broccoli and mustard greens are also good sources. The USDA consumption survey discovered that among preschoolers average calcium consumption for both poor and high-income children was slightly below recommended levels. Symptoms of calcium deficiency appear among middle-aged and older women, but are generally unrelated to economic class.

Iron

The most common nutritional shortfall among Americans appears to be iron deficiency—a problem we share with most other developed nations. As a key component of hemoglobin, iron is essential to the blood system's ability to absorb and deliver oxygen to the body. Periods of rapid body growth, such as infancy, adolescence, and pregnancy, increase the likelihood of iron deficiency, which can cause fatigue, impaired mental activity, and increased susceptibility to infection. Deficiency can be countered by eating foods rich in iron such as liver and other organ meats, egg yolks, raisins, dark leafy vegetables such as spinach, and legumes such as kidney beans, or by taking an iron supplement.

> *"Americans of all ages have diets rich in meat and protein in comparison with the rest of the world."*

During the early 1970s there was concern that iron deficiency was causing high rates of anemia among poor young children. In 1974, the Centers for Disease Control began monitoring anemia among low-income preschool children deemed to be at high nutritional risk. Among this group the prevalence of anemia has been more than halved, falling from 7.8 percent in 1975 to 2.9 percent in 1985. The anemia rates for poor children are now quite low, although still slightly higher than the anemia rates for middle-class children.

Part of the decline in anemia is a result of the expansion of the Women, Infants, and Children (WIC) food program beginning in the early 1970s. However, the CDC data show that between 1975 and 1985 the most dramatic reductions in anemia occurred among poor children prior to enrollment in WIC. Similar reductions in anemia occurred among middle-class children not eligible for WIC. These dramatic changes were the result of improvements in iron levels in the general food supply as well as changes in food selected for young children. These improvements included greater frequency and duration of breast feeding, increased substitution of iron-fortified infant formula for non-fortified milk, and increased use of iron-fortified cereals.

> *"Lower consumption of fruit among poor children did not result in vitamin C deficiency."*

Moreover, while CDC data from the mid-1970s show significant declines in anemia among poor children after those children began participation in WIC, CDC data from the 1980s show WIC playing a diminishing role. The difference in anemia rates among poor children prior to enrollment in WIC and the anemia rates of poor children after participation in WIC shrank between 1975 and 1985. This suggests that the improved level of iron nutrients provided to children in general has meant that WIC has played a less significant, although still important, role in reducing iron deficiency among the poor in recent years.

Body Structure

The effects of malnutrition are evident not only in blood chemistry but in a child's body structure as well. Thus, surveys of body structure are useful additions to food intake and biochemical studies as tools to detect malnutrition. Body weight relative to height, for instance, is the best indicator of adequate caloric intake. A child suffering from serious caloric underconsumption will exhibit low body weight relative to height—known as "thinness" or "wasting."

The CDC began monitoring wasting among poor children at risk of malnutrition in 1973. The CDC data show that thinness is not more common among impoverished children than among the general population. *Nutrition Monitoring in the United States*, produced jointly by the USDA and the Department of Health and Human Services in 1986, concludes that "wasting does not constitute a significant health problem" among impoverished children in the United States.

In NHANES II, the CDC also measured general body fat among poor and non-poor children through a "skinfold test." In this test a specific width of flesh is pinched together to produce a skinfold. The width of the skinfold is then measured with calipers that give a specific measure of the individual's body fat level.

Skinfold tests show that poor girls, on average, are plumper than non-poor girls. Poor boys, on the other hand, have slightly less body fat than more afflu-ent boys. But even in the case of poor and non-poor boys, the average differ-ence in skinfold thickness is roughly one one-hundredth of an inch. This amounts to a difference of around 2 percent or one-tenth of a standard devia-tion—a minute difference detectable only with very precise measurement.

The NHANES II survey did find that poor children were roughly 1 percent, or a half-inch, shorter than non-poor children of the same age. However, the sur-vey found no consistent evidence linking this lower height to lower levels of nutrition. The *Nutrition Monitoring Update* cautions that many factors other than food consumption may contribute to the relative shortness of poor chil-dren. For example, parents' height, genetically transmitted to their offspring, is the strongest determinant of a child's height. Poor children, on average, have shorter parents than non-poor children. Emotional disturbances due to unstable family structure also tend to slow a child's growth, and family instability is also more common among poor households. Smoking by a mother during pregnancy and exposure to parental smoking in the home during childhood can be an addi-tional cause of a child's stunted growth; both practices are more common among poor households. And low birth-weight, which is more common among poor children, has an effect on a child's height in subsequent years. . . .

Diets of Low-Income Americans Improving

Historical data show a consistent "upscaling" of the diets of low-income Americans over time. As of 1991, among the 20 percent of households with the lowest incomes, consumption of vegetables actually exceeds consumption among the general population in the mid-1950s. Low-income Americans today consume about 20 percent more meat, poultry, and fish than did the average cit-izen in 1955. And low-income consumption of meat, poultry, and fish is nearly 70 percent greater than the average per-capita consumption of these items in ur-ban households in 1948.

Beef consumption, often considered a symbol of diets of the prosperous middle-class, has shown a similar increase. Per-capita beef consumption among low-income households exceeds average consumption in the U.S. in 1955 by 35 percent. Most strikingly, per-capita beef consumption among the lowest economic quintile tops beef con-sumption among the most affluent 5 percent of urban households in 1948 by nearly a third.

> *"Low-income Americans consume about 20 percent more meat, poultry, and fish than did the average citizen in 1955."*

Consumption of frivolous items such as soft drinks is 100 percent greater among low-income persons today than among the general population in the mid-1950s. By contrast, inexpensive foods such as potatoes, bread, and flour are consumed by low-income individuals to-day at rates 25 to 50 percent below that of the general population in the 1950s.

The increasing levels of meat consumption and declining levels of grain consumption among the poor are further evidence that these households are not suffering from recurring hunger. Poor persons on average eat roughly the same amount of meat, poultry, and fish as do higher-income persons, with resulting protein intakes well above recommended levels. As noted, poor children actually consume more meat products than do higher-income children and have average protein intakes 100 percent above recommended levels.

> *"There is no evidence of widespread hunger and undernutrition."*

While meat is a good source of protein, it is an extremely expensive source of calories. Calories provided through inexpensive meats still cost roughly five times as much as calories obtained from grain products. It is simply not plausible that poor families would maintain the same level of meat consumption as high-income families while suffering, as FRAC contends, from recurring empty refrigerators and empty stomachs. If so, the empty stomachs could readily be filled through a slight reduction in meat purchases and an increase in less expensive although still healthful bulk foods. Indeed, many nutritionists would argue that reducing meat and increasing grain consumption would actually he healthier for most Americans, rich and poor.

In general, poor Americans, young and old, are well-nourished. The poor do not suffer from food shortages nor are they forced by penury to consume less healthy foods than the rest of Americans. There is no evidence of widespread hunger and undernutrition. To the contrary, the *Nutrition Monitoring Update* summary report, issued by USDA and HHS in 1989, concludes that among persons at all income levels: "The principal nutrition-related health problems experienced by Americans continue to be related to the overconsumption of some nutrients and food components, particularly food energy [*i.e.*, calories], fat, saturated fatty acids, cholesterol, [and] sodium." The report identifies five nutrition-related public health problems affecting U.S. citizens: obesity from excess calories; high serum cholesterol from excess consumption of fat, saturated fats, and cholesterol; hypertension promoted by high sodium intake; osteoporosis (loss of bone mass) from low calcium consumption; and anemia from low iron consumption. With the possible exception of iron-deficiency anemia, which is slightly more frequent among the poor, none of these health conditions can be attributed to poverty-induced undernutrition. . . .

The Best-Nourished Generation in History

At the turn of this century, as many as 10,000 Americans died annually from pellagra, a disease caused by vitamin B deficiency. Such diseases caused by undernutrition have today all but disappeared in this country. Nutrition-related health problems in the United States today are caused by obesity and consumption of unhealthy foods, not by food shortages.

The current generation of American children—even poor children—is undoubtedly among the best nourished in human history. Yet poor children do face devastating problems: escalating crime, disintegrating families, communities where the positive role models of working adults are often missing, and government schools that can no longer physically protect let alone educate them. But chronic hunger and widespread undernutrition are not problems for poor children. Perhaps the most regrettable consequence of FRAC's bogus hunger survey is that it distracts public attention from the overwhelming real problems facing poor children, problems desperately in need of creative solutions.

The Seriousness of Hunger in Rural Areas Is Exaggerated

by Dan McMurry

About the author: *Dan McMurry is an associate professor of sociology at Middle Tennessee State University at Murfreesboro.*

In January 1986, the Harvard Physician Task Force on Hunger in America published a report entitled *Hunger Counties 1986*. The main finding of this report was a list of the 150 counties with the "worst" hunger problem in the United States. In addition to attracting the attention of academics, the report had an intense impact on the media and politicians. Shortly after the report was released, newspaper and television crews swarmed over the counties listed in the report, pitting local officials attempting to defend their efforts to aid the needy in their counties against the damning statistics in the report, complete with the number from 1 to 150 the county had acquired on the "hunger list."

I found two aspects of the report troubling. First, and immediately apparent, was its strong antigovernment language. Second, because of the geographic distribution of the 150 counties and the criteria used to identify a county as a "hunger county," I suspected there were major errors in the methods used in the study. For example, the concentration of hunger counties in Montana and South Dakota and the virtual absence of any counties in Mississippi—the poorest state in the nation— on the list suggested improbable results.

In addition, about this time I had just begun a study of homeless persons, concentrating on the availability of "survival" services for them, particularly food. My scholarly expectation was that there was a critical shortage of food available for the homeless, especially for street people. After personal observation of the food situation in several cities, I had the biggest surprise of my career as a sociological researcher: I found no shortage of food in any of the cities. On the contrary, there was an overabundance of food available in all the locations I had

Abridged from Dan McMurry, "Hunger in Rural America: Myth or Reality? A Reexamination of the Harvard Physician Task Force Report on Hunger in America Using Statistical Data and Field Observations," *Sociological Spectrum* 11:1-18 (1991). Reprinted by permission of the publisher, Taylor & Francis, Bristol, Pennsylvania.

visited. This totally unexpected finding was to become part of a perspective I was to use to explain the distribution of the homeless in Tennessee and was to prove extremely controversial. Thus, if I could find *no hunger* among street people in Nashville, Tennessee, I had very serious doubts that Dr. Larry J. Brown [coauthor of *Living Hungry in America*] could find the biggest concentration of hunger in America in Eureka, Nevada.

The Study and Its Goals

When the report was released, I was teaching a class in rural sociology. Because a rural sociology class seemed to be a natural forum for studying hunger in America, I introduced the report as a class project. Each student selected two variables that were expected to correlate highly with hunger. Test variables ranged across social, economic, and cultural areas from unemployment rates and urbanization to average size of farms and abortion rates. The inconsistencies that the students found in the report justified further analysis. This viewpoint is the result of that analysis, which turned out to be a complete reexamination of the report.

At the outset, I intended to use three validity checks of the report. First was a recomputation of the data using the methods utilized by the author. In addition, I chose a number of variables that I assumed to be inextricably tied to hunger. I was going to check the compatibility of each of them with the reported "hunger score" of the counties. Finally, I was going to visit as many of the counties as I could on a planned trip to the western states the following summer. The goal was to determine, by independent investigation, the validity of the Harvard report: Would repetition of the study, with the addition of on-site investigation, support the findings of large numbers of hungry persons in the 150 counties?

The Methods of the Harvard Report

Because hunger is a physiological state, investigators use empirical indicators to "point to hunger." In the Task Force's research, the empirical indicators chosen to label a county a "hunger county" were (1) more than 20% of the county's population fell below the official poverty level and (2) less than one third of the eligible poor received food stamps. These were the only criteria used. No other conditions of the residents were taken into account, nor was there any consideration of the economic situation in the county. The restriction of the operational definition of hunger to the level of these two variables quickly draws suspicion to the validity of the research.

> **"I suspected there were major errors in the methods used in the [Harvard Task Force] study."**

Validity is the condition of measuring what one intends to measure. An investigation of hunger would be valid only if the project actually defined and measured hunger. Hunger research can be accurate, precise, and reliable without being valid. In addition, if studies measure something other than hunger, the report will be invalid. This appears to be a major problem of the report of the Harvard Physician Task Force on Hunger. The study seems timely, relevant, perhaps even generally accurate, but its validity is called into question. The report appears to measure something other than hunger.

The Poverty Level and Food-Stamp Participation

In the report, the 1980 census figures were used to indicate those counties in which more than 20% of the population earned below the official poverty level. A modification of the poverty level was made for each county, based on regional changes, to adjust the poverty figures to a 1984 level. Using the performance of several economic indicators from 1980 to 1984, an index was devised for each census region, and the result was used as a multiplier to adjust the 1980 poverty figure for each county in the region. Thus, the final poverty figure for each county was an estimate of the percent of the population living below the official poverty level in 1984. This method assumed that each county in a region would have undergone the same economic and population changes from 1980 to 1984. This is obviously incorrect.

"An investigation of hunger would be valid only if the project actually defined and measured hunger."

The estimates of the food-stamp participation rate were made by dividing the number receiving food stamps in each county by the number who were estimated to be eligible to receive them. The numerator, the number of persons receiving stamps in each county, was obtained from United States Department of Agriculture summary statistics. They are the only figures about which there is no question. The denominator, the number of persons eligible to receive food stamps in each county, was determined by taking 125% of the estimated number of persons living below the official poverty level in 1984. However, if the estimate of the size of the county population living below the poverty level is incorrect, especially if it is significantly overestimated, the fraction will be in error.

Although there are many questions that can be raised about the methodology the Task Force used to compute both the poverty figures and the food-stamp participation rates, it is not the concern of this viewpoint to pursue them. Many critics of the report included examination of the methodology, and the General Accounting Office (GAO) was asked by the Department of Agriculture to compile a report based solely on the soundness of the methods used. The GAO report was released in 1986 after my original reexamination and concerned itself solely with a technical discussion of the methods of the study, not with the presence or absence of hunger in the counties.

The Distribution of Hunger Counties

An alert reader of the report would immediately note that the hunger counties were concentrated in the Midwest, rather than in the South, where poverty rates historically have been the highest. Nebraska, Montana, and the Dakotas contain 66 of the 150 counties at highest risk for hunger, in contrast to only 7 in Georgia, Alabama, and Mississippi. This concentration of hunger counties in the Farm Belt presented a new and entirely different distribution of hunger in America.

> *"One would not expect counties in which the majority of workers were farmers and farm owners . . . to be among the hungriest areas in the nation."*

The element that combines with poverty to produce hunger in South Dakota, Montana, and Texas and not in Mississippi and South Carolina is the nature of farming in the West. Harding County, South Dakota, rated number four in the United States in the estimated extent of hunger, may be considered a typical case to explore the relation of farming to poverty.

Nearly 6 of every 10 workers in Harding County are engaged in agricultural jobs, and over 40% of all workers are self-employed. This source is the 1983 *County and City Data Book*, by the U.S. Bureau of the Census, which contains almost 300 variables for each county in the United States. It is the major source of social and economic data at the county level, and unless otherwise noted, all county-level data are taken from it. It is likely that these two categories—agricultural workers and self-employment—overlap, indicating a large proportion of farmers. In addition, the unemployment rate in Harding County was 1.7%; thus, almost everyone who wanted a job had one.

Identical situations existed in almost all of the counties in the farming states, which contained the majority of hunger counties. Haakon County, South Dakota, is similar to Harding County, having a large segment of the population working in agriculture and with many of the workers self-employed. In 1979, Haakon County had a per capita income of $4,924, and 20.58% of the population lived below the poverty level, which, combined, put the county at risk of hunger. Haakon County, therefore, with a large number of farmers, almost no unemployment, and a low per capita income, is still characterized by a high level of poverty.

One would not expect counties in which the majority of workers were farmers and farm owners (rather than farm laborers), and in which there were nearly no unemployed persons, to be among the hungriest areas in the nation. However, this is what the Task Force indicated was the case.

The average size of farms in Haakon County at the time of the report was 3,712 acres. The value of the average farm's land and buildings was $578,500. That is to say, the average farm in the county had a value of over one half million dollars. The average value of farms in Harding County, South Dakota, number four on the Task Force's list, was even higher: $711,600. These counties are farming counties, the population is almost totally white, most workers are farm owners, and the farms are large and very valuable. In addition, according to labor-force definitions, adult children of farmers and farmers' spouses are usually considered employed by virtue of being in a farming household. However, they are not salaried in the usual sense of the term. Thus, the farmers' income is divided by all family members to arrive at a per capita income figure.

What this procedure does, quite obviously, is to divide the average farmer's income by a factor of 4 to 10, depending on the size of the family. In addition, with almost no inmigration and a relatively large outmigration, particularly of young adults, the population of these hunger counties is made up of large proportions of "natural dependents." The rural population of South Dakota declined from 436,000 in 1950 to 370,000 in 1980, an absolute loss of 16%. During the 1960s, 53 of the 66 counties lost population; during the 1970s, 42 did.

Compared with counties with larger urban populations and fewer farmers, these counties contain many elderly and young persons, both groups generally considered economically unproductive. Nearly half of the population of hunger counties is composed of these natural dependents, compared with approximately 35% of more urban-type counties. For example, only 57% of South Dakota's total population is between 18 and 64 years of age, and for the rural population this figure drops to 54%. For the national population the percent is 62%, and in many urban and suburban areas it is close to 70%.

> *"If we examine the economic situation of the families in these counties . . . we find a much healthier set of numbers than the [Harvard] Task Force used."*

The effect of this unique demographic age composition is that it reduces the per capita income, *ceteris paribus* [if all other variables remain constant]. In addition, by the nature of an "intrinsic value factor"—a nonfinancial factor—which is attached to farm output, the per capita income is not a reflection of farmers' economic status. For example, well over half of the farms in Harding County had sales of over $40,000. It is unlikely that these farmers, living on extremely valuable farms, producing for market an average of $40,000 worth of goods, would dispose of these food products and the income without setting aside enough to feed their families adequately.

Nonfinancial Correlates of Poverty

If we examine the economic situation of the families in these counties apart from relying solely on per capita income for a given year, we find a much healthier set of numbers than the Task Force used to characterize these farming communities.

In these counties, almost all families own their homes; hence, they have no house payment and no rent. These families have been stable for years and few move. The houses are among the oldest, on the average, in the nation, and few homes have been built since the 1940s. In fact, several of these counties have the largest proportions of very old homes in the nation. Ten of the top 25 counties containing the most homes built before 1940 are hunger counties located in the Midwest. In Jerauld County, South Dakota, for example, 75% of all occupied houses were built before 1940. Hunger counties in Nebraska, Montana, Iowa, and North Dakota are also among the top 75 counties in the United States in the proportion of very old houses. As a consequence of the pattern of home ownership alone, the economic significance of per capita income, and subsequently the poverty level, dwindles as a realistic indicator.

> *"If one examines the size and value of farms, unemployment, home ownership, and average bank deposits, hunger becomes exceedingly suspect."*

By far the most unexpected measure of the economic condition of these counties is the exceptionally high per capita bank deposits. This measure is generally used to show the "economic well-being" of an area. On this measure, many of these Midwest hunger counties are among the most affluent in the entire nation. Using per capita bank deposits as an indicator of economic health, Haakon County, South Dakota, is at the same time the 24th hungriest county and the 21st richest county in the nation. With $11,957 average per capita bank deposits, ranking 21st of over 3,000 counties, Haakon County stands far above such places as Nantucket County, Massachusetts, and Westchester County, New York.

What emerges then is an economic picture of these areas that contrasts vividly with the gloomy portrait painted by the Harvard report. Rather than using the per capita income (the flaws of which we have already examined) to indicate a condition that creates the basis of hunger, if one examines the size and value of farms, unemployment, home ownership, and average bank deposits, hunger becomes exceedingly suspect. . . .

Eureka County, Nevada

To investigate the aspects of the areas that cannot be determined by secondary statistics, I contacted officials in several of the leading hunger counties. I now summarize what I discovered.

Eureka County, Nevada, leads the list of hunger counties in the United States. Less than 2% of the eligible poor receive food stamps in Eureka County, the worst showing in the country.

According to Marsha Elliott, Deputy County Clerk and Recorder for the county, the Boy Scouts were unable to find any needy to whom to deliver

Christmas food baskets. She stated that, after a thorough search and after lowering their standards of what was really a "needy, poor" person, the Boy Scouts finally located three individuals who accepted the baskets. Ms. Elliott said that "these turned out to be bar-type characters." She went on to add that she knew of no cases of hunger in the county. Her husband was a game warden, she said, and he would likely know of any hungry people in the area because his work took him all over the backroads of the county. She said, "He does not know of a single case of hunger in the county."

I asked her how a report could not only be wrong but err this greatly—to identify Eureka County as the worst in the country when officials in the county claim that there is no hunger there. Ms. Elliott indicated that the majority of workers are ranchers or miners, and that there are many retired people. The population is predominately masculine and many of the adults live alone. They are fiercely independent, according to Ms. Elliott, and "look out for themselves." In addition, with a note of finality, she said, "there is no place to get food stamps in the county, and no place will redeem them." There are only two grocery stores in the county, she added, and one of them is open only part-time.

Unique Geography and Demography

Eureka County, Nevada, floated to the top of the hunger list because of its unique geography and demography. It is a county the size of Rhode Island, with a total population of only 2,100. There are about 700 families. The Sheriff and I rode the roads of the entire county and saw where nearly every family lived. There is no county Human Services office where food stamps are available. The nearest movie theater is in Bishop, California, 170 miles away, and the high school students are bused to school 65 miles one way to Austin.

County officials in the other leading hunger counties had similar situations to report. None of the officials agreed with the Harvard report that their county had a problem of hunger, much less having one of the worst hunger situations in the nation. In fact, they all reported that hunger was not a significant problem in their area. "Oh yes," they said generally, "there are poor folks around here, but they're not hungry."

> *"Eureka County, Nevada, floated to the top of the hunger list because of its unique geography and demography."*

Reports from each county added some new perspective. In Buffalo County, South Dakota, the County Extension Agent, Ken Nelson, said that money went farther there than "back East." A poor person who might go hungry "in Boston or in North Carolina" might "get by pretty good here," he offered. The Manager for Petroleum County, Montana, second on the list, indicated essentially the same thing, as did Jane Brewster, Clerk and Recorder for Carter County, Montana. In addition to contradicting the Task Force listing by gathering economic statistics from these counties, my firsthand observation and interviews with informed residents also failed to uncover evidence of significant hunger. . . .

Not a Serious Problem

At first glance, it seems that there should be no controversy about the definition of hunger: Everybody knows what hunger is. However, that is certainly not the case. Obviously even the "experts" disagree on what hunger means and, most especially, how it can be measured. Unfortunately, in many of the past studies, such as the Harvard report, definitions of hunger have been used that confuse rather than inform. Hunger has come to symbolize deprivation, not necessarily to indicate malnutrition, and not just deprivation of food, but also of money and social status.

It has been the use of these sorts of "social" definitions of hunger that have led the most popular and influential studies of hunger to find such astonishingly large numbers of hungry people. They have confused hunger with need and deprivation. Quite often, hunger is used interchangeably with poverty. Critics of these studies point out that if hunger was as prevalent as is reported, the impact on health and mortality would be readily apparent, if not overwhelming. However, empirical evidence has not been located, even though there have been attempts to record the health effects of hunger.

According to the evidence of economic data and firsthand observations, hunger is not a serious problem in the areas that the report states are the worst hunger spots in the nation. In addition, these areas have performed their own investigations and likewise find no significant hunger problem.

Chapter 3

Can Technological Advances Increase Food Production?

CURRENT   CONTROVERSIES

Technology and Food Production: An Overview

by Scott Pendleton

About the author: *Scott Pendleton is a staff writer for the* Christian Science Monitor.

Cornfields blanket Iowa like a green ocean, making thoughts of famine seem as out of place as fleas on a goldfish. Yet John Ruan does worry about famine—so much so that he awards $200,000 each year to whoever contributes most to improving world food output.

"We can produce more population," the Des Moines businessman muses, "but not more land."

Our planet and its resources continue to shrink in relation to the burgeoning human population. Farmers must feed 5.3 billion mouths, and 90 million new ones each year—as much as another Mexico.

"Can We Do It?"

"The question is, can we do it?" asks Richard Harwood, a sustainable-agriculture expert at Michigan State University (MSU).

World food production must triple within 50 years to feed a peak population of 9 billion to 12 billion, says Dennis Avery, a senior fellow at the Hudson Institute. "I see it as a challenge," says Mr. Avery, who is considered the most optimistic forecaster of food production trends.

Less than a billion people inhabited earth 200 years ago, when English economist Thomas Malthus theorized that populations naturally grow at a faster rate than food supply, making misery and starvation inevitable. That scenario has unfolded in some poor countries. But Malthus did not foresee that economic development and modern birth-control techniques would curb population growth, nor that new agricultural technologies would boost food output, as has happened in much of the world.

Consider 1992's "International Human Suffering Index," compiled by the

Population Crisis Committee in Washington, D.C. In Denmark, the nation with the least suffering as measured by daily calorie supply, per capita gross national product, and other measures, population growth has slowed to zero. In Mozambique, where suffering is the greatest, annual population growth is a substantial 2.7 percent.

Thus, despite the currency of phrases like "world hunger" and "global famine," those conditions don't exist and probably never will, food resource experts agree. Starvation is local.

> *"Today, the world's people on average are better-fed than ever before, but vast numbers still go hungry."*

Today, the world's people on average are better-fed than ever before, but vast numbers still go hungry—786 million in the developing world, down from 941 million in the early 1970s, according to the United Nations Food and Agriculture Organization (FAO).

Several tasks lie ahead, agronomists agree. Political conditions that give rise to conflicts must abate. Agriculture must be put on a sustainable basis. Farm productivity must be enhanced and modern techniques disseminated. Economic development is essential to help the poor reduce their birth rates and afford a better diet.

The Political Challenge

In 1979 Tenneco West, then the agribusiness subsidiary of the Houston-based natural gas transmission company, set up a 3,000-acre mechanized farm in northern Sudan.

The country was being hailed as a potential breadbasket of the region because of its untapped land and water resources. Yields rose from half a ton of wheat per acre to two tons as the soil progressively improved. Tracy Park, the corporate vice president responsible for the farm, says it was able to feed 50,000 people in the region.

However, "you can't run a rational agriculture program in a country that's undergoing a civil war, not even if you're out of the immediate area where they're fighting," Mr. Park says. "You either can't get fuel, or supplies, or whatever it is you need." The company sold the farm to its employees in 1986.

And that is the story of starvation in Africa, says Avery. Except for the 1973 and 1983 droughts in Ethiopia, famine in Africa has been caused by shooting wars. . . .

The Sustainability Challenge

Farmers cultivate 3.7 billion acres—11 percent of the earth's land surface, according to the FAO. Is more available?

Lester Brown, founder of the Worldwatch Institute and the most pessimistic forecaster of food production trends, says the world farmland base stopped growing in 1980 and that "there's not much good crop land left to bring under the plow."

Avery says a billion acres of African wetlands and another billion of savanna with acidic soil could be pressed into service.

The FAO says that "with sufficient investment in drainage and irrigation," farmland could double worldwide. However, the FAO does not expect that. Rather, it forecasts a decline of up to 10 percent due to land degradation. Dr. Brown and Avery concur that erosion, salination, water-logging, and water table depletion will remove some farmland from cultivation.

> *"Farmers cultivate 3.7 billion acres—11 percent of the earth's land surface. . . . Is more available?"*

In addition, Brown notes, a United States government study found that air pollution can reduce crop yields by 10 percent. Elsewhere, studies have found that increased ultraviolet radiation, an effect of ozone depletion in the upper atmosphere, impairs important functions in rice and wheat. Research is continuing on the impact on yields.

Global warming, caused by the accumulation of "greenhouse" gases like carbon dioxide, would have an uncertain impact on total farm output.

Weather patterns would shift. High-value coastal farmland would be flooded. But carbon dioxide enhances photosynthesis and therefore crop production, says MSU's Dr. Harwood.

Though Brown argues that "part of the world's food output today is not sustainable," Harwood says the technological answers to many sustainability challenges are on the horizon.

Dennis Keeney, director of the Leopold Center for Sustainable Agriculture at Iowa State University, points out that the well-being of the farmer and his community are also part of the sustainability equation. And the trends toward large farms and mass-production of poultry, he notes, may not be for the best.

The Leopold Center found that a farmer could earn $29,600 from 1,000 acres of corn, but $47,300 from 400 acres of mixed corn and soybeans plus 120 pigs. If, like chickens, pigs are ever mass-produced, individual farmers might find it impossible to compete and, complains Dr. Keeney, "we lose the opportunity to be sustainable" as a business.

The Biological Challenge

Avery says that thanks to the "green revolution," which introduced fertilizer and high-yield crop hybrids to many developing nations, "we have effectively tripled the world's crop yields since 1960. We're farming almost exactly the same amount of land that we did then, in spite of the fact that we have twice as many people, and we're feeding them better."

Brown believes the revolution is over. "The nice thing about the period from 1950 to 1984 was, you just poured on more fertilizer," he says. But fertilizer use, which he argues has made its full impact, actually declined in the early 1990s. Part of the reason for the drop is that farmers are learning to apply smaller quantities of fertilizer directly where needed. Growth in per capita grain production has declined from 3 percent during 1950–84 to 1 percent since then.

"There are still a lot of opportunities for expanding food production, but they tend to be a little bit here, a little bit there—sort of more nickel-and-diming rather than the quantum jumps that we were getting from the enormous growth in irrigation from 1950 to 1978 or fertilizer from 1950 to 1984," Brown says.

James Hill, a senior FAO economist, says Brown has been making that prediction for years and has been proven wrong—so far. "However, the actual equation is correct. In sheer rational terms, there will be a limit to production," Dr. Hill says. "The question is, when is it going to occur?"

David Mengel, a soil and crop scientist at Purdue University, agrees that some technologies have given their full benefit. But he's counting on biotechnology to keep crop yields rising. "I'm not the pessimist that some other people might be," Dr. Mengel says.

The Economic Challenge

On the likelihood of raising output, Avery is as pessimistic as his counterpart at the Worldwatch Institute, though for a different reason. "Brown is saying that we can't produce more. I'm saying that there is no economic incentive to produce more," Avery explains. Countries with farm surpluses for export "are being shut out of virtually all of the growth in food demand" because countries desiring self-sufficiency put up tariffs.

In the last decade, world consumption of grain and oilseeds has risen 400 million tons, but trade is up just 29 million. Trade is supplying about 6 percent of the growth in demand for meat, he adds.

In the Western Hemisphere, Avery says, 50 million prime soybean acres go unused. Yet Indonesia just announced plans to clear 1.5 million acres of jungle to raise that crop—the very kind of hunger-related environmental depredation that Worldwatch has predicted.

With export markets uncertain, US farmers are seeking industrial customers for their food crops—turning corn into sweeteners and ethanol, for example. "This will drive the price of food up, which it is meant to do," Harwood says.

> *"Some technologies have given their full benefit."*

But what of the poor? In the US, Harwood says, rising food prices could mean more food stamps. A widening gap between the haves and have-nots could bring more Los Angeles–style social anarchy, he adds.

Avery says farmers in some parts of Africa could triple their corn production using high-yield varieties already in their possession. But they don't because their countrymen don't have the money to buy the output.

"You can see the problem [of malnutrition] is not primarily an agricultural one," Harwood says. Rather, it's one of wealth and income.

A recent World Bank report showed that 840 million people lived in 50 countries that experienced falling incomes during the 1980s. "The economic progress that should have been driving the demographic transition, the shift to small families, is just not occurring in a lot of these countries," Brown says. "Food output is slowing and population growth is not slowing. At least, not very much. That, I think, is going to get us in a jam before the end of this decade."

Avery, however, argues that the third world has gone 65 percent of the way to population stability in one generation. "We are set for more economic growth in poor countries than we have ever seen," he says, but he admits that Africa will have "a long, slow, desperately difficult struggle."

"I'm not predicting the end of hunger. I'm not predicting that governments will get perfect," Avery says. "I'm saying that there is no reason to have famine for lack of food production potential."

Technological Progress Increases Food Production

by Indur M. Goklany and Merritt W. Sprague

About the authors: *Indur M. Goklany is manager of science and engineering in the Office of Policy Analysis at the U.S. Department of the Interior. Merritt W. Sprague was formerly the director of the Office of Program Analysis at the U.S. Department of the Interior.*

Using as an example the historical increase in U.S. agricultural productivity, this viewpoint will show that—but for technological progress—all our forest-lands and croplands, including those that would have been only marginally productive, would have had to have been plowed to produce the quantities of food we produce today. The accompanying wholesale destruction of forests and other natural habitats and the reduction of biodiversity would have resulted in environmental problems that would have dwarfed those we face today and matched environmentalists' worst nightmares.

Increase Productivity of Land Use

The only way to feed, clothe, and shelter the greater world population that the future will inevitably bring—while limiting deforestation and loss of biodiversity and carbon dioxide sinks—is to increase, in an environmentally sound manner, the productivity of all activities that use land. [Forests are carbon dioxide sinks because they absorb and sequester carbon dioxide; their destruction is thought to increase atmospheric carbon dioxide, thus contributing to global warming.] Such increases are possible only within a legal, economic, and institutional framework that relies on free markets, fosters decentralized decision-making, respects individual property rights, and rewards entrepreneurship. Such an approach is the best hope for a world facing severe pressure on its land base, yet it has been noticeably absent from recent, much-publicized strategies that purport to lead us to sustainable development, conserve biological diversity, and combat global deforestation.

Abridged from Indur M. Goklany and Merritt W. Sprague, "Sustaining Development and Biodiversity: Productivity, Efficiency, and Conservation," *Cato Policy Analysis*, August 6, 1992. Reprinted by permission of the Cato Institute, Washington, D.C.

Technological change or progress, as used here, includes all the changes, on or off the farm, that have affected the economics of the supply of, demand for, and utilization of agricultural commodities. Included are changes in output due to changes in input; the introduction of new products and processes that have created new demands or reduced (or eliminated) demand for existing products and processes; and changes in lifestyles and tastes, themselves often the product of technological advances, that have affected demand for agricultural products. Thus, techno-

> *"But for technological progress—all our forestlands and croplands . . . would have had to have been plowed."*

logical change includes changes in machinery, seed varieties, fertilizers, pesticides, and other inputs; in management practices; and even in the land base. It also includes substitution of the internal combustion engine and electrical power for human, animal, and steam power as well as new and improved consumer products, derived from petroleum and other mineral resources, that substitute—to varying extents—for agricultural commodities used previously (e.g., synthetic fibers for cotton, flax, fur, and feathers). Anything that affects the market penetration of existing technology also constitutes technological change. In this viewpoint the sum of all such changes is considered technological change. Under that definition, technology that is available but has not been adopted for economic or institutional reasons does not constitute technological change.

To estimate how technological progress in the 20th century has influenced the amount of land used for agricultural purposes, one should ideally examine data from the 19th century, if not before. Because of data limitations, however, we have made calculations from 1910 data.

In 1910, 200 million acres were harvested to feed and clothe the U.S. population of 92.0 million. [Thirty-seven million acres were harvested to produce crops for export.] In addition, 88 million acres were harvested to feed 27.5 million horses and mules. (Had there not already been 468,500 motor vehicles in 1910, more land would undoubtedly have been needed for domestic purposes.) Twenty-four million of the 27.5 million horses and mules were on farms. Historical estimates of the amount of land required to feed horses and mules assume that nonfarm animals need one-third more feed than farm animals. Therefore, we estimate that 277 million acres were needed for all domestic purposes (including feed for horses and mules used to work the 200 million acres as well as for all nonfarm purposes), and 48 million acres were needed to produce crops for export.

The Results of Technology

In 1988 only 176 million acres of cropland were harvested to meet all the domestic needs of 246 million people. Had technology, its market penetration, and the U.S. standard of living been frozen at their 1910 levels, we would have needed to harvest 741 million acres to meet domestic needs, an increase of 565 million equally productive acres.

In 1988 about 40.7 percent (or 121 million acres) of U.S. cropland were harvested for export. If the average productivity of land (for purposes other than producing feed for horses and mules) had been frozen at the 1910 level, we would have needed 368 million acres to produce those exports. We also would have needed an additional 113 million acres to feed the horses and mules necessary to work the 368 million additional acres. Thus, if technology (and its market penetration) had been frozen at 1910 levels, in 1988 we would have needed to harvest about 1,222 million acres, rather than the 297 million acres actually used, to meet our domestic needs and produce the same amount for export.

To put the enormous requirement of 1,222 million acres into perspective, consider the fact that the total U.S. land area, including Alaska, is 2,271 million acres. Thus, over 54 percent of the entire U.S. land mass would have had to have been put to plow. Even that is a conservative estimate. Clearly, absent technological change, America would be in dire straits.

Thanks to technological change, we use *at least* 925 million fewer acres for crop production today than we would have without such change (Table 1). . . .

Reasons for Success

The principal reasons we are able to meet our expanded needs for food and other agricultural commodities for the domestic and foreign market with as

---

Table 1

Projected Acreage Necessary for Crop Production in 1988 If Technology Had Been Frozen at 1910 Level

Use	Acres (Millions)
Domestic food production	535
Horses/mules for domestic production and other uses	206
Exports	368
Horses/mules for export products	113
Total acres needed under a technology freeze	1,222
Acres actually harvested in 1988	297
Minimum additional acres required for 1988 production with no technological change from 1910 levels	925

Note: Calculations ignore land that is fallow or in cover crops. Generally, that amounts to about 10 percent of harvested land.

much, or less, land are the various technological and management changes that have occurred in each step of crop production and distribution, as well as in the supply of and demand for agricultural products. In particular:

• The internal combustion engine eliminated the need for horses and mules to provide transportation and to power agricultural machinery. If the horse and mule population had expanded in proportion to the human population, we would have needed 319 million additional acres just to produce feed for our horses and mules—more land than we currently harvest to feed our entire human population, as well as millions abroad. Thus, it would seem that horses and mules would be less "sustainable," even though they employ "renewable" fuels, than the internal combustion engine, which relies on "nonrenewable" fuels. (In 1910 there were about four people for each horse or mule. If it were possible to freeze technology at 1910 levels and still improve the general standard of living, it would be reasonable to expect that the number of horses and mules per capita would increase. That, in turn, would increase the amount of land needed for feed.)

• The widespread availability and use of agricultural fertilizers and pesticides and new cultivars have led to more intense land use and higher yields of quality produce.

• Additional irrigation capability; conversion of wetlands to highly productive farmlands through tile, levee, and drainage systems; and the development of more productive livestock

> *"Absent technological change, America would be in dire straits."*

and livestock confinement systems have increased yields relative to inputs of land and labor.

• Better management practices have increased productivity while reducing soil loss and improving the efficiency of water use; for example, more powerful tractors have allowed the use of deep tillage tools, which contribute to increased soil conservation.

• The advent of refrigeration in the home and in stores and advances in transportation have led to less spoilage and have reduced the need for deliberate overproduction.

• New and efficient processing technologies have resulted in better utilization of raw commodities (both agricultural and mineral) in the consumer markets for food, feed, and fiber products.

• An efficient infrastructure has developed to distribute and store agricultural products.

Each of those changes undoubtedly has had some detrimental effects on the environment. For example, agricultural fertilizers and pesticides pollute waters, and the draining of wetlands has contributed to loss of habitat for some species. . . . Instead of dealing with those familiar themes, the remainder of this viewpoint will address what is often ignored or forgotten: the beneficial effects of technological change on the nation's land resources and, in particular, on forest-lands, other natural habitats, and biological diversity.

Beneficial Effects of Technology

Clearly, technological change has enabled us to feed much larger domestic populations and to provide them with better nutrition. It has also helped the United States to supplement the rest of the world's food supplies. In addition, as the preceding calculations indicate, a major benefit of technological change has been the dramatic reduction in the amount of land that would otherwise have been converted to agriculture.

As projected above, at least 925 million more acres would have needed to have been harvested in 1988 if technology had been frozen at 1910 levels. To put that into perspective, an additional 925 million acres corresponds to

• over 11 times the total acreage currently managed under the National Park system (including Alaska),

• over 4 times the total acreage currently in the National Forest system (including Alaska),

• about 3 times the acreage of all cropland now harvested in the United States,

• over 4 times the total acreage of wetlands in the conterminous United States in the 18th century and 8 times the current area of wetlands, and

• over 180 times the area purchased by the federal government since 1965 using the Land and Water Conservation Fund at a cumulative cost of over $17 billion (in 1991 dollars). In the absence of technological change, increases in relative land prices would have reduced the amount of land that could have been purchased with the same level of funding. . . .

Not Enough Arable Land

The minimum of 1,222 million acres that would have needed to have been harvested would have

• exceeded total cropland and forestland in the United States (excluding Alaska) by 15 percent (those lands occupy 1,066 million acres) and

• required that at least 60 percent of the U.S. land area (excluding Alaska) be harvested for crops.

Although firm estimates of the amount of arable land in the United States are not available, one often-quoted estimate, based on the U.S. Department of Agriculture's National Agricultural Lands Survey, pegs it at 540 million acres. Clearly, there is not enough suitable land in the United States to have produced the same amount of crops

"The internal combustion engine eliminated the need for horses and mules to provide transportation and to power agricultural machinery."

actually grown in 1988 if technology had been frozen at 1910 levels. Moreover, as noted previously, the calculation of 1,222 million acres assumes that the last 925 million acres of harvested land would be as productive as the first 297 million acres. It also does not allow for land that may be idled or kept in cover crops. Thus, in the absence of technological change, much more than 1,222 million acres would have needed to have been harvested—unless famine claimed a large share of the population.

> *"Technological change has . . . helped the United States to supplement the rest of the world's food supplies."*

Land conversion of such massive proportions would mean that about the only areas left as National Parks, Wilderness Areas, or other reserved lands would be mountain peaks or virtual deserts unable to support any cultivation. The amount of forestland would also be reduced substantially, and the forest acreage left would be harvested more frequently. There would be even greater pressure to drain wetlands. On each of those counts, natural habitat and biological diversity would be the losers. Finally, such massive land conversion would almost surely result in higher net greenhouse gas emissions into the atmosphere.

Changes in Actual Area of Farmlands

So far we have considered only what might have happened had technology and agricultural productivity been frozen at 1910 levels. Let us now look at actual trends.

Between 1910 and 1969 there was not much change in total cropland acreage, whether used for crops or left idle. Pasture and grazing land, however, declined from 1,084 million to 886 million acres, a decline of about 200 million acres; unpastured forestland and woodland increased from 293 million to 406 million acres. (Because data in the same format were not readily available after 1969, this precise analysis could not be extended to a more recent year.) A substantial portion of the decline in pasture and grazing lands was also manifested as a decline of land in farms. Land in farms (not all of which is cultivated or cultivable) peaked in 1950 at 1,161 million acres. By 1987 it had dropped by almost 200 million acres, to 964 million acres. Thus, the land taken out of farms is more than twice all the land area currently used for urban and transportation purposes—83 million acres; less than half of the land that was freed was developed. Much of the 200 million acres freed nationally is now left to nature or managed as forestlands or woodlands.

The consequences of the reversion of land to nature as a result of the reduced need for farmland are quite apparent in some areas of the country. In New York, for example, there were 24 million acres of farmland in 1880; today there are about 8 million acres (i.e., a reduction of about two-thirds). That reduction in farmland is also matched by reductions in cropland: between 1949 and 1987 cropland declined from 13.0 million acres to 5.3 million acres, or by about 59 percent. Similar impressive reductions in farmland have been recorded throughout the Northeast: from 1880 to 1969, land in farms in that region was reduced from 68 million to 26 million acres, whereas in 1989 it stood at 23 million acres, also a reduction of about two-thirds since 1880. Between 1949 and 1987 cropland declined from 32.4 million acres to 13.3 million acres, or by 59 percent. Most of those lands reverted to nature or are managed as forestlands or woodlands; relatively little was built up. (The entire Northeast in 1987 had less than 10 million acres that were urbanized or used for transportation). As a result, wildlife is more abundant and varied today than it was at the turn of the century, and some species are making a comeback.

Progress Must Continue

During this century, technological progress has made it possible to limit U.S. land conversion to agricultural uses, thereby protecting natural habitats and biological diversity. That has been achieved by (1) greatly increasing the overall productivity of all agricultural activities (from planting to harvesting, processing, distribution, and storage); (2) making obsolete, due to the introduction of the internal combustion engine, the use of animals for transportation, industry, commerce, and agriculture; and (3) reducing the demand for certain agricultural commodities from what it otherwise might have been by producing economic substitutes from noncrop sources (e.g., synthetic fibers). A similar analysis done for the entire world would undoubtedly lead to similar conclusions. . . .

> *"Wildlife [in the Northeast] is more abundant and varied today than it was at the turn of the century."*

Over the next century, the world population is projected to more than double from the current 5 billion to between 11 billion and 15 billion. Moreover, it is hoped that the average economic well-being of that larger population will improve. Both factors would increase the demand for agricultural and forest commodities, as well as for land for livestock and settlements. If the population were to double and food production per capita were to increase by 0.8 percent per year [as United Nations statistics suggest], by 2050 food production would need to be 223 percent greater than it is today. If the demand for forest products caused by improved economic circumstances were to increase by 2 percent per capita per year, by 2050—all else (including technology) being equal—the demand for forest commodities would increase by 550 percent.

There simply is not enough productive land in the world to meet such increasing demands for food and forest products—unless there is continued technological progress. Such progress will be crucial to maintaining or improving the quality of life of all the societies of the world. The question, therefore, is not whether technological progress is inevitable, but rather, how do we ensure that it is? The primary issue surrounding deforestation and conserving biological diversity and carbon dioxide sinks is how to ensure that not all *productive* lands—including those that are marginal—are devoted to crops, forest products, grazing of livestock, and human settlements. How to manage productive lands that will not have been pressed into service to meet human demands, though important, is a secondary issue.

The continued opportunity for the societies of the world to benefit from technological change gives rise to the hope that standards of living and the quality of life can be maintained or improved. Improved economic conditions often go hand in hand with more stable population levels. . . .

A Global View

Good stewardship requires that all resources—energy, land, and all other natural resources—be used as efficiently and productively as possible. It would be ironic if well-intentioned actions and programs to improve the environment by limiting agriculture inputs only aggravated the threats to forestlands, other natural habitats, biological diversity, and carbon dioxide sinks. Instead, we need to take a global view of the consequences of actions that affect the productivity of land and support a more comprehensive, careful, and objective analysis of the benefits and costs of such actions.

Some people currently advocate an end to technological advances in the belief that such changes most often have greater adverse consequences than benefits for society. Others advocate less intensive land use for agriculture in the hope that somehow the result will be less total environmental damage while farm income is maintained and needed products are provided. The preceding discussion of the potential effects of having stopped the clock on progress in 1910 should offer some insight on the wisdom of taking such actions now. More significant, such an examination indicates the wisdom of placing increased emphasis on supporting environmentally sound technological change and improvements in agricultural productivity as the key to ensuring that sufficient *productive* land remains in the future for purposes other than fulfilling human needs.

> *"[Technological] progress will be crucial to maintaining or improving the quality of life of all the societies of the world."*

Finally, it should be noted that one consequence of low-input sustainable agriculture (LISA) is that more land would be devoted to crops than would be otherwise. The extra land used for agriculture will mean that much less for other species. What we need is not LISA, but HOSA—high-output sustainable agriculture—consistent with each farmer's maximizing his or her net income in a free-market environment. With equal emphasis on both the high-output and the sustainability criteria, in some situations HOSA may resemble LISA, but not the other way around.

Technology and Market Forces Can Increase Food Production

by Frances Cairncross

About the author: *Frances Cairncross is the environmental editor at the* Economist, *a weekly newsmagazine published in Britain.*

Environmentalists tend to be alarmists. They have to be, to get their voices heard. The day-to-day traumas of politics and economics—a coup here, a currency crisis there—seize the attention of policymakers and elbow aside, week after week, the slower pace of environmental change. Besides, many environmental changes, especially in the rich world, appear to threaten neither health nor wealth. If the fish vanish from a river or the city air becomes hazier, the costs—in anything more than emotion—may be slight. In the rich world, many more people almost certainly die in traffic accidents than from the side-effects of pollution. Moreover, the recession of the early 1990s has probably cost most rich countries more than all the environmental damage of the past 20 years.

Human Lives and Health

The costs of environmental damage in the poor world, though, are another matter. There, the damage has been accelerating and occurring on a scale never seen in most rich countries. Some of the costs are emotional: There will be plenty of sadness as pandas, black rhinoceros, tigers, gorillas, and elephants disappear from the wild—and perhaps from the planet—over the next generation. Unfortunately for those creatures, they are concentrated in parts of the world where land use is changing fastest and where the financial and administrative resources to protect them are least available. More important in many developing countries, however, are the environmental costs measured in human lives and health. Moreover, the immense predicted growth in population—almost all of it in the poor world—will put increasing pressure on natural resources. . . .

Abridged from Frances Cairncross, "Environmental Pragmatism." Reprinted with permission from *Foreign Policy* 95 (Summer 1994). Copyright 1994 by the Carnegie Endowment for International Peace.

The inevitable starting point is world population growth. That growth, spread unevenly across the globe, is likely to be behind almost all the challenges to the stability of the international system that have environmental origins. We face a world in which the current population of 5.3 billion will certainly double, may treble, and could conceivably quadruple before it levels out. In the second half of this century, world population has increased more rapidly than ever before, reaching a peak growth rate of 2.1 per cent in 1965–70. Since then, although the rate of growth has slowed everywhere except in Africa, the absolute size of the increase is still getting larger. In 1994 it was about 101 million, or more than the entire population of Mexico.

> *"The immense predicted growth in population . . . will put increasing pressure on natural resources."*

Will that growth continue? Recent experience suggests not. As a country grows richer, it reaches a point at which its average family size sharply diminishes. But the link between wealth and babies is not precise. If greater wealth causes fertility to fall as rapidly as it has done in Hong Kong, Jamaica, Mexico, and Costa Rica, then the world's population might level out at 10.1 billion. However, if it falls as slowly as it has done in Paraguay, Sri Lanka, Turkey, or Suriname, then it would stabilize at around 23 billion—and not until the end of the twenty-second century. Those figures assume, of course, that some sudden catastrophe, such as a war or an acceleration of the spread of AIDS and its associated diseases, does not alter current trends.

Population Densities

Because of the fall in fertility accompanying wealth, rapid population growth is concentrated almost entirely in the poorer countries. It is fastest in Africa, closely followed by Southeast Asia, not including China. That uneven spread of growth has dramatically changed the proportion of peoples from different parts of the world. In 1950, 33 per cent of the world's population lived in the developed countries. Today, that share is approximately 23 per cent. By 2025, it will fall to 16 per cent and will have been overtaken by Africa, which by then will have 19 per cent of the world's people. Southeast Asia—wherever its boundaries are drawn—already contains many more people than any other part of the world. Interestingly, the population of India will overtake that of China early in the next century. That forecast assumes that the economic boom in China, which is undermining China's "one-child" policy, does not lead instead to an acceleration in the country's fertility rate.

As populations grow, people will live at ever-greater densities. The World Bank's *World Development Report 1992* notes that only Bangladesh, South Korea, the Netherlands, and the island of Java now have population densities of more than 400 people per square kilometer [or more than 1,036 per square mile]. By the middle of the next century, one-third of the world's people will probably live at such densities. Given the current trends, the population density of Bangladesh will rise to an unimaginable 1,700 people per square kilometer [or 4,400 per square mile]. . . .

Monster Cities

One important side-effect of population growth in developing countries will be the emergence of monster cities. Even in developing countries, cities will house a growing proportion of the population. They will be difficult to run, and potentially politically dangerous.

The World Resources Institute reports that only 3 per cent of the world's inhabitants lived in urban areas in the mid-eighteenth century. By the 1950s, that proportion had risen to 29 per cent; today, it is more than 40 per cent; and by 2025, 60 per cent of the world's people are expected to be living in or around cities. Almost all that increase will be in what is now the Third World. Because it is the young who tend to move to the cities, populations of the megalopolises will be even younger than populations of the developing world as a whole.

Many cities in developing countries are already a close approximation of hell on earth. They will get worse. Mexico City, which had 17 million inhabitants in 1985, will have 24 million by the end of the century; São Paulo will jump from 15 million to 24 million. It will be hard to provide those cities with the services needed to maintain even a moderately healthy environment. The percentage of people without clean water has remained virtually unchanged over the past decade, despite a steep rise in the numbers of town-dwellers being supplied. The absolute number of people without sewerage has sharply increased. Removing solid waste is an even greater challenge, made worse by the presence of many small enterprises, often within houses, that may be carrying out highly polluting activities generating toxic waste. . . .

> *"Many cities in developing countries are already a close approximation of hell on earth."*

Solving the problems of cities will drain the budgets of governments in the developing world. To keep city-dwellers quiet, governments must ensure that they are fed, that they have water, and that money is invested in infrastructure. In many developing countries, the current tension between town and country will be exacerbated by such demands, as farmers increasingly feel they are being milked to maintain urban living standards.

Raising the Yield

Anybody who predicts a Malthusian crisis in the next century must remember what has happened over the past two decades. [Malthus said population would grow at a faster rate than the food supply.] The warnings of catastrophe that were popular in the early 1970s were followed by years in which world food

128

output rose faster than population. For instance, India's population grew on average by 2.1 per cent between 1950 and 1990; its food output grew on average by 2.7 per cent. As a result, India now exports food. The global trend conceals some countries that have become increasingly hungry, such as Bangladesh, Nepal, and most countries of sub-Saharan Africa. But World Bank estimates suggest that it would be technically possible to feed a world population of 11.4 billion people with a daily diet that provided 6,000 calories of "plant energy" (grain, seed, and animal feed) a day. That is roughly twice the calories in the typical diet in South Asia today.

In a sense, then, there is enough food: not only for today's population, but for one twice as large. Such calculations, however, rely on a sizable increase in yields in developing countries. Such increases are theoretically possible: Cereal yield in the United States at the start of the 1980s was 4.2 tons per hectare [2.47 acres] of harvested area, compared with 1.5 tons for fertile Kenya or 2 for hungry Bangladesh. For a growing number of countries, increasing yields will be the only way to raise food output, as the growing population competes for cropland.

Higher Yields vs. Habitat Conversion

The alternative to increasing yields is to increase the amount of land taken into cultivation. That usually means destroying forests and cultivating ever-steeper hillsides. Quite apart from the implications for wildlife habitats, such policies are frequently unsustainable. Marginal land is usually marginal precisely because it has traditionally been considered too fragile for permanent cultivation. Tilling it increases the danger of erosion, landslides, and floods. It is also likely to produce lower yields than land already in cultivation.

The conversion of habitat into farmland is the main cause of species extinction. That may not in itself be a cause of global insecurity; however, the United States has already used trade controls against countries that hunt whales and dolphins. Might some rich countries be tempted to use trade sanctions against poorer countries that fail to protect the wildlife the West loves?

The yield from farmland can be raised either by using more fertilizers and pesticides or by bringing more land into cultivation. Raising the yield from the sea, however, will prove harder. Since 1989 the world marine catch has stopped increasing. Throughout the 1980s, catches of the most valuable species, such as cod and halibut, were lower than they had been the previous decade, even though the capacity of world fishing fleets was greater. Catches were maintained by a rising take of less-valuable fish, such as pollack and anchovies. Fish are the most important source of animal protein in many developing countries. If the yield of wild fish has reached (or passed) its maxi-

"To keep city-dwellers quiet, governments must ensure that they are fed."

mum, any increase in the supply of fish will have to come from aquaculture. Unfortunately, that has so far proved an expensive way to mass-produce fish.

The pressure of population on world food supplies is unlikely to lead directly to sudden famines. Those are more often caused by some other disruption, such as civil war or drought, in a country where food supplies are already inadequate. More likely is that in some countries, mainly in Africa, a growing share of the population will either be permanently malnourished or else seek to emigrate.

> *"For a growing number of countries, increasing yields will be the only way to raise food output."*

Countries do not, of course, need to be able to feed themselves. Hong Kong does not; neither does Singapore. But countries that do not grow their own food must pay to import it. Some developing countries, such as India, have a sufficient entrepreneurial base to produce exports to pay for any necessary food imports. Countries such as Burkina Faso do not.

Water

In many parts of the world, the most sought-after resource will not be agricultural land, but water. A growing number of countries are reaching the point where the availability of water will seriously constrain agricultural expansion and industrial development. Within countries, quarrels over the availability of water will sour relations between country and town. And where watersheds are shared by several countries, the availability of water will become a source of political tension.

Three parts of the world are particularly short of water: Africa, the Middle East, and South Asia. In each of those areas, rainfall is low. For example, India is already using half the rain that runs off land into rivers and lakes, and half as much again from underground wells and springs. By the year 2025, India is likely to be using 92 per cent of its freshwater resources.

The way Indian water is used is typical of many developing countries. Industry uses only about 1.4 cubic kilometers of water a year. Domestic demand is double that. Livestock and power stations each use 3 times as much. But in India irrigation uses 360 times as much water as industry. Worldwide, 70 per cent of the world's freshwater is used for irrigation, and the share is higher in poorer countries. The use of irrigation has been essential to the increase in food output over the past 20 years. Although only a fifth of the world's cropland is irrigated, a third of the world's food now comes from irrigated land.

It would certainly be possible to irrigate the same amount of land with much less water. As much as a third of all irrigation water is wasted: Channels are unlined and water seeps away. It will be essential to find more frugal ways to irrigate for two reasons. First, irrigation can easily do irreparable damage to farmland. As water soaks into thin soils, it flushes salts and minerals to the surface.

When the water evaporates, those particles remain to create a thin, poisonous crust. More and more irrigated land is losing the battle against such salinization. Second, as industry and cities grow, they too need water. Governments in places as different as California, China, and Egypt face politically awkward problems of diverting water from the country to cities, where it can be more productively used. One of the things that differentiates water from food and energy is that it is not usually marketed: Without a price increase to signal growing scarcity, users have little incentive to invest in more efficient technologies. . . .

Market-Driven Change

The best hope of stretching resources to meet demand is likely to lie in technological change, spurred on by the forces of the market. If . . . food starts to run out, prices will rise and make producers more willing to increase supplies and buyers look for ways to economize. In the long run, such price changes will balance the supply of and demand for privately owned natural resources, but price changes may cause sudden shocks to the world economy and will certainly have large distributional side-effects. Importing countries will be impoverished and exporters enriched.

However, even if the market helps share out those resources that are privately owned and exploited, it will not deliver a cleaner environment. That can be done only by government intervention. The market, left to its

> *"As much as a third of all irrigation water is wasted. . . . It will be essential to find more frugal ways to irrigate."*

own devices, will frequently aggravate environmental harm, as is dismally evident in southern China today. But government intervention, in the form of environmental regulations or "green" taxes, is more easily accomplished in industrial countries with a long tradition of administrative activity than in developing countries where government institutions may still be relatively primitive. As a result, the environment is most at risk in countries that combine rapid economic growth with fragile governmental institutions.

Where government is willing and able to intervene, technological change can help deliver dramatic improvements in environmental quality. The rich countries have greatly reduced the most dangerous air pollutants—sulfur dioxide particulates such as soot and dust—partly by changing from open fires to central heating and from the direct use of coal to a greater use of electricity. They have also enormously improved the quality of their water. Some developing countries are beginning to follow their example. As countries grow richer, they tend to demand rapid improvements in those kinds of pollution that most harm human health.

Modern Agricultural Practices Are Beneficial

by Dennis T. Avery

About the author: *Dennis T. Avery is a senior fellow and director of the Center for Global Food Issues at the Hudson Institute, a public policy research organization headquartered in Indianapolis, Indiana.*

The environmental movement is valid and important. Environmentalists are forcing us to recognize that we are increasingly capable of—and responsible for—saving natural resources. Nevertheless, though they recognize the problems, they do not always see clearly the solution strategies. In the case of agriculture in particular, they have come to exactly the wrong policy solutions.

Mankind is at the most critical moment in environmental history. What we do as people and societies in the next decade will determine whether we have a more crowded but sustainable world to bequeath to future generations—or whether we will bring on the very apocalypse of famine and wildlife destruction that the gloomiest environmentalists have envisioned. Our decisions on agriculture and forestry will be the most crucial of all, because they will govern how we use two-thirds of the earth's surface. They will dictate the habitat—or loss of habitat—for 95 percent of the earth's wildlife species.

"Think Globally"

So far, we are making the wrong decisions, for the wrong reasons, based on the wrong information. The environmental movement was never more correct than when it coined the slogan, "Think globally and act locally." But today's environmentalists are not thinking about farming and forestry in global terms.

Land, one may argue, is the scarcest resource of all. We need it to produce our food and timber. It is increasingly in demand for human recreation. Now, in addition, we recognize an almost unlimited demand for land as wildlife habitat. Virtually every bit of wildlife habitat is important. Agriculture and forestry are the only sector where we can "create" more land without sacrificing the environment. High yields are the only way to do it.

The environmental movement, however, has been recommending exactly the opposite strategy—low-yield farming. That would almost certainly trigger the plow-down of huge tracts of wildlife habitat as people attempt to avoid famine.

The yields from traditional and organic farms [which use biological and mineral materials for fertilizing soil and combating pests and diseases] are too low to feed people and still protect wildlife.

In the case of forestry, most environmentalists are similarly recommending low-yield forest management and the non-harvesting of trees. That would leave us with fewer trees and less wood—and reliant on more polluting alternatives (like steel) for construction needs. High-yield plantation forestry on a few acres is a key to having lots of forest products and still having lots of wild forests and wildlife.

> *"[Low-yield farming] would almost certainly trigger the plow-down of huge tracts of wildlife habitat as people attempt to avoid famine."*

Much of the green movement has also opposed international trade in general, and farm product trade in particular. They fear that trade will weaken environmental initiatives and threaten small traditional farmers. However, the lack of trade in agriculture and forestry is likely to mean losing big tracts of wildlife habitat in some parts of the world, while safe and renewable farming resources are wasted in other places. The key problem region will be Asia, which will be nine times as densely populated per acre of farmland as North America in the year 2050. . . .

The Importance of High-Yield Agriculture

- The world cannot save its wildlife without high-yield agriculture [using seeds that produce large yields] and the careful use of farm chemicals.
- The world cannot afford to do without high-yield plantation forestry *for its environmental benefits* in preserving truly wild forests free from logging pressures.
- Rising crop yields (and thus more food security) haven't encouraged more births; on the contrary, they seem to bring the number of births per woman down more rapidly.
- The methods used to achieve high yields in farming and forestry are already far safer for the environment and for people than the so-called "green" alternatives. There are major risks involved in organic farming. For humans, the organic farming risks include higher cancer rates from unseen natural toxins in untreated grains and oilseeds. They also include higher prices for fruits and vegetables, discouraging the fruit and vegetable consumption that can cut cancer rates in half.
- For wildlife, the low yields of organic farming—and resulting habitat loss—far outweigh the occasional, and unfortunate, losses of wildlife to

pesticides. When we factor in these risks, organic farming is the high-risk solution for both people and wildlife.

• For small, traditional farmers, the risk is being condemned to a short, harsh life of toil, disease and ignorance—while raising large, poverty-driven families that destroy forests and erode fragile soils.

Conversely, we should be able to feed, house and clothe 10 billion people on less land than we use for farming and forestry today if we:

• Aggressively pursue yield-enhancing agricultural and forestry research. New research is especially important for the Third World, which cannot yet afford to pay for it. Biotechnology is particularly important in both field and tree crops since it represents our biggest reservoir of unexploited new high-yield strategies.

> *"Organic farming is the high-risk solution for both people and wildlife."*

• Use the best and safest land to produce our field and tree crops. The yields on the best land are often twice as high as on the poorer land. That means much more uncropped land can be left to wildlife and recreation. Equally important, there is far less biodiversity on the best and safest lands; biologists theorize that the easy environments allow a few major species to dominate (like the bison, wolf, and prairie dog on our Great Plains). A square mile of rain forest may contain more species than the entire Great Plains.

High-yield farming is not a matter of putting small farmers out of business, anywhere in the world. A planet that must roughly triple the output of its food system has no interest in putting any farmers out of business. The question is where we invest to expand.

High Yields for a Better Future

Several of President Clinton's appointees (not in the Department of Agriculture) reacted to my [writings] about high-yield agriculture by saying, "Oh, that high-yield stuff is how we *used* to do farming. Now we have found a better way."

The old way of producing food has been around since before Chief Massasoit taught the Pilgrims how to fertilize their corn with fish. It is called low-yield farming.

The environmental movement has not brought forward any breakthroughs in food production.

Organic farmers, who after all are essentially low-yield, traditional farmers, have not suddenly discovered how to produce lots of extra food. In fact, they are recommending we produce less.

Similarly, biological pest controls are making some progress in controlling a few pests in a few places, but there is little likelihood that they will replace much of our chemical pest control. Biological controls are too narrow and too uncertain.

Integrated pest management (IPM) [which involves a limited use of chemicals along with other methods such as crop rotation and biological controls] is also useful, and more producers are using more of it. However, it is not a way to replace pesticides, but rather a way to make them more effective.

Finally, composting and organic fertilizer can only add marginally to our plant nutrient supply. Organic farmers cannot replace the huge quantities of chemical nitrogen and mined phosphate without clearing huge tracts of land for green manure crops—thus sacrificing wildlife habitat.

Nor can the environmental movement bring down the world's population growth trends much more quickly than they are already coming down. The Third World's birth rates have already come more than 60 percent of the way to stability, essentially in one generation. We have a fighting chance at re-stabilizing population at 8 billion people and as early as 2035—mainly because of economic growth and TV. But that won't preclude the need to essentially triple the output of the world's agricultures.

> *"The environmental movement has not brought forward any breakthroughs in food production."*

No one is delivering a vegetarian world. Tropical forest is already being cleared to grow low-yielding soybeans for broiler chickens. Big dams are already being built to irrigate more feed grains for hogs. Crop residues are already being stolen to feed more dairy cows to produce more milk, despite the long-term risks to soil productivity.

Obviously, the rising food needs of the world must be met this year, and next year, and the year after that. The key question—and one that the environmental activists and organic buffs refuse to answer—is this: "How many million acres of wildlife habitat are you willing to clear to have chemical-free farming?"

The question of high-yield farming is no arcane or historical debate. Its answer will almost certainly determine the future of the world's wildlife, and probably the futures of billions of people as well.

Unfortunately, it has been tough to get a public hearing for the high-yield viewpoint. It might have been easier if Paul Ehrlich had published his 1968 book, *The Population Bomb*, before Rachel Carson wrote her powerful indictment of pesticides (*Silent Spring*) in 1962. If we had truly become concerned about population before we got frightened of pesticides, we might have been more open to the benefits of high yields. But Rachel Carson got there first. One might say she poisoned the well of public opinion against fertilizers and pesticides.

Low Risk from Chemicals

We know now that manmade chemicals are no more dangerous than natural chemicals. Most chemicals, both natural and manmade, seem to be dangerous to rats in high-dose testing. But high-dose rat tests, as most scientists will admit, overstate the risk to human beings from *all* chemicals.

We also know now that Ms. Carson's fears of widespread human cancer from pesticides have not been borne out. When we adjust for the increasing age of our population, there has been *no* increase in nonsmoking cancer rates as the use of pesticides has spread.

Nor do we have any examples of pesticides threatening wildlife species—or even any major wildlife *populations*. Quite the opposite, in fact. We have pesticides helping to raise crop and tree yields instead of having to plow down wildlife habitat. Every naturalist writing about potential extinction of wild species is worried about three things: habitat, habitat, habitat. Pesticides help protect the habitat.

> *"How many million acres of wildlife habitat are you willing to clear to have chemical-free farming?"*

Fortunately, the environmental movement no longer needs to indict farm chemicals to justify its existence. The environmental movement has demonstrated its own vital validity. The fact that the movement got its start in the aftermath of *Silent Spring* should not dictate environmental policy recommendations today, when we know so much more about the ecology, and about cancer; and when the pesticides themselves have gotten so much safer.

Such relatively new compounds as the sulfanylureas and the glyphosates are no more toxic than aspirin, need only a few ounces per acre, and can be used around such sensitive species as trout and quail with no harm.

Even given such chemical safety, my claim is not that farm chemicals have zero risk. Rather, I claim that *the major wildlife benefits they offer far outweigh the very small and declining risks they may contain*. . . .

Slowing World Population Growth

It's a surprise to many, but high-yield farming seems to help slow down population growth.

The countries that have made the most progress in raising their grain yields have also made the most progress in bringing down their birth rates. Producing more food *has not* aggravated the world's population problems. In fact, the world's population growth rate began to trend down in the very year that the world gave the Nobel Peace Prize to Dr. Norman Borlaug [a geneticist who developed high-yield varieties of grain] (1970)—in the wake of the Green Revolution.

It is entirely reasonable that higher grain yields should be a leading indicator of lower birth rates. They help produce higher standards of living. They help give parents confidence that their first two or three children will live. More grain makes people more confident that they will be looked after adequately in their old age.

Furthermore, countries generally do not develop cities and urban industries until they have ample food available to feed nonfarm populations. Urban populations almost always have sharply lower birth rates than rural ones, in every culture, and on every continent.

We've known for a long time, of course, that higher yields have been associated with low birth rates in the First World:

- America's corn yields have increased 152 percent since 1950, compared with an 89 percent rise in our population. U.S. births per woman are at 2.1, exactly the long-term replacement level.
- French wheat yields have risen 195 percent in the same period, while its population has risen 38 percent. The French fertility rate is now 1.8, below replacement.

The same association seems to hold in the Third World as well:

- India's rice yields have risen 135 percent, and its wheat yields have more than doubled, against a population increase of 149 percent. India's births per woman have fallen from 5.8 to 3.1, with virtually all of the reduction achieved since the beginning of the Green Revolution.
- Indonesia's rice yields are up 160 percent, against population growth of 142 percent. The fertility rate of a *Moslem population* has fallen dramatically, from 5.5 to 2.4 births per woman.
- Emerging Chile has boosted its corn yields by more than four-fold, and easily accommodated a population increase of 130 percent. Births per woman have fallen *in a Catholic country* from 4.0 to 2.1.

> *"High-yield farming seems to help slow down population growth."*

- Zimbabwe has long had the best corn-breeding program in Africa. Corn yields among its traditional village farmers have roughly quadrupled, matching the fourfold expansion of its population. Zimbabwe's births per woman started dropping sooner and have come down more sharply than most Sub-Saharan countries, from 7.7 to 3.5.
- China's rice yields have risen 150 percent since 1950, outgaining a population increase of 114 percent. China's births per woman are down to a very low 1.9, well below replacement. China has also been famous in recent decades for a harsh policy against large families. However, China's dense population has unquestionably driven both its population policy and the establishment of one of the Third World's best agricultural research systems.

Unsuccessful Farming Leads to More Births

It may seem counterintuitive, but the countries which have had less success in raising grain yields have also kept the highest birth rates:

- In Ethiopia, grain yields have more than doubled (120 percent) but the population has increased 178 percent. The fertility rate *increased* from 5.8 in the 1970s to 7.3 in 1993.

- Kenya's corn yields have risen 47 percent, but its population has risen more than 300 percent! The fertility rate was 8 children per woman as recently as in 1970. The population growth rate hovered near 4 percent (one of the highest rates in the world) until the end of the 1980s. A crash family planning effort by the Kenyan government has recently helped start the fertility rate downward more rapidly.
- Ghana's rice yields have risen only 24 percent since 1950, while the population has increased more than 300 percent. The fertility rate is still 5.4 births per woman, down from 6.7.
- Rwanda's corn yields have risen only about 25 percent, while its population has increased 250 percent. (Yields for the important potato and bean crops *have* risen significantly.) Births per woman have come down from 7.8 but are still at 4.9.

The lesson is clear. High-yield farming helps bring birth rates down. Cutting off high-yield farming research and discouraging the use of fertilizer in the world will hamper our progress toward restabilizing population.

If the world opts for low-yield farming (or simply fails to support a whole-hearted push for higher-yield farming) it will take longer to stabilize the population. Low-yield farming is likely to produce more population growth, not less.

But the First World hasn't learned this yet.

The Senate Hearing

In March 1994, I debated Lester Brown, one of our most prominent environmentalists, at a Senate hearing. For years, Brown and his Worldwatch Institute have been predicting famine and environmental disasters due to population growth. They have also contended that agricultural research and higher yields could not meet the food challenge facing the world. They have argued, instead, for population "management." The occasion for our debate was a hearing of the Senate Agricultural Appropriations Committee on the world food outlook. The chairman was Sen. Dale Bumpers (D-Ark).

Brown predicted that the world was headed for massive famine and chaos. Of course, he has been predicting these calamities virtually every year for 25 years. To date, the big famines have never appeared. Bumpers called Brown a "genius" and noted that he himself didn't think the world could sustain more than 2 to 3 billion people (roughly half of our current world population).

When my turn came, I testified that there is no need for famine in the world's future. The reasons: First, high-yield agriculture is raising crop yields much faster than population growth. Second, high-yield farming has already tripled the output of land and water in farming since the 1950s, during the very period when Brown has been wrongly predicting famine. Third, plant breeding, biotechnology, and other

> *"There is no need for famine in the world's future."*

knowledge advances continue to permit higher and higher crop yields, even in the most advanced countries. Fourth, if we *did* get famine, it would only be after starving people had destroyed virtually all of the world's wildlife in last, desperate efforts to keep their children alive.

The question was not whether we would feed more people. The real question was whether we would feed the world's extra people from a few acres or a lot of acres. Wildlife would be the key beneficiaries of our success—or pay the supreme price for our failure.

I said that there was every reason to believe that if Bumpers' Agricultural Appropriations Committee kept funding high-yield agricultural and forestry research, we would be able to feed the doubled-and-restabilized human population of 2050 and beyond—*and* have at least as much room for wildlife as the planet has today.

I was astonished at the Senator's reaction. "Mr. Avery," he said, "your testimony makes me sorry I convened this hearing." Sen. Bumpers seemed suddenly depressed—by the idea that we wouldn't have famine!

Bumpers had apparently been contemplating a big, mechanistic, guilt-free famine solution to end the world's population growth. Meanwhile, his Senate committee was proposing to cut funds for the international agricultural research which could help produce more food quickly. The funding, instead, was going to provide more condoms and pills for the Third World—though these were unlikely to have any significant impact soon enough to stave off famine or wildlife losses. . . .

Preventing Famine and Saving Wildlife

Thanks to high-yield farming, . . . we do not need to induce mass famine, nor force abortions upon the unwilling. . . .

Nor do we need to accept the loss of any significant wildlife, wildlife habitat or key environmental resources. We can create the new resources we need from our increasing knowledge of the natural world—and use more intensively the natural resources already supporting humanity.

The loss of high-yield farming, by contrast, would mean famine for billions; and destruction of more wildlife than most of us can imagine.

For nothing.

Biotechnology Can Enhance Food Production

by Laurent Belsie

About the author: *Laurent Belsie is a staff writer for the* Christian Science Monitor, *a daily newspaper.*

Two plants sit side by side in a greenhouse.

One is healthy and untouched by pests.

The other is leaf-eaten. Having bored a small, brown hole through one of its cotton bolls, a worm now sits drowsily on the inside of a blossom.

"That's going to make zero cotton," says Rob Horsch, manager of crop transformation for Monsanto Company's agriculture group in St. Louis, Missouri.

What's the difference between the two plants? Biotechnology.

The first plant is a new bioengineered variety that's unappealing to pests.

A Silent Revolution

Twenty years after the green revolution, which boosted wheat and rice yields dramatically in parts of the developing world, biotechnology is preparing to boost production again. The biotech revolution, if one can call it that, will be far different from the green revolution that preceded it.

"It's going to be more like a silent revolution than a bomb," says Luther Tweeten, professor of agricultural economics at Ohio State University.

"The green revolution did one good thing. It helped third-world farmers produce more food," says Rebecca Goldburg, who is a senior scientist at the Environmental Defense Fund, an environmental group based in New York.

But it also pushed farmers into using pesticides, chemical fertilizer, and irrigation that, in some cases, caused environmental harm.

"We have to worry a lot more about the appropriateness of what we are doing this time around," Dr. Goldburg says.

It's hard to call biotechnology a revolution. Despite the hype from supporters and detractors, its initial impact will be modest. Although biotechnology will affect a wider range of agriculture than the green revolution ever did, commercial products will take years to get to the marketplace. Scientists can only manipulate simple traits of plants at the moment. In the end, the technology will probably have a greater impact than the green revolution. But it will be cumulative, not a dramatic one-year burst of productivity.

"We will look back and call it a revolution," Dr. Horsch says.

Wary Consumers

The scientific breakthroughs are only half the battle. A study prepared for the United States Department of Agriculture suggests that public education will be crucial for the technology to be a commercial success. Consumers are wary.

Bioengineered bovine somatotropin—or BST—is a prime example. BST is a growth hormone that occurs naturally in cows. Researchers have created a bioengineered version that can boost and prolong a cow's milk production by an average of 5 to 20 percent when introduced into a cow's system.

Some Midwestern farmers, horrified at the prospect of more milk flooding the market, have mounted an effective protest that has put Monsanto and other BST producers on the defensive. Agriculture economists and pharmaceutical companies have countered by touting BST's benefits. Consumers will pay less for dairy products, they say.

The reality is more mundane than either side cares to admit.

Monsanto estimates that if 40 to 50 percent of US farmers use the product on 40 to 60 percent of their cows, US milk production would go up 5 percent. Professor Tweeten calculates that if 80 percent of farmers adopted BST—an optimistic assumption—the average US family would save $9 a year.

"A lot of people think BST is a revolution," Tweeten says. "It's no big deal."

All of biotechnology is that way. It will be years before advances match the annual gains made through plant breeding and other traditional agricultural techniques. Those traditional advances typically add $2 billion a year to US national income, Tweeten says. Even when fully implemented, bioengineered BST might add $1 billion a year in national income. Thus, it will take 20 BST-like advances every decade just to match the progress of today's farmers and processors.

> *"[Biotechnology] will probably have a greater impact than the green revolution."*

Besides the economic impact, there are other biotechnology concerns. Animal-welfare advocates worry that BST will put added stress on cows. Biotechnology's best-known opponent, Jeremy Rifkin, helped organize a supermarket boycott of milk produced using the bioengineered BST. The US Food and Drug Administration (FDA) already has ruled that milk from bioengineered BST is safe for human consumption. It has yet to rule on BST's impact on animals. [The FDA declared BST safe for cows in November 1993—ed.]

Other bioengineered products are also under fire. When the FDA announced in May 1992 that it would not require labels on genetically altered foods, Mr. Rifkin gathered more than 20 famous chefs and food gurus to publicize those foods.

The flap has sensitized even biotechnology's most ardent defenders.

"I would never have guessed that you would have to defend in all public arenas such bioscience applications," says Clifton Baile, director of research and development at Monsanto's animal sciences division. If he had to do BST over again, "now I would look to see what a Green would say."

"Genie Is Out of the Bottle"

Public debate is necessary, even if it slows down biotechnology advances, says Marshall Martin, professor of agricultural economics at Purdue University. But he doubts that biotechnology research will stop in its tracks if BST is not successful.

"The genie is out of the bottle," he says. After BST will come PST or porcine somatotropin and, after that, a whole range of new products.

At a research farm of the Illinois Agriculture Experiment Station, supervisor Bill Fisher stands in the middle of dozens of squealing pigs. Some are long, lean US hogs; others are fatty, wrinkled varieties from China. "We would just as soon not have this package," Mr. Fisher says, slapping the hairy back of a 2½-year-old Chinese sow. The Chinese hogs carry only half the meat per pound that US varieties do. But they have one very desirable trait: Instead of farrowing 8½ pigs per litter, the US average, Chinese sows give birth to an average of 11½.

"Advances in bioengineered grain will be important to keeping up with the world's food demand."

Researchers here are using various biotechnology tools to try to reproduce that trait in US hogs. In some cases, gene-mapping has been used to determine which hogs to use for traditional crossbreeding. In others, scientists have merged parts of Chinese and American embryos and transplanted them into Chinese sows, which gave birth. The result: transgenic pigs.

The transgenic pigs look the same as traditional crossbred varieties. Researchers hope that by the year 2000, they will have created a new breed of lean, high-litter hog. If they could increase the average litter by just one pig, the boost would put millions of dollars into the pockets of Illinois farmers alone.

Don Holt, director of the experiment station, says that the BST milk controversy has had little impact on his PST pork program. "The sensitivity to milk will always be greater because it's fed to babies," he says. Some biotech supporters say it's unfortunate the industry chose BST as its first commercial agriculture product.

Animal agriculture—even if it is bioengineered—won't increase the world's food production. It only increases the variety of what people eat. By one estimate it takes seven times as many resources to provide nutrients through beef as it does through grain. Thus, advances in bioengineered grain will be important to keeping up with the world's food demand.

The world today raises enough food to feed itself, says Professor Martin of Purdue. Starvation continues because of poor distribution. Countries are unable or unwilling to pay for food imports and get them to their populations. The world could probably get by during the next 50 years without the benefits of bioengineering, he adds, but the earth would be stretching its resources to do it.

> *"To adapt biotechnology to the developing world, special research efforts are needed."*

Benefits for Developed Nations

Most of the commercial research in bioengineered crops will benefit the developed world more than the developing one. At Monsanto, for example, researchers are busy creating plants that are more resistant to insects, viruses, and pesticides. These traits would allow farmers to use fewer pesticides in smaller quantities without losing current production. That should help the environment, especially in developed nations where farmers have the resources and training to take advantage of the technology.

Monsanto and Calgene of Davis, California, are working on such products as tomatoes that ripen slowly when picked. That way, commercial growers could pick them when they're flavorfully pink and still get them to market before they're overripe.

For the developing world, the effects are mixed. Mexico, Jamaica, and a few other countries are already using bioengineered BST commercially. Some observers, such as Dennis Avery of the Hudson Institute, suggest China may be the biggest beneficiary of PST long-term. Some 85 percent of China's meat is pork.

But PST researchers caution that new biotech products often require new production methods. When Dr. Baile of Monsanto visited China, he found that PST was much more applicable to China's lean export hogs than to the fatty ones common in the countryside. Dramatic changes in culture and in agricultural production would be needed for rural China to take advantage of the technology.

Sweet-Potato Project

To adapt biotechnology to the developing world, special research efforts are needed. For example, sweet potatoes are an important subsistence crop in many parts of Africa, but they're not well researched because they are not a big commercial crop. Under a special project, funded jointly by Monsanto and the US

Agency for International Development, a scientist from Kenya is using the company's gene-transfer technology to develop virus-resistant sweet potatoes.

African farmers can lose up to 75 percent of their crop because of viruses. If the project works—and the strain is properly distributed—African farmers one day could see significant production gains.

But here, as elsewhere in biotechnology, that hope is at least a few years away.

Modern Agricultural Methods Threaten the Food Supply

by Eugene Linden

About the author: *Eugene Linden is a writer for* Time *magazine.*

Bent Skovmand is not exactly a household name, but he has more to do with the welfare of the earth's 5 billion people than many heads of state. As a plant breeder at CIMMYT, the internationally funded agricultural research station in El Batán, Mexico, he spends his days in silent battle with threats to the world's wheat crop. Recently Skovmand discovered a rare strain of wheat from eastern Turkey that is resistant to the Russian aphid, an invader that has so far cost American farmers $300 million. By using the Turkish strain to develop hearty new hybrid wheats, CIMMYT breeders may help growers outwit the aphid.

Unfortunately the strains of crops that seem to have almost magical qualities are becoming ever harder to find. As farmers go for the highest possible yields these days, they all want to use the same kind of seeds. Individual crops share more genetic material, and local varieties are vanishing. Moreover, as the explosive growth of the world's population causes more farmers to turn more forest land into fields, wild species of plants are getting wiped out. Potentially valuable food sources are lost—forever—before they are even discovered. The world is losing a marvelous diversity of genetic material that has enabled the plant kingdom to overcome pests, blights and droughts throughout the ages.

Plant breeders have used this genetic diversity to help fuel the green revolution and keep agricultural production ahead of population growth. But as the raw material of the revolution disappears, the food supply becomes more vulnerable to catastrophe. Skovmand, for one, is not optimistic about the prospects for the coming decade. "The world has become complacent about food," he says. "In the 1970s the surprise was that India could feed itself. In the coming years the surprise may be that India can no longer feed itself."

Eugene Linden, "Will We Run Low on Food?" *Time*, August 19, 1991, ©1991 Time Inc. Reprinted by permission.

Ever since Thomas Malthus' 1798 *Essay on the Principle of Population* proposed that human fertility would outstrip the ability to produce enough food,
human ingenuity has consistently belied such predictions. Books such as Paul
Ehrlich's *The Population Bomb* in 1968 and the Club of Rome's 1972 study *The
Limits to Growth* raised fears that unchecked population growth might lead to
mass starvation. Later in the '70s,
Lester Brown of Washington's
Worldwatch Institute argued that the
world's farmers were already pushing
the practical limits of what good
land, high-yield crops, irrigation and
artificial fertilizers and pesticides
could deliver.

> *"The world is losing a
> marvelous diversity of genetic
> material that has enabled the
> plant kingdom to overcome
> pests, blights and droughts."*

The Malthusians, however, have consistently underestimated how much the
technological wonders of the green revolution—along with the ability of farmers to make good money growing crops—can spur food production. Ehrlich and
Brown have long predicted that food prices would rise as agricultural production fell short of demand, and they have been wrong. India, where 1.5 million
people died in a 1943 famine, became a grain exporter by 1977, even as it doubled its population. Farmers planting short, seed-laden wheats developed by
Nobel laureate Norman Borlaug at CIMMYT had to post guards to protect the
riches in their fields.

Beginning in the mid-'80s, however, the momentum of the green revolution
slowed dramatically, especially in parts of India, China and Pakistan. In India's
Punjab state, yields of rice and wheat have begun to flatten despite increasing
reliance on fertilizers and better use of water. Elsewhere in Asia, rice researchers have failed to raise yields significantly for more than two decades.
Hidden costs of the green revolution have begun to surface all around the
world: the amount of irrigated land, which produces 35% of the food supply,
has been declining in per capita terms. One reason is that fields become poisoned with salts left behind when irrigation water evaporates. Looming in the
future are the unknown agricultural impacts of global changes such as ozone
depletion in the upper atmosphere and the greenhouse effect. . . .

The combination of both immediate and long-range threats to the food supply
has brought back the old alarming questions: How much longer can the world
deliver adequate food to human numbers relentlessly expanding at the rate of
91 million a year? Is it possible that the Cassandras will soon be right?

Many agricultural experts are taking doomsayers more seriously. A new cause
of concern is the steady loss of genetic diversity, which has made the food supply less stable and reliable than in the past. With farmers growing similar crops
in similar ways, diseases and droughts have more impact than they would if
planters grew a diverse array of crops. Vice President Albert Gore is convinced
that the decline of diversity is one of the greatest threats facing world agricul-

ture. "We may see a significant number of crops become functionally extinct," he says, "enjoying bumper crops until one day the hammer falls in the form of a blight they cannot handle."

According to economist Peter Hazell, who conducted a study of crop volatility for the International Food Policy Research Institute, the likelihood of major food shortfalls has doubled during the past four decades. India, for instance, relies heavily on one type of fast-growing wheat, called sonalika, that is susceptible to several diseases. One epidemic in this crop could wipe out India's entire grain surplus.

Plant breeders can provide India with wheat strains resistant to the pests that threaten sonalika, but, says Michael Strauss of the National Academy of Sciences, "this is not a battle you win just once." Disease germs and insects continually evolve, developing resistance to pesticides and seeking out vulnerabilities that enable them to penetrate crop defenses.

A mix of strains minimizes this damage. But more and more of the world's basic crops now share genetic material. Most high-yielding wheats and rices derive their short, sturdy stature from just a few ancestors. While these genes may be tough, the genes transferred with them may contain a hidden vulnerability that could allow pests to lay waste to huge areas. Observes plant breeder Garrison Wilkes of the University of Massachusetts at Boston: "Imagine what a burglar could do if he got past the front door of a building and found that all the apartments shared the same key."

> *"Beginning in the mid-'80s . . . , the momentum of the green revolution slowed dramatically."*

One promising solution to this problem is for breeders to draw genetic material from a wide variety of sources so that bugs and blights are forced to breach many types of defenses. The new tools of biotechnology allow scientists to identify particular genes and thus predict which strains will exhibit such desirable characteristics as disease resistance or drought tolerance. Crossing many varieties can then create the best possible mix of traits. Entomologist John Mihm and CIMMYT geneticist David Jewell are combating a corn borer that costs tropical farmers as much as 50% of their crop. The two scientists hope one day to create hybrid corn with resistance from a maize local to Antigua as well as the phenomenal defenses of Tripsacum, a wild grass that is related to corn.

Although plant scientists rely on traditional crossbreeding, they are experimenting with actual genetic engineering. Eventually they hope to take individual genes from one strain and put them into the cells of another. Researchers expect to isolate genes from plants that have found ways to cope with ultraviolet radiation, drought, salty soils and other changes future crops may face as a result of mankind's meddling with the earth and atmosphere.

But such techniques will gradually have poorer results if the genetic catalog scientists work with is shrinking. When so many farmers switch to the most popular strains, their wild ancestors and traditional crops that have become adapted to local conditions for centuries (called land races) can easily disappear. Urban development paves over traditional crops and good soil, because cities have usually grown up near the richest land. Calvin Sperling, the U.S. Department of Agriculture's chief plant explorer, believes coastal development along the Mediterranean may have already caused the disappearance of many land races of beets. And war almost always takes a toll. . . .

Agriculture's main defense against the loss of diversity has been the establishment of seed banks, which collect and preserve crop strains. International agencies have helped set up a worldwide network of eight banks that hold myriad varieties of seeds for 25 important food crops. These international centers serve as vital backstops for national seed collections, which are sometimes carelessly maintained.

No one contends that these seed banks can completely halt the diversity drain. While impressive collections have been built for such major crops as wheat, corn and rice, efforts to accumulate samples of vegetables and lesser-known cereals have been much more spotty. During times of unrest, people have raided and eaten seed collections. . . .

Another strategy for preserving diversity is to encourage farmers to maintain a variety of traditional crops. But the global movement of people into cities creates tremendous pressures on farmers to grow uniform, easily transportable crops. This situation will only get worse. By 2000 there will be about 400 cities with more than 1 million inhabitants each, containing one-sixth of the world's population.

The rise of megacities in the developing world also thwarts agricultural policies that would stimulate food production in the countryside. Mindful that governments get overthrown by city dwellers and not farmers, many Third World regimes artificially lower crop prices to placate their urban populations. In Egypt, livestock growers find it cheaper to feed their animals subsidized bread than to produce the grain themselves. This absurdity is unlikely to change, because a past attempt to hike the price of bread produced riots in Cairo.

Such unrest may become more frequent in the coming years. Donald Winkelmann, CIMMYT's director general, notes that a decade ago, India's farmers could thrive even as wheat prices dropped, because production costs fell faster. Now it is harder to lower costs and, Winkelmann says, "India may not be able to count on cheap

> *"Disease germs and insects continually evolve, developing resistance to pesticides and seeking out vulnerabilities."*

food as it has in the past as an element of industrialization." He expects crop prices to rise after mid-decade, as demand increases faster than supply.

Lester Brown has renewed his earlier predictions that world population is reaching the limit of what the planet's land can support. Per capita food production is already declining, he points out, in Africa and South America. Ethiopia has suffered its tragic famines, Brown contends, partly because the country's population has outstripped the productive capacity of its fields. But World Bank analysts disagree, arguing that Ethiopia's agricultural failures stem more from the policies of the recently ousted Mengistu regime, which paid farmers rock-bottom prices and created no incentive to conserve resources.

> *"[Genetic engineering] techniques will gradually have poorer results if the genetic catalog scientists work with is shrinking."*

Just Faaland, the director general of the International Food Policy Research Institute, maintains that what Brown sees as limits are really only impediments: "It's true that fertilizer yields have stopped growing, that crops are more vulnerable to pests, and it has become more difficult to find arable land and water, but we can move these limits. It is not reasonable to project a logical and necessary catastrophe." Dennis Avery of the Hudson Institute in Indianapolis goes further in his new study *Global Food Progress 1991*. He argues that financial investment, not fertile soil, is now the limiting factor in food production. Idle and underutilized cropland in the U.S. and Argentina alone, he says, could feed an extra 1.4 billion people.

When it comes to predicting food prices and supplies, the optimists so far have a much better track record than the pessimists. But few experts would deny that as the human population grows, threats to the food supply become ever more dangerous. And mankind is losing the weapons to fight those threats, as it allows the irreplaceable diversity of the plant kingdom to disappear.

Modern Agricultural Practices Are Destructive

by E.G. Vallianatos

About the author: *E.G. Vallianatos is the author of* Fear in the Countryside *and* The Power of the Powerless Third World.

North American agriculture is the grandest experiment ever to bring nature and culture under authoritarian control. The plight of the farm workers is the first symptom of decay—that this massive experiment is itself out of control. Now, in the last few remaining years of the twentieth century, we also see that more and more 'family farmers' are pushed into the decay of the farm workers. . . .

Agribusiness corporations are in charge of US farming and food: the top seven US agribusiness corporations—Cargill, RJR Nabisco, Safeway, Continental Grain, Mars, Southland, Supermarkets General—had an income in 1989 of $106.4 billion. And Cargill, the giant food company, with revenues in 1989 of $43 billion, was first in 1988 and 1989 in the private corporate world of the US.

"Something Is Wrong"

Agribusiness corporations are also laying waste the American countryside: just three organisations—Cargill, ConAgra and Iowa Beef Processors—control the vast meatpacking industry, with sales in 1987 of about $47 billion. The effects of this enormous concentration of power are toxic to the environment and dangerous to society, particularly to farmers, ranchers, packing-house workers and rural communities. Close to one-third of the US has been set aside for the grazing of cattle; about one-half of all farms raise livestock feed, and cattle drink as much as half of all potable water in the country. To get a pound of feedlot-finished beefsteak, it is necessary to start with 5 pounds of grain, about 2,500 gallons of water, close to 35 pounds of eroded topsoil, and the energy equivalent of a gallon of gasoline.

John Helmuth, chief economist for the committee on small business of the US House of Representatives from 1979 to 1987, warned in 1990 that

Abridged from E.G. Vallianatos, "Agri-Cultural Madness," *Race & Class*, vol. 34, no. 1, July/September 1992. Reprinted with permission.

the consolidation of economic power in the meatpacking industry has resulted in (and is resulting in to a greater degree every day): lower prices paid to farmers and livestock producers; lower wages and deplorable working conditions for meat industry workers; serious questions about the quality and nutritional safety of meat; and higher prices paid by consumers. When an industry drives its best small- and medium-sized companies into bankruptcy, which cattle producers and farmers are driven into bankruptcy by lower and lower prices, when workers are treated like animals and injured and maimed for life, and consumers are charged higher and higher prices for minimum quality, often unsafe meat, something is wrong.

The agribusiness corporations have so much power that they own most of the land and people—not that they buy and sell rural folk, but they come close to that. They determine both the price the farmer gets for his crops and what the farmer's next crop will be. Thus, the chains of dependence between the farmers and agribusiness corporations have created a colonial system that is camouflaged under the pervasive myth of family farming. . . .

Given this cultural madness and the single brutal fact—the huge and rapid seizure of power by agribusiness corporations—everything else falls in place in the vast but tottering empire of US agriculture. The rapid increase of mechanical and chemical power—the value of machinery and chemicals jumped from 25 per cent to more than 50 per cent of the resources used for farming in the last thirty years—led to a rapid multiplication of those who left

> *"Just three organisations . . . control the vast meatpacking industry."*

the land. Thus, from the 1950s to 1980s, more than 15 million men, women and children were forced to abandon their homes in the country for the cities. Also, the mechanisation of agriculture made farms bigger. The size of the average farm increased from 200 acres in the 1950s to 400 acres in the 1980s. And that bigness and the use of ever larger and more powerful machines changed a way of life to an industrial system of production. Which is to say, the care of human beings for the land, the tradition of growing a variety of crops, the craftsmanship and ecological wisdom of the small farmer, maintaining a healthy society in the countryside, had to make room for giant corporate factories producing a single commodity, mining human communities, land, water and the environment. Agricultural factory farms stretch as far as the eye can see, their huge machines and aircraft dominating the unsettled and lonely landscape.

Handicaps from Technology

And yet not merely the corporate structure, but also the very nature of farm technologies constitute another Achilles' heel in this super-sophisticated giant agriculture. Insects, weeds and disease, for instance, destroyed 31 per cent of the crops, worth $27 billion, in the 1940s. That damage in the 1980s was hovering around $80 billion, since 'pests' and disease continue to wipe out 34–37 per cent of the farmer's crops. One such 'pest', the Colorado potato beetle, is practically indestructible precisely because the farmer's most advanced technologies, pesticide chemicals, have changed that beetle's genetic make-up. And there are now some 500 arthropods (insects, ticks and mites) that resist the killing power of one or more insecticides. Practically all of the *Anopheles* mosquitoes capable of transmitting malaria to people are immune to insecticides thrown against them—in eighty-four countries. Malaria is coming back, with debilitating and often fatal consequences for hundreds of thousands of human beings in Asia, Africa and Central America.

The other great handicap of giant agriculture is that the farmer, often getting on in years and calling himself 'grower', is no longer efficient in what he does because, in many cases, he spends too much borrowed money on his machines, petroleum, chemicals, land, information. This means that when he harvests rice, for instance, he barely breaks even—each calorie of what he grows is already mortgaged by a calorie of technology and energy he uses for his production. That is one reason why many of these farmers are going out of business so fast. And the only 'farmers' who make it are large corporations—linked both to the science of the land grant universities and to the subsidies of public works and legislation—which convert their rural real estate and capital into monoculture factories, ploughing huge tracts of land into profitable cash crops.

Such monoculture factories contaminate the gods' water of mercy—ground water. For example, from about the late 1960s to 1980, both the raising of cattle and corn zoomed in the fertile Big Spring basin of northern Clayton County, north-eastern Iowa. The number of cattle increased by about 30 per cent and the number of acres growing corn increased by approximately 40 per cent. But then, during the same period, the amount of nitrogen fertiliser the farmers of the Big Spring basin spread over the land rose by about 250 per cent. That profligate practice has had consequences. Corn can use so much nitrogen fertiliser, the rest is simply lost in the environment. And, in the case of these Iowa corn farmers, they wasted 50–75 pounds of fertiliser per acre. In the Big Spring basin that extra 50–75 pounds from each acre goes down to the ground water. Once in the water, nitrogen fertiliser becomes nitrate, a chemical potentially toxic to human beings. And, from the 1960s to 1980, the nitrate found in the water of the Big Spring basin increased by 230 per cent. That is, the more nitrogen fertiliser the farmers fed their corn, the more nitrate ended up in their drinking water.

> *"Agricultural factory farms stretch as far as the eye can see, their huge machines and aircraft dominating the unsettled and lonely landscape."*

Is there any wonder that 'farmers' like these are not strong where they should be? In seeing that their fertile soil continues to be fertile and in the efficiency of what they do? Pressures to produce as much as possible leave no room for the care of the land. And they falsely believe that the mountains of food they force out of the land will go to feed hungry peasants.

Spreading the Risk of Famine Thin

But the peasant in the Third World rarely sees American food. He persists in his ancient ways alone, often against terrible odds. The peasant goes on with life, raising not much bread from his strip of land, yet everything he does is efficient. For instance, for each calorie of work that the Filipino rice peasant puts into his tiny farm, he harvests 16 calories of food. Contrast this to the rice farmer of Louisiana, who just about gets back what he puts into that huge farm marvel of science technology, land and rice.

> *"Pressures to produce as much as possible leave no room for the care of the land."*

The 'modern' farmer has much to learn from the peasant who practises a gentle if 'primitive' form of agriculture: the peasant does not try to squeeze every ounce of fat from the land because experience has taught him that such exploitation would hit him back with a vengeance. Apart from the catastrophe of drought, he can expect wholesome food coming to him year in and year out when he applies the manure of his animals over the good land, letting some of the soil rest, always planting a variety of crops, spreading the risk of famine thin, praying only to the local gods for sunshine and rain. Thus he puts back into the soil everything he takes out. That way, he guarantees the permanence of what he does. And what he does is more than raise crops. Agriculture for the peasants is life, religion, civilisation.

The Threat of Modern Practices

I said in my 1976 book, *Fear in the Countryside*, that western agricultural technologies in the tropics were dangerous because they made it possible for the urban and rural elites to increase their oppression over the peasant. Ten years later, in 1986, several Third World intellectuals meeting in Penang, Malaysia, confirmed my conclusion—in fact, they went much further. In 'The Penang Declaration on Science and Technology', they said this:

> The resources, techniques and practices of the Third World in the fields of agriculture, irrigation, forestry, animal husbandry and fisheries are in immediate danger of being wiped out under the impact of policies favouring modern western practices in all these areas. The new practices that are being introduced are inherently incapable of efficiently utilising the resources available in the Third World countries and sustaining the Third World populations. These practices are adversely affecting the productivity of land and are destabilising the ecological balance. They are worsening the dependence of the Third World on the industrialised countries for knowledge, techniques and in-

puts in areas where indigenous knowledge and resources are capable of, and were till recently, meeting the needs in a satisfactory fashion.

Darrell Posey, an American anthropologist who has been living with he Mebêngôkre Indians of Brazil since 1977, has nothing but praise for the scientific knowledge of these forest people. He said, in 1990, that the Mebêngôkre

> use a precise knowledge of insect behaviour to control agricultural pests. For example, they deliberately place nests of 'smelly ants'—*mrum kudja* (of the genus *Azteca*)—in gardens and on fruit trees that are infested with leaf-cutting ants (*Atta spp*). The pheromones of the 'smelly ants' repel the leaf-cutters. These protective ants are also prized for their medicinal properties. The highly aromatic scents of the crushed insects are inhaled to open up the sinuses.

> The Indians cultivate several plants containing extrafloral nectars, often on the leaves or stems, which attract predatory ants to serve as bodyguards for the plant. Banana trees are planted to form a living wall around their fields, because predatory wasps nest preferentially under the leaves. . . .

Another westerner, the English agricultural scientist, Sir Albert Howard, author of the 1940 classic study of Indian agriculture, *An Agricultural Testament*, once observed that, in his twenty years or so of research in India, he learned agriculture from the Indian and the Chinese peasant: 'My new professor—the peasants and the pests. By 1919 I had learnt how to grow healthy crops, practically free

> *"The resources, techniques and practices of the Third World . . . are in immediate danger of being wiped out."*

from disease, without the slightest help from mycologists, entomologists, bacteriologists, agricultural chemists, statisticians, clearing-houses of information, artificial manures, spraying machines, insecticides, fungicides, germicides, and all the other expensive paraphernalia of the modern experiment station.'

In a sense, Howard was saying that fertile land gives birth to disease-free crops which should then be able to nourish healthy animals and people. And his great discovery was simply to do what the Indian peasant was doing for countless centuries with infinite patience and trust in the fertility of his land, with plenty of love and not less animal manure. Howard grabbed at that idea with a passion. He tested the peasant's gentle methods endlessly. 'Large-scale results coming in a growing torrent from all over the world', he said, 'show that the ephemeral method of manuring, by means of chemicals and the resulting *survival of the weakly plant bolstered up by poison sprays*, are bound to be swept into the oblivion which they merit' (emphasis added).

The Power of Toxic Sprays

Howard, of course, is right. But for the western science mandarins to accept such a judgement would be tantamount to treason. Enormous energies, resources and ethical standards have been sacrificed to the idols of 'clean' agriculture—and the chemical sprays that make it possible.

The real power of toxic sprays is the power they bestow on industrial farmers to control and expand their conquest of large pieces of land. The most lethal of them—the nerve gas toxins known as organophosphates—were born in the heat of battle in the 1940s. They continue to be potent weapons of war.

> *"The real power of toxic sprays is the power they bestow on industrial farmers to control and expand their conquest of large pieces of land."*

That power is the single most important reason why these poisons were and continue to be so integral a part of any effort to industrialise farming in the United States and, through US technical assistance, to do the same thing in the Third World. And, despite the devastating ecological effects of these aggressive practices, they are still standard measures of modernity, efficiency, privatisation and progress in any development project funded by the US government and international financial institutions like the World Bank.

Scientists in the US, for instance, have known since the 1960s that these toxic agricultural sprays have a special affinity to race and class—they are anthropocides [killers of human beings] in general but they cause more adverse deleterious effects on people of colour and people who do not have a balanced diet; that is, hungry and poor human beings. American migrant farm workers—who are primarily black, Chicano, Latin American and Asian—lose at least twenty years of their lives in their hazardous and seasonal labour.

Toxic Countryside

In a strange, science-fiction, ghoulish way, not merely the farms themselves but the entire countryside of America is becoming toxic. In one paradigmatic example, city teenagers get convulsions for hand weeding soybeans, while their rural friends are unaffected for doing the same thing. Does this mean that young agricultural folk are developing a 'tolerance' for a poisoned environment which causes medical consequences to young persons from a city? Is agriculture becoming the ultimate testing ground for race, class and biology?

In the early 1980s, several researchers from the Center for Rural Affairs, Nebraska, studied the farming practices that have the blessings of science, the very technologies that are making American agriculture the envy of the world. They say:

> The changes that have taken place in American agriculture in the span of two generations are staggering. Principally, these changes have constituted an industrial revolution on the farm, the application of standard technology to natural systems, the substitution of chemical for biological processes, and the replacement of diversity with uniformity. . . . If you farm in Iowa the chance of dying from multiple myeloma [a cancer affecting the bone and bone marrow] is about 48% greater than that of the general population; from lymphoma

[a cancer attacking the lymphatic system] about 26%; and leukemia [a cancer of the blood] about 24%. You are also more likely to die of lip, stomach or prostate cancer. . . . If you live on a farm in Minnesota, you're more likely to die of brain cancer than either urban residents or people who live in rural areas but not on farms. . . . The evidence has been mounting that pesticide use has increased farmers' rate of death from various cancers.

The Farmers' Dope Drugs

Yet, in high-tech agriculture pesticide poisons are supreme. They kill weeds, insects, fungi, rodents—and all other living things. But they also have a cultural, behavioural, impact on the farmers, their users. S.E. McGregor, a biologist with the US Department of Agriculture, says that insect poisons, insecticides, 'are like the dope drugs. The more they are used, the more powerful the next one must be to give satisfaction—and therein develops the spiralling effect, the pesticide treadmill. The chemical salesman, in pressuring the grower to use his product, practically assumes the role of the "dope pusher". Once the victim, the grower, is "hooked", he becomes a steady and an ever-increasing user'.

The utterance of this blasphemy took place in 1978, when this distinguished honey-bee expert was retiring from his government post. In 1987, another biologist, Robert Metcalf, professor of entomology at the University of Illinois and inventor of carbamates, nerve-gas toxins used as insecticides, said, 'The short-sighted and irresponsible use of pesticides . . . is producing strains of monster-bugs that are resistant to our chemical weapons. Some strains of insects . . . have appeared that are resistant to nearly everything in our chemical arsenal. . . . It is difficult to see how anyone can remain intelligently optimistic about the future of chemical control. The outlook is dismal—and getting worse'.

> *"The short-sighted and irresponsible use of pesticides . . . is producing strains of monster-bugs."*

The Industrial Food Production System Harms Poor Nations

by Gary Kline

About the author: *Gary Kline is an associate professor of political science at Georgia Southwestern College in Americus.*

Even in these times of keen global competition, U.S. agriculture is admired and envied around the world for its dynamism and its bounty. Agriculture continues to provide much of the cheer in our otherwise gloomy trade picture. It occupies a central place in the psychic landscape of this predominantly urban nation which yet cherishes its images of the sturdy, hard-working family farmer. Not surprisingly, its exponents have made this powerful image a model for the world, and particularly for the so-called less-developed, or Third World, countries.

Wasteful Methods

The abundance and astounding productivity of American agriculture since the Second World War led to a complacence: most critics, conservative and liberal alike, disagreed on the details of policy only, but did not challenge the basic structure since this would seem to be arguing with success. But our bountiful food system is predicated on massively wasteful, energy-intensive methods which cannot be sustained over the long term and which threaten the environment and its ecosystems.

The specialization and monoculture of today's commercially profitable farms require large amounts of chemicals and energy. As opposed to traditional agricultural techniques, industrial farming, with its heavy reliance on chemicals, destroys the soil's organic matter, leaving land hard and more erosion-prone and causing more rapid evaporation of moisture. This, in turn, necessitates a spiralling application of energy, chemicals, and water to offset what would otherwise be a decline in productivity. Likewise, planting one crop season after

Abridged from Gary Kline, "Food as a Human Right," *Journal of Third World Studies*, Spring 1993. Reprinted with permission.

season increases vulnerability to pests, requiring more chemicals for protection, leading to more-resistant pests and to a need for more and stronger chemicals. Indeed, the major producers of herbicides have been trying to develop more herbicide-resistant, not more pest-resistant, strains of crops so as to allow farmers to apply larger doses to their crops.

Larger farm machinery militated in favor of larger farms. Those that could afford to make bulk purchases of industrial inputs had the advantage over smaller farms that could not.

> *"Our bountiful food system is predicated on massively wasteful, energy-intensive methods."*

Similarly, farmers increasingly produce for markets dominated by a relatively few processors and distributors. With the integration of farming into national and world markets, larger farms have been favored and smaller farms often overlooked or neglected by the giant food processors and marketers. The same holds true with respect to financing, which larger productive units find more readily available and at lower rates. Therefore, quite productive, small to medium-sized farms have not been as *commercially* viable as the large.

Agricultural programs and policies reinforced cultural preferences for certain crops and foods, encouraging specialization in supported produce and thus the whole pattern of capital-intensive industrial farming. Our traditional emphases on science and technology, on struggle and mastery over Nature rather than harmony and husbandry and careful conservation, on bigness, and on individual interest over the commonweal led agricultural research and extension services to promote capital-intensive farming. High-yielding varieties of plants (HYVs) developed by agribusiness have displaced traditional varieties and reduced the crop and genetic diversity of the plants that we depend upon, thus making our food system more vulnerable to diseases, pests, weeds, and climatic factors. Moreover, HYVs require more water, fertilizers, and other chemicals in order to thrive, without which they can yield far less than the traditional varieties.

Profit vs. Nutrition

Extensive food processing and product differentiation contribute to value-added and, thus, to corporate profits. To the same end, advertising has been employed to shape consumer tastes and generate demand. Typically, these food products are highly processed and in many cases virtually all of the nutrients and natural flavors have been eliminated. Sometimes artificially produced nutrients are re-introduced and almost always artificial flavors and preservatives, salt and sugar are added. The objective, of course, is principally to arrive at a commercially successful product, one that will have a considerable shelf-life and that can hold up under the rigors of transportation and processing.

Government policies have generally attempted to establish a favorable business climate and have countenanced market concentration by largely ignoring antitrust legislation. Supermarkets today are therefore filled with a bewildering variety of products, most of them supplied by a handful of giant corporations.

Included among the costly consequences of this system, waste of energy and other resources (as in over-processing and packaging) rank very high. This increases the price of food and production resources and results in greater maldistribution as the poor are out-bid by the rich. But this food system also produces a dubious quality of nourishment. While a food system's prime objective should be to satisfy society's nutritional needs, this goal has been subordinated to a profit-oriented logic engendering energy- and capital-intensive methods, emphasis on productivity and growth, and other dynamics which frequently undermine the objective of serving basic needs. Consequently, even in the U.S. the nutritional needs of humans are not met though our silos are bursting with a surplus. It is a system, then, which is highly efficient at producing profits, but only occasionally and incidentally efficient in terms of resources-usage, distribution of food, meeting nutritional needs, producing salubrious community effects, and conserving the environment.

Uneven Bargaining

Nevertheless, this is a system with its own dynamic of self-aggrandizement, a powerful impulse to extend its logic and methods everywhere. So it remains a potent model, influencing agricultural policies in the lesser-developed countries and justifying expansion of U.S. corporations globally. U.S. trade and tax policies have encouraged investments abroad while foreign aid has been used to secure markets, to deal profitably with domestic agricultural surpluses, and to foster a kind of dependence. In addition, programs like the Overseas Private Investment Corporation [a U.S. government agency that provides assistance to American investors in Third World countries] have reduced the risks for transnational corporations (TNCs). Though the scheme of supply and demand in a market system has always erroneously presumed a fundamental equality of participants, such policies have secured rather consistent advantages in the market for the giant corporations over Third World nations. This results in uneven bargaining between nations and peoples, which over time becomes relatively more unequal.

Political scientist George Kent notes, "bargainers do not move to an equilibrium at which the benefits are equally distributed, but instead move apart, with the gap between them steadily widening." In the skein of trade between the developed and

> *"Expansion of the U.S. [agricultural] model has entailed a growing concentration of landownership."*

Third World nations, then, the pattern of unequal bargaining results in subtle advantages for the stronger traders and disadvantages for the weaker parties to the exchange. That is, the poor tend to get poorer and the rich richer. While the logic of the U.S. food system is congenial to the use of food to help the balance of trade and as an instrument of foreign policy, it offers little succor to those without *effective* demand (i.e., the poor who most need it).

Though the colonial system [through which the industrialized nations controlled much of the Third World's resources and markets] is now formally defunct, a pattern of unequal bargaining still results in subtle advantages for the stronger traders (viz., the developed nations) and disadvantages for the weaker parties to the exchange (usually the former colonies). There is a growing gap between rich and poor in virtually every market-oriented (perhaps "corporate-oriented" would be more apt) society, as well. An examination of the pattern of trade in food reveals that the industrialized Western countries are net food importers; and even the U.S., with its vast surpluses, chronically has become a net importer of food from many lesser-developed countries.

> *"Fully one-half of the world's seriously malnourished live in just five market-oriented countries: India, Bangladesh, Nigeria, Pakistan, and Indonesia."*

With about one-quarter of the world's total population, the rich countries consume almost three-quarters of all the food produced. The average North American consumes 2888 pounds of grain yearly, mostly in the form of meats, milk, eggs, and alcoholic beverages. In the U.S., almost half of all harvested cropland is sown in feed crops and animals ultimately eat about four-fifths of the grain. The average Asian, on the other hand, eats less than 488 pounds of grain per year, mostly in original form. Still, we find 36 of the world's 40 most impoverished countries actually *exporting* food to the United States.

Concentration of Landownership

For many countries, expansion of the U.S. model has entailed a growing concentration of landownership and its corollaries: increased landlessness and unemployment, lower wages and income, and grinding poverty and hunger. Four percent of the world's landowners possess half of the cropland and in many countries ownership is more concentrated. This suggests why we continue to find disheartening statistics about the quality of human existence even as production grows and wealth accumulates. Agricultural markets globally have become more concentrated, dominated by fewer and fewer TNCs. This undermines the autonomy of governments responsible for dealing with social and economic problems: agribusiness TNCs tend to establish production priorities and this generally means orienting resources to meet the needs of the more lucrative markets of the richer, industrialized countries.

India, for example, has in recent years routinely harvested grain surpluses, but the per capita consumption of calories and protein has declined. As Third World countries have pursued export-oriented strategies for development, the quantity and quality of affordable food has deteriorated for the world's poor. Hunger correlates closely with one's economic status, sex, and skin color: even in Ethiopia, rich white men do not go hungry. Market-oriented, industrial agriculture means that the affluent may casually outbid the poor and redirect protein-rich fishmeal from starving children to their pets. Not surprisingly, then, we find that fully one-half of the world's seriously malnourished live in just five market-oriented countries: India, Bangladesh, Nigeria, Pakistan, and Indonesia.

Notwithstanding the image of the U.S. as the "breadbasket of the world," Americans have become dependent on a food system which distorts markets, trade, resource usage, and priorities in much of the rest of the world. U.S. exports do not generally go to feed the needy, but rather the relatively affluent who have effective demand. More than half of U.S. grain exports go to feed animals for production of meat for affluent consumers, mostly in the rich countries. Developed countries receive more than two-thirds of U.S. farm exports. By and large, the debt-ridden Third World countries do not receive food from the U.S. Unless specific nonmarket-oriented policies override the system's tendencies, value in all its forms will continue to flow disproportionately to the "haves" within countries and among countries and increased trade will merely reinforce the pattern of privilege.

"Free Market" Delusion

Advocacy of the power of the "free market" to efficiently allocate food and agricultural resources and justly distribute costs and benefits becomes mere delusion, or fraud, where the requisites of a free market are absent. The market is already a highly structured system of power. The magnitude of the human misery and hunger worldwide belies the simple "free market" solution with its industrial food system. The problems are acute and urgent. More than one billion people, mostly in the Third World, are chronically hungry and about twenty million starve to death annually. Every day about 68,888 human beings die of hunger and the great majority of these are children under the age of five. If one adds to these figures the number of children and adults who succumb due to hunger-related illnesses, the picture appears bleaker

> *"Every day about 68,888 human beings die of hunger and the great majority of these are children under the age of five."*

still. Between 1988 and 1993, hunger has taken the lives of more people than all the wars, revolutions, and murders occurring during the past 150 years.

Reasons for Optimism

This, however, is no natural disaster. The situation viewed from another angle gives one reasons for optimism. In order to feed all of the seriously malnourished children of the world, in excess of the minimum calories necessary to sustain life, we would have to lay claim to less than one percent of the world's annual yield of cereals. World grain production amounts to about five pounds per person per day, or about three times the minimum required to support life. Nor does this take into account the substantial and varied nongrain sources of sustenance: vegetables, fruits and nuts, meats and fish, roots and tubers.

Prior to the colonial period, most Third World countries had need-oriented, traditional food systems whereby, in the words of Karl Polanyi, "distribution of material foods [was]

> *"Traditional societies practiced systems of agriculture which were ecologically sophisticated and diverse."*

ensured by noneconomic motives." Starvation was unusual because available food supplies were widely shared and starvation became a problem only when the entire community or region experienced a severe shortage. Moreover, "societies that now suffer endemic food shortages were, on the whole, food-abundant societies in precolonial times," claims Susan George, who notes with grim irony that "deprivation on today's scale is a thoroughly modern phenomenon. Humanity has taken several thousand years to reach its present state of underdevelopment."

Traditional societies practiced systems of agriculture which were ecologically sophisticated and diverse. They tended to preserve the fertility and productivity of the land by striking an environmental balance through practices such as crop rotation and fallowing. This made them reliable, as crop and genetic diversity provided greater security against the onslaught of diseases, pests, and climatic irregularities. However, traditional agriculture was decisively undermined by a system aimed primarily at the production of wealth rather than the direct satisfaction of the food needs of the community. Europeans and North Americans came to regard the peoples of the Third World as primitive, despite their success by many standards. These colonies were viewed as sources of primary commodities and as potential markets for the processed goods of the manufacturing countries, all within the context of a profit-oriented world system.

Cash Crops

Land, labor—everything became a commodity valued primarily for what it could contribute to profits. This drove the price of land increasingly beyond what most people could afford; and it shifted use toward production of cash crops [crops produced primarily for market] rather than staple foods. Millions, then, have become landless and their numbers cannot be absorbed either in the countryside, where rural employment has shrunk due to the growingly concentrated and capital-intensive agriculture, or in the cities, where shanty-towns and squalor signal the human costs of underdevelopment. Mounting numbers of people, through no fault of their own, have neither the resources to produce their own food nor the income needed to purchase it. Furthermore, capital-intensive TNCs have undermined the option to generate desperately needed employment through labor-intensive techniques.

In alliance with aid agencies and financial institutions, agribusiness TNCs have encouraged cash-cropping, which thrives at the expense of basic food crops and claims scarce resources like credit, energy, and fertilizers. This drives up the cost of food such that the poor must increasingly resort to lower-nutrition substitutes for their normal fare, or they do without.

Landownership has become concentrated due to these market forces. Drawn helplessly into the cash economy, small farmers have been neglected by agricultural researchers and planners guided by the Western model: inputs from seeds to irrigation systems to credit have been directed toward the farmers of means, since the model assumes that larger farms will account for most of the production. Similarly, agribusiness firms responsible for buying and processing farm produce have overlooked small farmers as not worth the bother. The Western model of development has also generally given priority to industrial and urban development over rural development. Though Third World populations are overwhelmingly rural, the concentrated urban centers have usually been given more attention since they are potentially more clamorous and destabilizing.

Control Withheld

While the "transfer" of this industrial model of food production implies a transfer of control, actual control is seldom relinquished by the TNCs, but is jealously guarded so as to insure continued dominance. For example, while many of the valuable genes that have been engineered for commercial purposes have been brought from the Third World, the U.S. has so far refused to comply with the U.N. Food and Agriculture Organization in its calls for a sharing of benefits with the developing nations. The U.S. has been loath to jeopardize patent rights and ultimately control and profits.

In his foreword to Susan George's *Ill Fares the Land*, Robert Borosage of the Institute for Policy Studies writes: "The transfer and promotion of technological solutions tends to increase inequality of power and wealth, concentrate land and resources in the hands of the few, [and] displace the many." The corporate focus is on production and the needs of the system rather than upon consumption and the needs of the people. But this view fails to confront the spectre of growing inequality and the marginalization of millions. Aggregate measures of production and market value have clouded considerations of distribution, nutritive value, participation of rural peoples in the economy, and other qualitative concerns.

> *"Mounting numbers of people ... have neither the resources to produce their own food nor the income needed to purchase it."*

Though productive both in terms of employment and providing staple foods, small farms have been left economically inviable. That is to say, the market-oriented food system has already undermined and uprooted most modest-scale, communally based, need-oriented, environmentally sensitive food systems developed over many generations. Environmentally sensitive (i.e., complex) and economically simple food systems have been displaced by giant, environmentally simple (thus, more vulnerable) and economically very complex food systems (also more vulnerable). Ultimately this robs people of their ability to feed themselves and their families, their self-reliance, their own powers, and their dignity. Even land reform is insufficient to effect a genuine improvement so long as credit, channels for marketing commodities, and other aspects of the system continue to reflect the dynamics of unequal power, wealth, and bargaining position intrinsic to the Western market-oriented model.

Biotechnology Is Dangerous

by Liebe F. Cavalieri

About the author: *Liebe F. Cavalieri is an environmental science research professor at the State University of New York and the author of* Double-Edged Helix: Genetic Engineering in the Real World.

Today we are exposed to a continuous stream of scientific discoveries that are unveiling all kinds of secrets regarding the structure of matter and the basic mechanisms of life. One of these "breakthroughs" has given us the Flavr Savr tomato [a tomato genetically engineered to retain freshness]. This and other genetic engineering feats are the subject of this viewpoint. What else can genetic engineering do? Do we need it? Are there any side effects? Can the same ends be accomplished in other ways? These questions need to be answered before we commit an important segment of the economy to a pathway that could lead to a fiasco from which . . . it is hard to escape.

Genetic engineering is a new means of genetic modification quite unlike the old type, where the aphorism "like begets like" applies: A rose gives rise to a rose. It has ushered in a new era of manipulative biology, making it possible to create truly novel organisms by combining the hereditary determinants, or genes, of unrelated organisms with no holds barred. Cow genes have been inserted into bacteria; human genes have been inserted into mice; flounder genes have been inserted into tomatoes; chicken genes have been inserted into potatoes; virtually all types of combinations have been tried already. Such heritable manipulations reach in an unknown fashion indefinitely into the future. This radically new power has implications not only for the occupants of this planet but for the planet itself. Although genetic engineering can be applied to any organism, I will focus on its use for the modification of microbes and plants. Once released into the environment, these organisms are most difficult to control, and they sometimes act in unexpected ways. . . .

Molecular biologists in the early 1940s . . . were driven by scientific curiosity

Abridged from "Economic Brinkmanship" by Liebe F. Cavalieri. This article appeared in the December 1994 issue and is reprinted with permission from *The World & I*, a publication of the Washington Times Corporation.

to try to find answers to basic questions about the way genes work. After painstaking effort over several decades, the researchers discovered a new technique that provided a way of joining genes in the test tube and reinserting them into an organism. It was soon evident that the method could be used to create organisms with combinations of characteristics that could not arise by natural means, resulting from novel gene combinations.

> *"Cow genes have been inserted into bacteria; human genes have been inserted into mice; flounder genes have been inserted into tomatoes."*

This method, sometimes called recombinant DNA technology because the genes are made of DNA, was a breakthrough of momentous proportions, sending shock waves throughout the community of molecular biologists. The old, classical rules, which restricted mating and genetic exchange to members of a species, didn't apply anymore. Elated scientists realized that the discovery would lead to entirely new and uncharted areas. Because the technology could rapidly create genetic arrangements resembling changes that might occur naturally over eons through evolution, Nobelist David Baltimore proclaimed that "we can outdo evolution."

At another level, entrepreneurs foresaw marketable products. Despite Nobelist Walter Gilbert's insistence that "scientists will be in charge," large corporations are playing the power role. . . . Corporate giants have already begun to get into the act in all areas of biotechnology, paving the way for a complete takeover of the industry. The bottom line is fast becoming the only basis for decisions.

A Genetically Engineered Microbe

Microbial pesticides have come to the forefront in the last several years, following the advent of recombinant DNA technology. The expectation is that they will replace chemical pesticides, which are becoming increasingly ineffective and have been shown to be injurious both to human health and to various ecosystems. A typical example now under development is a bacterium that lives inside the corn plant, called *Clavibacter xyli cynodontis* (abbreviated Cxc). Cxc has been converted to a microbial pesticide by inserting into it the gene for an insect toxin from another bacterium (*Bacillus thuringiensis*, often referred to simply as Bt). Corn seeds are impregnated with the genetically engineered Cxc, and, as the corn plant develops, the bacteria spread throughout the plant. When a common caterpillar, the European corn borer, feeds on the corn plant, it ingests the genetically engineered Cxc as it tunnels through the plant and is killed or incapacitated.

There are problems, however. First, the corn borer will eventually develop resistance to the Bt toxin, rendering the genetically engineered microbe progressively less effective. Whether the lethal blow is delivered by a genetically engineered Cxc or by a chemical spray is irrelevant: *Development of resistance is a constant, unsolvable problem that stems from the basic nature of insect populations.* The best that can be done is to delay its onset.

Second, my own research shows that the use of microbial pesticides, either natural or genetically engineered, can have unexpected results. In a case study I find that, under certain field conditions, the European corn borer population, in the presence of a microbial pesticide, can oscillate wildly from year to year, sometimes reaching population peaks far higher than if no pesticide had been applied and therefore doing more damage.

The Union of Concerned Scientists, the Environmental Defense Fund, and the National Wildlife Federation have been critical of the small-scale field tests that have been carried out by the company (Crop Genetics International) that is developing Cxc as a biopesticide. They are concerned about the natural and mechanical dispersal of Cxc in the field. The presence of the agent in corn plant residues and soil, which come in contact with other insects, has not been adequately investigated; nor has the possibility of transfer of the toxin gene from Cxc to related bacteria in the environment (genetic exchange does occur between related species). The killing of nontarget insects, many of which are beneficial, could cause significant ecological disturbances.

Genetically Engineered Crops

In the genetic engineering of plants, herbicide tolerance is currently the holy grail. In general, herbicides kill food crops as well as weeds. A crop with herbicide tolerance would be resistant to weed killers in quantities considerably larger than are now used. The crops survive, all the weeds die, and the herbicide manufacturers make a killing. Incidentally, the developers of herbicide-tolerant crop seeds include Monsanto, DuPont, Rhone-Poulenc, and Hoechst: All are major producers of herbicides. This is part of a new agricultural trend in which seeds and chemicals are controlled by one industry, allowing large corporations to sell both as an interdependent package. Of the world's seven leading pesticide firms, five are also ranked among the world's twenty-five largest seed companies. This toehold on agribusiness has monopolistic tendencies, to say the least.

> *"The use of microbial pesticides . . . can have unexpected results."*

Crops can be made tolerant to herbicides by inserting genes into them that will nullify the effects of the herbicide. The added genes could act by breaking down the herbicide or reducing the plant's sensitivity to it. An example of the former is the herbicide-tolerant cotton created by Calgene, containing a gene for an enzyme that degrades the herbicide Bromoxynil. Alternatively, a gene could be inserted that produces an essential cell component, already present, that is destroyed by the herbicide, so that the plant will produce more of that component than the herbicide can destroy. Among the crops that have been rendered herbicide-tolerant are corn, soybeans, cotton, sugar beet, peanuts, wheat, sorghum, and tobacco.

The use of these genetically engineered (transgenic), herbicide-tolerant plants is not risk free. There is the possibility that the transgenic crop itself might become a new weed. For example, the inserted gene may work by causing enhancement of seed germination in early spring, so the crop plant gets a jump on later-germinating weeds. But it will also compete with other, slower-germinating crops that may be planted subsequently in the same fields, in effect acting as a weed. New weeds could also arise if the engineered plant pollinates related wild plants. A number of crop plants have weedy relatives that could thereby become resistant to the herbicide.

> *"The transgenic crop itself might become a new weed."*

There is also the inevitable problem of resistance, just as there is with microbial pesticides. Weeds eventually develop resistance to herbicides as a result of their continual application. Under these circumstances, more and more herbicide must be applied; finally, the herbicide-tolerant strategy breaks down when both the crop plant and the weeds have become resistant to very high amounts. The harmful effects on human health of weed-killer residues in food crops and water escalate in parallel.

Toxic Substances

Herbicides are, in general, toxic substances. Anything that kills one form of life is likely to have an effect of some kind on other forms. For example, the effects on U.S. troops of Agent Orange, the herbicide used in the Vietnam War, are well known. Related chlorphenoxy chemicals, still in use in the United States, have been shown to cause nerve damage and to increase the risk of lymphatic cancer. Another type of herbicide, represented by paraquat, has been implicated as a possible cause of Parkinson's disease. Other herbicide types can cause birth defects, nerve damage, acute poisoning, headaches, and rashes.

Not only humans are at risk. Ecosystems are vulnerable because wildlife habitats such as bird sanctuaries are sensitive to foreign chemicals, which invade them through contaminated groundwater.

The corporations that are developing herbicide-tolerant plants maintained early on that the plants would reduce herbicide use and hence decrease risks to human health, although chemicals would still have to be used. They argued that plants were going to be made tolerant to new, "benign" pesticides. From a physiological standpoint, however, "benign" is a nebulous concept. It could mean that, for example, no rash or headache is evident after exposure. But so-called silent genetic mutations might occur, showing no clinical symptoms for years but eventually resulting in cancer. "No observable effects" is not a reassuring statement in this context.

Moreover, not all the resistances to which tolerance is being developed are "benign." Included are such war-horses as 2,4-D, an agent known to cause cancer. A case in point is the cotton engineered to be tolerant to Bromoxynil, which is classified by the Environmental Protection Agency as a developmental agent, giving rise to birth defects in animals. Bromoxynil-tolerant cotton presents a clear and present danger. Cottonseed oil is widely used in prepared food, but it is not controlled by the Food and Drug Administration (FDA) because cotton is not primarily a food crop. Consequently, the herbicides used on it can slip without notice into our food, exposing us to chemicals known to be dangerous.

Altering Metabolism

Yet another sort of problem can arise in any genetically engineered plant or other organism. The foreign gene that is inserted may alter the metabolism of the modified organism in unforeseen ways. A cliché applies inside the cell: Everything is connected to everything else. A single change may have many consequences in addition to the one intended. Such pleiotropic effects are hard to predict because they depend not only on the inserted gene but also on its location in the resident DNA and on the actions of other genes. In food crops, genetic engineering can pose a number of potential risks to consumers. The FDA has published the following statements in the *Federal Register:*

> *"The foreign gene that is inserted may alter the metabolism of the modified organism in unforeseen ways."*

• "Toxicants ordinarily produced at low levels in a plant may be produced at high levels . . . as a result of genetic engineering."

• "Another unintended consequence of genetic modification of a crop may be a significant alteration in levels of important nutrients. In addition, changes may occur in bioavailability of nutrient due to changes in form of the nutrient or the presence of increased levels of other constituents that affect absorption or metabolism of nutrients."

• "It is possible to introduce a gene for a protein that differs significantly in structure or function, or to modify a carbohydrate, fat or oil, such that it differs significantly in composition from such substances currently found in food."

• "Proteins transferred from one food source to another might confer on food from the host [recipient] plant the allergenic properties of food from the donor plant. The sensitive population [those who are allergic to the substance] is ordinarily able to identify and avoid offending food. However, if the allergens [allergy-causing substances] were moved into a variety of a plant species that never before produced that allergen, the susceptible population would not know to avoid food from the variety."

For a sensitive individual, the result could be fatal. The lesson is that food derived from genetically engineered plants should be identified as such and should be viewed with caution. Before it is placed on the market, we need to be sure that it has been thoroughly evaluated in terms of nutritional value, possible low-level toxicity, and possible allergic threats. . . .

What Is the Real Problem?

There is a myth going around that genetic engineering of food crops will solve the problem of world hunger. In fact, most of the genetic engineering now being practiced for commercial purposes does not aim in that direction. Food crops such as cowpeas and cassava, which are most commonly used by the 1.1 billion undernourished people of the world, are largely ignored. The seeds of engineered crop varieties are expensive, and the crops require heavy subsidies in the form of fertilizers, pesticides, and irrigation. Poor farmers in underdeveloped countries will not be able to afford them. The real factor that limits the world's food supply is the loss of cropland through overexploitation, desertification, soil erosion, and conversion to habitable space. Diminishing agricultural land, coupled with population growth and inequitable trade and land-use practices, is responsible for world hunger.

Far more important than the addition or removal of genes from a handful of species is the preservation of the vast biodiversity that already exists. The destruction of centers of biodiversity and the replacement of primitive crop varieties, some of which have been nurtured for perhaps ten thousand years by native peoples, are causing species extinction at a rapidly accelerating rate. We are destroying the repositories of irreplaceable raw genetic material, the stuff of evolution necessary for improvement of crops.

When the corn blight destroyed a major portion of the corn crop in the southwestern United States in 1970, agronomists looked for wild varieties with corrective genes that could be introduced into the afflicted varieties. It seems to me that we are morally obligated to preserve the biodiversity of the earth. Biodiversity, unlike other natural resources, is a very fragile entity, qualitatively different from aquifers, fisheries, timber forests, and the ozone layer. All these resources can be renewed, or somehow repaired, albeit with the passage of much time and effort. But the loss of biodiversity is forever.

We often hear the phrase "we are borrowing the earth and its resources from our children and their children." Should we be concerned with the effects of present-day genetic-engineer-

> *"There is a myth going around that genetic engineering of food crops will solve the problem of world hunger."*

ing decisions on future generations? In our quest to find solutions to our current pressing problems, we are all too anxious to resort to technological fixes that provide temporary solutions but do not take into account the complexity of natural systems. Is it right to divert our creativity to serve the short term and the privileged while ignoring possible long-term damage?

To achieve ecological sanity, I believe that a good starting point would be a workable policy for sustainable agriculture. There already have been successful experiments using alternative agricultural practices to replace chemicals.

A recent report of the National Research Council of the National Academy of Sciences emphasizes the development and use of alternative farming systems as a means of increasing productivity and decreasing environmental damage. Greater diversity of crops will play a role in the development of a sustainable agriculture; the importance of new strains of today's major crops, whether classically bred or genetically engineered, will recede. Practices such as intercropping, cultivation of natural predators, animal/plant integration, crop rotation, constant monitoring for pests, and pheromone trapping will reduce the need for chemical fertilizers and pesticides. The National Academy of Sciences estimates that pesticide use could be reduced 75 percent in ten years without loss of productivity. More research is needed on benign methods like these. Sustainable agriculture is an essential goal for a viable future. It's time to put the emphasis on the real means that will get us there.

"The loss of biodiversity is forever."

Chapter 4

How Can Hunger and Famine Be Reduced?

Reducing Hunger and Famine: An Overview

by Robert S. Chen

About the author: *Robert S. Chen is the director of interdisciplinary research at the Consortium for International Earth Science Information Network (CIESIN) in Saginaw, Michigan, and an adjunct professor in the Alan Shawn Feinstein World Hunger Program at Brown University in Providence, Rhode Island.*

Since the early 1960s, global food production has been sufficient to meet the basic needs of the world's population. Although the number of people worldwide has nearly doubled during the intervening three decades, dire Malthusian predictions that population growth would outstrip food supplies and lead to more frequent and severe famine have not come to pass. Enough food is grown each year to feed a world population substantially larger than we have now.

Nevertheless, food security for much of the world is fragile. During the past few years, global carry-over stocks of cereals have dropped as low as 17 percent of annual consumption—the minimal 2-month supply considered "safe" by the Food and Agriculture Organization of the United Nations (FAO). Between 500 million and one billion people lack access to enough food for survival or work, and hundreds of millions suffer from malnutrition and related health problems. Famine continues to threaten millions of people throughout Africa who suffer from drought, displacement, and war. Chaos and conflict in Eastern Europe have led to the displacement of more than one million people and forewarn of hungry times ahead.

Pessimism and Optimism

Thus there is room for both pessimism and optimism about the future of hunger. Is the world in peril of returning to the food crises of the 1970s? Will regional conflicts, economic instability, and environmental degradation cause a resurgence in famine, refugee migrations, and chronic hunger and poverty? Or are we in a transition during which economies, ecosystems, borders, and people

Robert S. Chen, "Hunger Outlook: Peril or Promise?" *Forum for Applied Research and Public Policy*, Winter 1993. Reprinted with permission.

must sort themselves out before the world resumes its long-term progress towards greater food security and prosperity?

Evidence exists for both scenarios. For example, fewer large countries now may be vulnerable to famine than in the past, but more small countries are plagued by famine and other disruptions to food systems—largely because of violent conflicts. The number of refugees and other displaced people continues to rise; at the same time, however, the potential for repatriation is unprecedented in the wake of peace accords in Central America, eastern and southern Africa, and Asia. The proportion of world population suffering from chronic hunger and poverty is in decline, but the absolute number of hungry and poor in at least some regions remains stagnant and could increase.

> *"Are we in a transition ... before the world resumes its long-term progress towards greater food security and prosperity?"*

Such mixed signals suggest that actions taken now could determine whether progress in reducing hunger continues or falters in the long run. It is therefore important to examine key trends affecting world food security and the options available to alter them.

Population and Production

Recent demographic data suggest that fertility rates have declined less rapidly than expected in a number of developing countries. As a result, the United Nations projects that world population will increase to more than 6 billion people by 2000 and to between 7.6 and 9.4 billion by 2025. The share of population in less developed countries is expected to increase from 77 percent in 1990 to 84 percent in 2025.

Between 1980 and 1990, total food production increased about 10 percent in developed countries and 39 percent in developing countries. This translates into about a 3-percent per-capita increase in developed countries and a 13-percent increase in developing countries. Such aggregate figures hide the fact that many countries in Africa, Latin America, and Asia have experienced declining per-capita food production during the past decade.

Keeping up with population growth will require continuing increases in food production. According to one set of estimates, world cereal consumption would need to increase by nearly half over 1985 levels by 2010 and double by 2050 to provide a minimal diet to all the world's people. In the developing world, consumption would have to double by 2010 and triple by 2050. These estimates assume no change in diet or income distribution. Changes in income growth rates and diets could necessitate even higher levels of per-capita production and consumption.

Such large consumption increases are not implausible: they require an annual per-capita growth rate of about 0.5 percent per year through 2010 and 0.1 percent from 2010 to 2050. This compares with an average annual growth rate of about 0.9 percent from 1950 to 1985.

Soil and agricultural experts, however, have raised doubts about whether past progress in improving crop yields can be maintained in the future, especially for crops important in developing countries. Thus it is an open question whether increased agricultural production will be able to meet the needs of consumption in the next century.

Critical Factors

Traditional Malthusian concerns have focused on the potential mismatch between explosive population growth rates and modest increases in food production. However, other factors also may be critical to future food security, especially at the regional level, including land and water resources; environmental change and degradation; income distribution; dietary needs and preferences; and the protection of groups vulnerable to hunger.

Land and Water Resources. A major obstacle to increased food production is the limited availability of land and water resources. In Africa and Latin America, much of the production increase during the past several decades has come from the expansion of agricultural lands. Much of the remaining reserves of arable land, however, can only be exploited through extensive deforestation and large capital investments. Reserves of arable land are much smaller in Asia and the Middle East and would require large quantities of water to bring them into production. China and India already use four-fifths of their stable freshwater supplies, and many other developed and developing regions face constraints in water quantity and quality. The expansion of urban areas, soil erosion, salinization, and desertification annually remove millions of hectares of arable and irrigated lands from food production. As a result, future increases in food production will have to come primarily from higher crop yields and more intensive use of existing cropland.

Environmental Change and Degradation. A wide range of environmental problems affect the food system. Soil erosion, salinization, droughts and floods, air and water pollution, acid deposition, and heavy metal and radioactive contamination are among the world's most persistent environmental headaches. Each carries important implications for local, regional, and even national food security. In the former Soviet Union, for example,

> *"Keeping up with population growth will require continuing increases in food production."*

the Chernobyl nuclear accident and environmental degradation around the Aral Sea demonstrate that regional environmental problems can affect large populations and key food-production areas. Millions of people and their livelihood are affected each year by floods and drought. Many of these environmental hazards disproportionately affect the poorest and hungriest populations who, in their desperate efforts to survive, may become trapped in a downward spiral of impoverishment and environmental degradation.

Global Concerns

Potential global environmental changes caused by human activities add yet another layer of complexity to questions of future food security. First, it is important to recognize that global warming may lead to an array of environmental changes. How these changes—directly or indirectly, singly or in combination—may affect food production, distribution, and consumption is uncertain.

Second, actions to prevent uncertain long-term environmental changes may have important near-term impacts on agricultural production and related human activities. Restricting deforestation, for example, in many areas would conflict with expansion of agricultural lands. And efforts to stabilize emissions of greenhouse gases such as methane, nitrous oxides, and carbon dioxide could force limits on biomass burning, livestock grazing, rice-paddy production, fertilizer use, irrigation practices, and agricultural energy and water use. There is no guarantee that these preventive measures will succeed in averting or slowing environmental changes. In fact, it is possible that even after such measures are taken, some adaptation to a changing environment would still be necessary.

> *"Potential global environmental changes caused by human activities add yet another layer of complexity to questions of future food security."*

Income Distribution. Data on how food and income are distributed within countries are limited. Studies by the United Nations and World Bank indicate that about 15 percent of the world's population, or nearly 800 million people, lack access to enough food to meet their basic nutritional requirements for survival and child growth. One-fifth of the world's population, or more than 1 billion people, are too poor to obtain the calories they need for work. At the other end of the scale, one-quarter of the world's population in developed countries effectively consume more than 40 percent of the global production of food calories and command more than 85 percent of world income.

Long-term trends suggest that poverty will decrease and access to food will improve. However, the World Bank estimates that the number of poor people will increase throughout the 1990s in most regions of the developing world. The total number of poor may level off by 2000, but even this somewhat promising forecast conceals major projected increases in poverty in Africa and Latin America that likely will be offset by declines in Asia.

Dietary Needs and Preferences. Consumers in many parts of the developed world have begun to limit or even reduce their consumption of animal products, mainly for health reasons. Lower growth in livestock production implies decreasing demand for feed grains and, therefore, lower grain prices, with presumably positive consequences for consumers but negative consequences for farmers. However, it seems likely that present trends towards higher meat and dairy consumption in the developing world will continue for some time, given the low consumption rates now prevalent.

"Even modest gains in world meat and dairy consumption could have significant effects on future food demand."

Even modest gains in world meat and dairy consumption could have significant effects on future food demand. Each calorie of meat or dairy product requires as much as 3 to 8 (or more) calories of feed grains to produce. Projecting these dietary improvements into the future suggests the need for even higher growth rates in food production.

Social Policies

Protection of Vulnerable Groups. A key contributor to improvements in food security in recent decades has been the development of social policies to protect people who lack the income or resources to obtain enough food. Mechanisms include the social welfare systems and policies found in developed countries and the efforts of international agencies and non-governmental organizations to provide early warning of famine, emergency relief, and development assistance in the developing world.

Contrasting trends are evident in the developed and developing worlds. On the one hand, there is increasing recognition and acceptance of the basic human right for each person to have access to enough food to ensure survival and enjoy reasonable protection against the ravages of hunger. In many instances, aid institutions have expanded their ability to supply humanitarian assistance, despite recalcitrant governments, and to improve the effectiveness and efficiency of their operations.

On the other hand, in many countries economic disruptions and adjustments of the past decade have called into question long-standing ways of providing basic entitlements. The resulting dilemma is evident in efforts to give a "human face" to programs designed to restructure a country's economy by reducing the cost and availability of social welfare programs. Such transformations are found not only in the developing world but in the countries of the former Soviet bloc as they move from centrally planned to market-oriented economies. What form of social "safety net" will replace state guarantees of employment and food security is not certain.

In the long run, there are important unknowns about the world's willingness to continue to accept refugees and migrants, provide food and other forms of aid, intervene in intra- and inter-state conflicts, and sustain social and economic safety nets. For example, present food aid flows are only half that necessary to stabilize food prices in the poorest developing countries, and needs are expected to multiply in the near future. Significant increases in aid resources will be required to meet burgeoning humanitarian needs in Somalia, southern Africa, eastern Europe, Cambodia, and many other regions. Is the world up to the challenge?

An Optimistic View

More optimistically, it is also possible that food security could improve significantly as a result of specific initiatives at international, national, and subnational levels. For example, 140 countries have signed the Convention on the Rights of the Child, a world declaration on the survival, protection, and development of children. The convention's goals include "optimal growth and development in childhood, through measures to eradicate hunger, malnutrition and famine."

Other initiatives include a major United Nations' program to end the "hidden hunger" of nutrient deficiencies by 2000, the World Food Council's Cairo Declaration, and a non-governmental call-to-action, the Bellagio Declaration on Overcoming Hunger in the 1990s. The Bellagio Declaration asserts that at least half of existing hunger could be eliminated by 2000 through a combination of existing tools and modest new resources. In addition to eliminating nutrient deficiencies as a public health problem, it contends that it is possible to end deaths due to famine, cut malnutrition among women and children in half, and make substantial reductions in rural and urban hunger.

Fundamental Changes Needed

In the long run, however, solving the perplexing and inter-related issues of poverty, conflict, and hunger is more problematic. For many impoverished people, fundamental changes in economic and social structure—both within and between countries—may well be a prerequisite to food security. This may be true not only for the world's poorest and hungriest peoples but also for those living in wealthier countries who no longer enjoy guaranteed access to adequate food supplies. Whether a sufficient change in course can occur without substantial social disruption or violent conflict remains to be seen: the ongoing transition in the former centrally planned economies may be an early test.

> *"There are important unknowns about the world's willingness to . . . intervene in intra- and inter-state conflicts."*

Nevertheless, the underlying constraints are clear. To keep up with expected rates of population growth, food production must increase at a steady pace into the next century. To improve diets, even faster growth may be needed. Although the required rates of growth in production are not unprecedented, they may be difficult to sustain over the next several decades in light of the diverse resource and environmental constraints at both regional and global levels.

Improving access to food also will be difficult. One approach to reducing hunger is to reduce poverty, but the complete elimination of poverty is a daunting and lengthy task. In the interim, it makes sense to strengthen entitlements to food and to increase access to the resources needed to produce food. To succeed, this alternative may require overall economic growth and a shift in emphasis from aggregate production increases to a more equitable distribution of food and income.

Under the rubric of "sustainable development," a consensus is growing on the need to integrate environmental and developmental priorities. One approach to putting this concept into operation lies in the emerging field of "industrial ecology"—an attempt to meld the tools and concepts of environmental science, technological innovation, and the social sciences into a coherent framework for improving the ability of people to manage the Earth's resources and environment. This and similar efforts are essential not only to "save the planet" but to ensure that the long history of human suffering caused by hunger will come to a permanent end early in the next millennium.

U.S. Aid for Development Can Reduce Hunger

by Sharon Pauling

About the author: *Sharon Pauling is a policy analyst for Bread for the World, a Washington, D.C., organization that attempts to influence U.S. policies affecting poor and hungry people worldwide.*

Overall, foreign aid is unpopular and threatened. However, foreign aid programs designed to reduce poverty, protect the environment and meet humanitarian need—that have long been the focus and concern of church groups—are especially threatened.

The election of President Clinton and new appointments in the State Department and the Agency for International Development finally provided the opportunity for church groups and non-governmental agencies to turn the administration's attention to the problems that have long afflicted US foreign aid. At the same time, new assaults on aid to developing countries arose from shifting interest to Russia, and, in the United States, the rising federal deficit and other pressing domestic needs. . . .

Transforming Foreign Aid

In the midst of eroding public support for foreign aid, tens of thousands of Christians across the United States have been raising their voices in support of making foreign aid work—not slashing it. The past failures of US overseas assistance really to make a difference in the lives of poor people have been widely criticized.

Bread for the World (BFW), through its 1993 Offering of Letters Campaign, "Many Neighbors, One Earth: Transforming Foreign Aid," mobilized churches across the denominational spectrum and generated some 90,000 letters. Christians, affirming the interdependence of the world's communities, poured letters into Congress that stressed the importance of aid that helps poor people and recommended ways to fix a flawed program.

Sharon Pauling, "Foreign Aid: In Need of Fixing," *Christian Social Action*, March 1994. Reprinted with permission.

The theme of "Many Neighbors, One Earth" is indeed consistent with the policy of The United Methodist Church, which has long asserted in its Social Principles that "God's world is one world" and (in its resolution on *The United Methodist Church and Peace*) that assistance programs "must be designed to respond to the growing desire of the developing world to become self-reliant." In the Social Principles The United Methodist Church applauds international efforts to develop a more just international economic order in which the limited resources of the earth will be used to the maximum benefit of all nations and peoples.

> *"Christians across the United States have been raising their voices in support of making foreign aid work—not slashing it."*

In Pursuit of Self-Reliance

During 1987, as civil war raged in southern Sudan, Mrs. Toma Aboi and five other women in the government-held town of Juba were determined to provide their families with an adequate diet. They pooled their resources and also sought help from the AMUPE Project, a local grassroots self-help organization, to create a small groundnuts enterprise. The project was approved and funded by the Trickle-Up Program, a US private organization, and the women were able to improve the standard of living for their families. According to the women, they were better able to afford food, as well as more adequate health care, they learned basic business skills, and they felt better about their future.

In nearby Kenya, at the height of the drought in 1984, villages were weakened from poor harvests, overgrazing and deforestation. A cooperative whose members represented the affected villages met for several months to plan a water system. The African Development Foundation, a US government agency, provided a $300,000 grant to help build an irrigation and storage system. The members planned a project to replenish the trees lost to years of cutting. Now, water is easily accessible for washing and cooking, cattle are healthy and producing enough milk to be sold in the market, and forests are being restored.

Self-help initiatives such as these are being carried out all over the developing world—in Africa, Asia and Latin America. Signs of hope are present despite the problems of long-running wars, repression, recurring drought, undernutrition, urban sprawl, environmental deterioration, inadequate access to health care and clean water and a growing gap between rich and poor. People at the grassroots are engaging in self-help activities and organizing for greater participation in decisions that will affect their futures.

Unfortunately, US foreign aid programs, driven largely by the super-power rivalry of the Cold War, have contributed more to the problems than to the solutions. Security-related assistance has often overshadowed development assistance and even the latter has often not reached poor people at the grassroots.

Chapter 4

Defining Priorities

The end of the Cold War presents the United States with opportunities to shift its foreign aid goals away from meeting short-term political objectives toward promoting peace, sustainable development and democracy. The Clinton administration is challenged with the task of breaking from the past and revamping foreign assistance.

Church groups and other NGOs [non-governmental organizations] are urging the administration to give priority to foreign aid that helps people meet their own basic needs, improve their livelihoods, protect the environment, resolve conflicts and participate in economic and political decision-making at national and local levels. Many administration officials have been responsive to this message and have engaged NGOs—though only those based in Washington—in an unprecedented dialogue on the future of foreign aid.

In its foreign aid reform proposal, the Peace, Prosperity and Democracy Act, released in February 1994 [and later killed in committee], the Clinton administration narrowed the many and still somewhat contradictory objectives of US assistance and proposed five goals: (1) fostering sustainable development, (2) building democracy, (3) promoting peace and security, (4) providing humanitarian assistance and (5) promoting trade and investment.

On the positive side, "fostering sustainable development" appears as the first of the five goals, and resources for sustainable development pro-

> *"Security-related assistance has often overshadowed development assistance."*

grams would be protected from use for short-term emergencies. However, in a number of respects the bill fails to give sufficient priority to sustainable development:

• The bill would cover only certain bilateral economic and military assistance programs. Other foreign aid programs, including food aid and aid channeled through the World Bank and multilateral development banks, fall outside the proposed reform. Yet many of these programs have undermined sustainable development by widening the gap between rich and poor and by failing to protect the environment. Thus, the reform proposal may not be sufficiently comprehensive.

• The bill overlooks the question of whether all goals are compatible with sustainable development. As a result, programs serving other goals might work at cross-purposes with the goal of sustainable development. For example, the Agency for International Development might support programs helping small farmers in, say, the Philippines, adopt sustainable agriculture methods that minimize the need for chemical inputs; at the same time OPIC, a US trade promotion agency, might be extending assistance to a US company to expand its market in that country in fertilizer and pesticides.

• The section on sustainable development does not give sufficient emphasis to poverty reduction as a key element of sustainable development. It fails to make reference to key strategies for reducing poverty, such as the equitable distribution of income and assets or land reform.

• Although the bill recognizes the Agency for International Development, it makes this agency "subject to the supervision and direction of the Secretary of State." This clause could mean the continued subordination of development assistance to political, military, or commercial interests—a major failing of development aid in the past.

Post Cold War Politics

The Clinton administration is faced with twin challenges. Not only should foreign aid be reprioritized, but the new demands of a post Cold War era—e.g. peacekeeping missions, democratization in the former Soviet Union and elsewhere, disasters worldwide, the Middle East peace and population stabilization—may have to be met with the same or fewer resources. Public support for overseas spending has eroded with the end of the communist threat and the worsening of domestic problems. For example, many US citizens feel that rising unemployment, greater numbers of families on the poverty rolls and a high federal deficit mean that the United States should spend less overseas. Thus, it is possible that the crisis over aid funding could outweigh and overtake the reform process.

Fortunately, the end of the Cold War has meant a decline in financial and military assistance that helped dictators or insurgent groups, most notably in Africa and Latin America. However, people in the countries of these regions that received security assistance for so long rightly fear that they will be abandoned just when they need development assistance the most. Recently, development assistance has declined precipitously while economic assistance to Russia has dramatically increased and security aid to Israel and Egypt has been maintained.

The trend toward favoring Russia and Eastern Europe at the expense of poorer regions began at the end of the Bush administration, and the Clinton administration is continuing this trend. The administration boasts that its reform proposal replaces specific country interests with broad strategic objectives. The reform bill, though, makes major exception for countries that enjoy, as State Department officials routinely put it, a "special relationship" with the United States—namely Russia, Israel and Egypt.

> *"Many [foreign aid] programs have undermined sustainable development by . . . failing to protect the environment."*

In 1994, assistance to Russia was raised to $2.5 billion and $5.2 billion was maintained for Israel and Egypt. As the peace process in the Middle East advances, the United States plans to maintain these high levels of aid to the Middle East and possibly even increase them in order to reward progress toward peace.

Trends Are Not Promising

Bread for the World and many other groups believe that the United States should also pursue a "special relationship" with the poorest people of Africa, Asia and Latin America. This should be reflected in the level of resources committed to promoting sustainable development in these regions, but recent trends have not been promising.

In 1993, of the $1.4 trillion budgeted for federal spending, only $14 billion was appropriated for foreign aid—less than 1 percent. In September 1993, Congress voted to cut foreign aid levels by $1 billion, including $200 million for sustainable development programs. Later, Congress further reduced 1994 foreign aid levels by another $340 million, including $104 million in development assistance, to help meet the costs of the California earthquake.

The administration's budget proposals for 1995 included recommendations for increases for most programs, but the proposals included decreases in programs that most directly serve poor and hungry people. Food aid for emergencies and development programs were slashed by $169 million. Another $67 million was cut from funding programs in such areas as health, child survival, education, housing, microenterprise and agricultural production. At a time when increasing numbers of people across the world have been forced to flee their countries, the administration has proposed a decrease of $37 million in refugee assistance.

> *"In September 1993, Congress voted to cut foreign aid levels by $1 billion, including $200 million for sustainable development programs."*

In view of budget constraints and changing interests, Clinton's promises of support to fledgling democracies in the developing world are beginning to ring hollow. To the leaders of five Central American countries, Clinton promised, "The United States will be there as your partner to help. We will not make the mistake of abandoning this region when its dramatic recovery is not yet complete." However, assistance to Latin America may be cut by as much as 50 percent.

When Secretary of State Warren Christopher announced that the Clinton administration would establish a new relationship with Africa, he credited the end of the Cold War for providing the impetus for change. He said, "Thankfully, we have moved beyond the point of adopting policies based on how they might affect the shipping lanes next to Africa rather than the people in Africa."

US development assistance to Africa, though, has already been cut by $16 million for 1994 and the administration proposes further cuts. To the outrage of Africa's supporters, the Clinton reform bill dropped the authorized funding designation for the Development Fund for Africa. Without this protection, established in 1988, assistance to Africa is very vulnerable.

Supporting Aid That Works

A continuous wave of public support for addressing long-neglected human needs could encourage policy makers not only to revamp foreign aid to make it more effective but also to resist further aid cuts. People are right to be concerned when aid does not meet appropriate objectives. They should have been troubled when, as in 1993, less than one-third of foreign aid was spent on programs and activities that met sustainable development objectives by helping to reduce poverty, protect the environment and meet humanitarian needs. It is absolutely critical that foreign assistance that helps to reduce hunger and poverty not be cut, but expanded.

US interests in a more prosperous, stable world would be helped, not hurt, by this approach. By promoting participatory, sustainable development, the United States would be helping to protect the global environment, addressing the causes of conflicts and famine that require costly solutions, and stemming the tide of refugees who flee political and economic instability. Reprioritized foreign assistance would also be encouraging grassroots economic development and, thereby, create future markets for US goods.

In testimony before the House Foreign Affairs Committee, BFW President David Beckmann said, "There is a compelling self-interest behind promotion of sustainable development overseas, but the reasons must go beyond self-interest. Hungry and poor people are part of our global community. We have a moral obligation to help them help themselves. Their suffering is our pain, and their prosperity and well-being will be ours as well."

A fiscally responsible Congress need not contribute to deficit spending or support good foreign aid at the expense of needed domestic programs. Rather, Congress should tap into the defense and intelligence department accounts as well as aid to Israel and Egypt. It is important that the United States support democratization efforts in the former Soviet Union and peace in the Middle East. It is more important that US assistance help to break the cycle of hunger, poverty, war and environmental deterioration worldwide.

A Wide Variety of Foreign Aid Can Reduce Hunger

by Cynthia P. Green

About the author: *Cynthia P. Green is an independent consultant specializing in international development issues.*

The good news about the race between food and population growth is that the massive famines predicted for the 1970s and 1980s did not materialize, thanks largely to the Green Revolution and foreign aid. The bad news is that, despite spectacular progress in both food production and fertility reduction, the threat of famine and the reality of widespread malnutrition remains.

A False Sense of Complacency

Why hasn't this problem been licked? Basically, we were lulled into a false sense of complacency. At the macro level, the situation looked promising. Food production has kept pace with population growth since 1961 in all regions of the world except sub-Saharan Africa.

This rosy scenario, however, did not extend to the poorest countries. There, the rate of population growth was nearly double the increase in food production between 1961 and 1977. During the 1980s, per-capita food production fell in 29 of the 43 low-income countries, including 22 African nations.

A comparison of rates also masks the fact that the total number of hungry people is rising. Because of population growth, more people are malnourished today than in the early 1970s. Nearly one in every three Africans and more than one in every five Asians do not eat enough to lead fully productive lives. Malnutrition not only saps physical strength, but it also harms children's learning ability and increases vulnerability to disease and infection.

In theory, all the world's people could be fed from the world's present level of food production. In reality, at least one-fifth of the world's people lack the means to grow their own food or purchase adequate food supplies.

Much food is wasted. Farmers cannot transport their crops to markets, and

Cynthia P. Green, "Too Many People; Not Enough Food," *Forum for Applied Research and Public Policy*, Winter 1993. Reprinted by permission.

some food rots in storage facilities or is eaten by rodents. This situation is complicated by myriad government policies controlling prices for farm goods, distribution of agricultural products, import tariffs, goods for export, and investments in rural areas.

Simple Truths

Abstract discussions of food supplies often neglect to point out the obvious. People need to eat regularly to survive; food supplies must be available and affordable; and a healthy, varied diet is needed for children to develop normally and adults to work productively.

Increased food supplies do not necessarily translate into more people fed and better diets among the neediest because much of the additional food is consumed by middle-income consumers who use their increased spending power to improve their diets. For example, food demand is projected to increase by 4 to 5 percent annually in most countries. Population growth accounts for about half of this increase.

In many countries, the poor remain unable to afford adequate diets. As their numbers increase, farm plots become increasingly smaller as they are subdivided among successive generations. Families try to grow crops on marginal land unsuited to farming because of low rainfall, poor soils, or hilly terrain. Tropical forests are cut to create cropland, but the weak soils cannot support crops for more than a few years.

As population density grows, people are not able to migrate over large areas and leave land fallow for 15 to 20 years—the time needed for the forest to regenerate and replenish the soil. Thus, the world's poorest billion people are destroying their habitats in a desperate struggle for survival.

As if these problems were not formidable enough, they are occurring at a time of unprecedented increases in human numbers. Most developing countries can expect their populations to double in 20 to 30 years, even if fertility rates drop, because the next generation of parents is already born.

Since 1950, when death rates plummeted due to improved sanitation and health care, world population growth has doubled (see Figure 1). World population continues to increase at a magnitude unprecedented in history, despite a drop in the rate of growth. The United Nations' 1992 projections estimate that the world's present population of 5.5 billion will rise to 8.5 billion by 2025 and 10 billion by 2050.

Startling in their magnitude, these projections are nevertheless optimistic. They assume an all-out family planning effort leading to a 2-child family average worldwide by 2050, down from today's average of 3.3 children per woman. The high projection, which assumes an average of 2.5 children per

> *"At least one-fifth of the world's people lack the means to grow their own food or purchase adequate food supplies."*

woman by 2050, reaches 9.4 billion people in 2025 and 12.5 billion in 2050. Alternatively, an average of 1.7 children per woman produces 7.8 billion people in 2050.

Would achieving this low projection avert massive famines? Probably not. Expert "guesstimates" of the total number of people the Earth can feed vary widely, ranging from 2 billion people with diets comparable to the United States and Europe, to an infinite number supported by as-yet-uninvented technologies.

Figure 1. World Population Growth

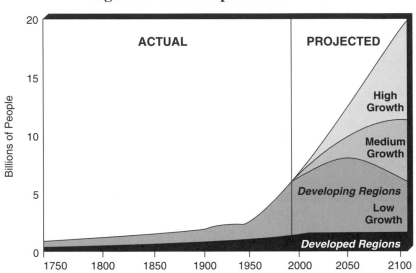

A detailed review by B. Gilland of crop-yield estimates and other data places the maximum world's carrying capacity at 7.5 billion people. World population is expected to exceed this level within 25 years.

Many developing countries already have exceeded their carrying capacity. Based on an analysis of soil and climate conditions, the United Nations Food and Agriculture Organization (FAO) concludes that more than half of the developing countries (64 out of 117 studied) will be unable to feed their populations by 2000 at present levels of subsistence farming. And with vastly improved inputs, such as full mechanization and use of agrochemicals, high-yield seeds, and crop mixes, 19 countries still will not be able to feed their people on a sustained basis.

Increasing agricultural production rapidly enough to keep pace with population growth is a tall order. For example, the Aswan Dam expanded Egypt's arable land by about 33 percent. However, it took a decade to build, during which time the country's population rose by 25 percent. As a result, per-capita food production hardly changed. Moreover, sprawling cities have gobbled up more than 10 percent of Egypt's most productive farmland since the early 1960s.

Introducing new technologies and making necessary social and economic changes to support increased crop production take time. For example, Europe and Asia developed intensive farming practices over two centuries. Because of the demands of its rapidly growing population, Africa has only one-sixth as much time to make the transition.

> *"The world's poorest billion people are destroying their habitats in a desperate struggle for survival."*

Some countries have sought to blunt the impact of population growth by relocating families to undeveloped areas. This approach, which has proven expensive, also has had mixed success. Furthermore, it does not address population growth problems.

For example, in 1970, Sri Lanka embarked on an ambitious scheme to resettle one-tenth of its population in the interior. Two decades later, nearly four times as many people have been added to its population, and the land's productivity is in jeopardy because the hillsides are bare and vulnerable to severe erosion.

Environmental Destruction

Population trends are not the only worry. Increasing food outputs above today's levels may be difficult. Today's practices, productive as they are, may not be sustainable in the long term because of massive environmental destruction. Limiting factors include:

Finite arable land. The amount of land converted to cropland each year is about equal to the amount removed from production due to soil erosion, dryness, salt deposits, or water saturation. Large amounts of land are being taken over by housing, roads, and industry. Prospects for increasing cropland are limited, because most of the unused land has weak soils or receives insufficient rainfall.

Reduced soil fertility. The push to grow more food leads farmers to abandon traditional soil conservation measures and cultivate fragile areas, such as steep hills and dry rangelands. With intensive cultivation, soil nutrients are depleted and valuable topsoil often is washed or blown away.

Water shortages. Irrigation is the key to increased crop yields and multiple crops in semi-arid areas. However, prospects to increase irrigation are dim because most countries in Africa, the Middle East, and north Asia will face serious water shortages within 35 years.

Chemical pollution. Increased crop yields will require heavier use of agrochemicals, including fertilizers and pesticides. These chemicals seep into the water supply, contaminate produce, and kill plants and animals needed to maintain balanced ecosystems.

Dwindling energy supplies. High-yield farming technologies use copious amounts of oil to run machinery and manufacture agrochemicals. As oil supplies become scarcer and more costly, energy supplies will need to be reallocated to maintain present crop yields. A doubling of world food outputs would require a three- to four-fold increase in the amount of energy expended for agriculture.

Global climate change. A warming of the Earth's atmosphere may reduce the productivity of the world's major grain-growing areas. These areas would not necessarily be replaced by regions with a warmer climate due to soil quality and terrain. Under the most pessimistic scenario, assuming a 10-percent decline in grain production and unfavorable climatic events every three years, severe grain shortages would take place every five years.

Air pollution. Additional thinning of the stratospheric ozone layer and an increase in acid rain will not only harm plants but also fish and farm animals.

Developing Countries

The sum total of these factors is likely to hit developing countries hardest, because most cannot afford to import large quantities of food, pay higher prices for energy and raw materials, or introduce technologies to overcome environmental limitations (such as building dikes to preserve coastlines, piping water over mountains or deserts, desalinating or purifying water, and providing alternative energy sources on a large scale). Even if developing countries could afford imported food, reliance on external food supplies creates economic difficulties when prices increase and currency values fluctuate. Distribution systems also may break down, causing shortages.

> *"More than half of the developing countries . . . will be unable to feed their populations by 2000."*

Mexico, one of the success stories of the Green Revolution, provides a good example of the challenges facing developing countries. Between 1950 and 1984, its population more than doubled and grain production quadrupled. However, grain production has leveled off because some croplands are worn out. Despite this loss, Mexico will need to feed 70 percent more people within 35 years.

As human settlements expand and more land is taken over to grow food and meet other needs, other species are crowded out. Ecosystems of plants and animals uniquely adapted to a particular area are destroyed. This destruction is occurring on such a large scale that many species disappear before they are even identified by scientists and their value to humans can be assessed.

Today, people use about 40 percent of the planet's food resources on land (solar energy captured by plants, known as net primary production), through direct consumption, agriculture, and human settlements. If world population grows by 50 percent as is projected by 2020 more than half of land-based food resources would be consumed by humans. Even more alarming, food production potential has been reduced by 13 percent since the early 1950s.

Wake-Up Call

Lack of dramatic news reports on famine should not obscure two facts: too many of the world's people go hungry, and population growth and food production remain on a collision course. Efforts to alleviate hunger and slow population growth have been more successful than anyone dared hope two decades ago. And yet they have been inadequate—given little political support, underfunded, and hampered by inept government bureaucracies. Too often, donor agencies have let domestic politics override humanitarian considerations and sound programmatic judgment. The task of the 1990s is to persuade policy makers to look beyond parochial political skirmishes to the larger issue of human survival.

What can U.S. policy makers do to turn around the present situation?

Family planning. One in five women in developing countries is in need of family planning services, and one-fifth of all births in developing countries are unwanted. To reach the fertility levels of the United Nations medium population projection will require five times the amount of foreign aid the United States currently provides to overseas population and family planning programs.

Technology transfer. Many developing countries could benefit from advanced technology such as high-yield seeds, water-conserving irrigation, and renewable energy generators. Foreign aid programs can provide the expertise and equipment to improve food production, distribution, and storage.

Support farmers. Farmers in developing countries—many of them women—need access to credit, basic supplies, and sound technical advice. Income-generation projects have multiple payoffs for communities and families.

Expand assistance. Other types of foreign aid, including health care, schools, nutrition education, and environmental protection, can improve the quality of life and contribute to better health and smaller families. The amount of foreign aid spent on development assistance, compared to military and economic aid, is small. For example, only 2 percent of U.S. foreign aid is allocated to population assistance.

> *"The push to grow more food leads farmers to abandon traditional soil conservation measures."*

The 1990s will be a crucial decade in determining whether humans limit their numbers humanely or through widespread famine and suffering. Will succeeding generations look back on this era as a time of enlightenment and compassion (albeit in our own self-interest), or as a time of short-sighted greed and self-absorption?

The time to act is short. We can heed the warning bells or passively wait to see if the worst predictions come true.

Food Aid Programs Do Not Reduce Hunger

by Tom Bethell

About the author: *Tom Bethell is a writer and Washington correspondent for the* American Spectator, *a conservative journal.*

Several months ago, the *Village Voice* carried an unusual story about Somalia on its cover: "The Famine Food Created," by Michael Maren. In October 1993 he spoke at the Cato Institute, his talk billed as "Good Intentions Gone Awry." I decided to find out what he had to say.

He turned out to be a quietly spoken man of 37 who over the years has worked for the Peace Corps, Catholic Relief Services, and the U.S. Agency for International Development. He has spent time in India, Kenya, Ethiopia, and Somalia, and to say that he had become disillusioned about food aid would be putting it mildly.

Neglected Story

His message was shocking and newsworthy, but almost wholly neglected by the U.S. news media: the free food that year after year is dumped in these African countries undermines the local agriculture and so causes famines when rainfall is below normal. The famine in Somalia was caused by the food that for years had been unloaded at the docks of Mogadishu. "Food is killing people, and that must stop," Maren said.

Somalia has enough arable land to feed itself even in the worst drought, he said. Briefly, in 1987, Somalia actually exported food. The country has no "population problem." It has a total of 6 million people in a country the size of Texas. The problem is that free food undermines the market for locally grown food.

On January 13, 1993, there was an article on the subject by Alison Mitchell in the *New York Times*, but I think it was the only one they published that year. Here is how it began:

> GENALE, SOMALIA—In this country of hunger, Faadumi Abdi Arush is cursed

with corn. She has corn stored away in barrels, corn stacked in sacks, corn to be tossed away as chicken feed. Mrs. Arush survived Somalia's civil war, and she and the farm hands on her large holding even managed to tend her fields, producing a bountiful harvest of corn four months ago.

But when she took her crop to the market, she found that the infusion of food from relief agencies was cutting demand. With food prices falling in a bottomless tumble, no merchant wanted to risk buying her corn and then see the prices tumble still lower, she said.

"Nobody is interested," said the slender 52-year-old farmer, pointing in exasperation to the piles of corn already gone bad that had been thrown on a tarpaulin for chicken feed. "Everybody has his own relief supply."

This is the paradox of famine and famine relief. The international charity that stopped starvation eventually can become a problem in itself, threatening to destroy what little remains of the local farm economy.

Mitchell went on to note that the price of rice in Somalia was said to be the lowest in the world, having fallen to $5 for a 110-lb. bag—less than half the price in the U.S. She added that "some relief agencies are starting to fear that the relief food will now cause another cycle of dependency by depressing the food market and making it unprofitable for farmers to farm." The principal relief agencies are CARE, Catholic Relief Services, World Vision, and Save the Children. Says Willet Weeks of Save the Children: "Prolonging free food distribution as the need is diminishing is a sure recipe for prolonging the famine."

The Effects of Aid

To understand the problem that food creates, it is necessary to go back in time before the emergency arises. Most food aid—about 90 percent of it—is distributed in places where there is no famine and, of course, where there are no reporters or TV cameras. This is the invisible part of the exercise, and the crucial part. It is here that native self-sufficiency is undermined, day by day. This is happening in many countries in Africa right now: for example, Zaire, Rwanda, Burundi, Mali, Burkina Faso, Senegal, Ivory Coast, Togo, and Ghana. And no doubt many more. These are simply the countries that Maren reeled off

"The problem is that free food undermines the market for locally grown food."

when I asked him to name the countries where free, non-emergency food is being distributed. In any given country, Maren told me, CARE or Catholic Relief Services or World Vision have routine programs: "School feeding programs, where they give food to children; mother-child health programs, where they give food to women with kids at clinics; and food-for-work programs, where they dump food on people for digging holes, things like that: digging wells, building roads." These projects tend to be make-work. Maren identifies one in Mogadishu: "Food-for-work consists of giving people empty garbage bags and then trading a bag of food for a bag of trash." This is doomed to turn into a scavenging exercise, he says, "with people looting garbage trucks as they once looted food convoys."

Relief Organizations and the Media

Meanwhile, in Somalia, as in other countries not yet known to the media or "the international community," local agriculture and self-sufficiency is undermined, sack by free sack. Once there is a drought or a civil war in which the normal channels of food distribution are disrupted, there is likely to be a famine. Then the relief organizations will telephone their friends in the news media and show up with more food—this time in a true emergency. The television crews will get the starving-children footage they need to make the evening news. And the relief organizations will be depicted in a very favorable light, alleviating on camera the starvation that their earlier off-camera efforts had helped cause.

Maren points out that news organizations are likely to be dependent on the relief agencies when they arrive in a new famine area for the first time. In March 1993, Maren gave a speech to the Camel Breeders, a group of Cornell University graduate students who are preparing to work in international development. The speech was reprinted in *Harper's* in August 1993. Here's an excerpt:

> *"Most food aid . . . is distributed in places where there is no famine."*

> Historically, the press has been willing to uncritically accept whatever image of Africa the western vanguard has been selling. In the case of the PVOs [private voluntary organizations, such as CARE] the press has bought their line because reporters are as dependent on aid organizations as the organizations are on them. It would have been impossible, for example, for the press to cover Somalia without the assistance of PVOs. There's no Hertz counter at the Mogadishu airport and no road maps available at gas stations. If a journalist arrives in Africa from Europe or the United States and needs to get to the interior of the country, PVOs are the only ticket. Journalists sleep and eat with PVO workers. When they want history and facts and figures, they turn to the PVOs. In press coverage of Somalia or almost any other crisis in Africa, it is always the PVOs who are most often quoted and are regarded as the neutral and authoritative sources—as if they have no vested interest in anything but the truth.

Where do these organizations get the food that they give away? Mostly from the U.S. and Canadian governments, and from the European Community. Farm price supports generate food surpluses in Western Europe and North America, which then pile up in storage depots. In the Eisenhower years it dawned on someone that giving the food to foreigners would rid us of embarrassing surpluses and perhaps even give foreigners reason to love the Yanks for a change. Shipping interests got into the act. If the (unionized) price was right, they'd be happy to ship grain from Port Arthur to wherever. So it was agreed that half the food would be transported in U.S.-flagged ships. Thus Public Law 480 was born—Food for Peace. It has turned out to be one of the more conspicuously harmful components of the U.S. foreign aid program. About half of the food aid worldwide comes

> *"Because of price supports, too much food is grown here. It is shipped abroad, and as a result too little food is grown there."*

from the U.S.—about $1 billion worth a year. It gives new meaning to the phrase "global economy."

Because of price supports, too much food is grown here. It is shipped abroad, and as a result too little food is grown there. Next there are famines. Pictures are shown on television, and the man in the White House feels compassionate. He sends a military escort to ensure that the food gets delivered. Some of the soldiers are killed and they in turn are shipped back to the U.S. Food for Peace began in 1954 but it didn't really get going until the 1960s. At that point Africa was still self-sufficient in food production. In April 1993 the *Economist* noted:

> Each year throughout the 1980s, western donors spent $1 billion shipping millions of tons of food to the hungry in Africa. It saved many lives. Yet by the end of the decade the proportion of African children who weighed too little because they ate too little increased. And the amount of food that Africans grew per person fell. Africans began to ask: Is food aid part of the problem?

In a 1984 article in the *Wall Street Journal* ("Free Food Bankrupts Foreign Farmers"), James Bovard pointed out that "per capita food production in Africa has decreased 20 percent since 1960, and PL 480 donations have helped governments perpetuate the destructive status quo." Aid officials try to argue that giving Africans wheat doesn't discourage the local production of sorghum—as though the provision of one form of grain doesn't discourage the production of another. As Bovard put it, if the Department of Agriculture really believed that giving away food has no effect on local farmers, presumably the Secretary of Agriculture wouldn't mind "if the European Economic Community sent over a billion pounds of cheese to feed all the hungry Americans they hear about." Our farmers have the clout to prevent such shipments. But the free food we send abroad goes to countries where the farmers are politically powerless. And the never-ending stream of food keeps them that way. Agencies such as CARE and Catholic Relief Services (CRS) are in effect government contractors and should be viewed as such.

Funding Relief Programs

Illustrating the point, Maren (when I spoke to him later) pulled out a copy of CARE's annual report at random. In 1986, CARE's total revenues were $401 million, 65 percent of which were agricultural commodities and ocean freight donated by governments. For CRS, that percentage is higher—between 80 and 90 percent, Maren estimated. The dominant incentive for these groups is to sign up as many people as possible for free food. They "fight like Coke and Pepsi" to expand their share of the donated food: their jobs depend on it.

A "crystal moment" in Maren's career came when he was working with CRS "in a famine situation in northwest Kenya." At a meeting in Nairobi, an American woman with CRS stood up and said: "We have to take advantage of this famine to expand our regular program." Keep 'em hooked, in other words. "When I'd return to Nairobi every few weeks," Maren told his Cornell audience, "my boss . . . had only one question: How many more recipients did you sign on? More recipients meant more government grant money, which meant we could buy more vehicles and hire more assistants."

Leftists and Conservatives

It's interesting that this is a story about the dangers of subverting markets, yet it has been told almost exclusively by the left. Maren himself comes from a leftist background. For years now the left has been issuing warnings about the problems caused by food-dumping in the Third World. Frances Moore Lappe writes about it. The aid literature is full of it. The BBC broadcasts it (Maren can get on British but not American television). Conservatives seem to have overlooked the argu-

> *"The dominant incentive for [relief] groups is to sign up as many people as possible for free food."*

ment almost completely. P.T. Bauer, a leading critic of foreign aid, missed it, and I am not aware that Milton Friedman has written about it, although it intensifies his claim that there is no such thing as a free lunch: when they do exist, free lunches may well be harmful to your (future) health.

Maren and Bovard think the explanation is that leftists are more likely to be out there in the field. They know what's going on. Conservatives don't really believe in "development" anyway, and aren't too excited about one more story of good intentions gone sour. They can point to the moral—doing good with other people's money is likely to do harm—but they don't have the facts (and typically aren't interested in reporting either, which is why there are so few conservative journalists). Leftists have the facts, but of course they shrink from the moral. Maren is one who does not.

Empowering Poor Women Can End Chronic Hunger

by Freedom from Hunger

About the author: *Freedom from Hunger is a private, nonprofit organization headquartered in Davis, California, that works to eliminate the causes of chronic hunger through development projects.*

World hunger is chronic and it is widespread, a fact of life for millions in developing as well as developed countries.

Media attention focuses on massive efforts directed to famine relief in such countries as Somalia, Ethiopia, Bangladesh, and Kurdish Iraq. Yet hunger is not primarily the result of food shortages caused by wars or natural disasters. Indeed, hunger and food surpluses often exist, as in the United States, side by side.

Today, when the knowledge and the tools to eliminate world hunger lie close at hand, one billion of the world's population live in households too impoverished to obtain the food they need to work.

The Chronically Hungry

The chronically hungry share common characteristics. They are poor, they have little access to services, and they lack political power. Many live in remote rural areas and are members of ethnic minority groups. The vast majority live, and die, in the developing countries of Africa, Asia, and Latin America.

But chronic hunger reaches a tragic scale even in the United States where one in eight children is reported to suffer from hunger.

Driven by the discomfort, weakness, and pain caused by lack of food, the chronically hungry are unable to participate in any human endeavor beyond the struggle to survive. Undernourishment brings listlessness, muscle wastage, and a reduced capacity for learning or work; a legacy that perpetuates their poverty. Hunger demands their undivided attention. And hunger claims their children as its most vulnerable victims.

Each day, worldwide, 40,000 children under five die from malnutrition and infection, deaths that are preventable.

In response to what UNICEF's [United Nations International Children's Emergency Fund] Executive Director James P. Grant calls "a silent holocaust," the largest gathering of world leaders in history convened at the World Summit for Children in September of 1990 at the United Nations. The 71 leaders who participated in the Summit identified the enhancement of children's health and nutrition as a "first duty and a task for which solutions are now within reach."

> *"Undernourishment brings listlessness, muscle wastage, and a reduced capacity for learning or work."*

The Summit singled out with urgency the situation of girls and women who bear a major share of the burden of poverty and are more frequently undernourished than men and boys. And the participants recognized the critical role women play in their families' nutritional well-being through their traditional roles in agricultural production, food production, childbearing, and child care.

Today's knowledge and unprecedented international resolve actually hold out the promise of eliminating chronic hunger, and preventing its return, among the world's children and their families.

The past few decades have seen major advances in our understanding of the origins and causes of hunger, successful attempts to improve nutrition and rapid progress in the battles against childhood and nutritional diseases. Development groups have forged partnerships with nongovernmental and grassroots organizations and a worldwide logistical system to deliver emergency food aid has been put in place.

Self-Help for a Hungry World

But aid is only a short-term solution to breaking the cycle of hunger if it does not change the conditions that prompted the need for the assistance in the first place. It is only when the poor can feed themselves and their children that there can be any hope for improved health and longevity, viable family units, increased agricultural production, literacy, economic growth and diversification, stable democratic institutions, human rights and environmental restoration and protection.

Self-help for a hungry world is the motto and the mission of Freedom from Hunger. Our goal is to empower the poor to eliminate chronic hunger. We do this by developing and testing model programs that provide the poor with resources and knowledge that enable them to overcome the immediate causes of chronic hunger and malnutrition. . . .

Our experience has taught us that providing the poor with the resources and information they need to make their own informed choices is the key to ending chronic hunger. Because women are a principal if not the sole economic support of themselves and their children and are responsible for ensuring adequate food supplies, Freedom from Hunger believes that promoting self-help among poor women is the most effective way to permanently improve the health and nutrition of their families.

To meet the needs of hundreds of millions of the world's poorest women, Freedom from Hunger acts as a catalyst for change, working together with funders and local organizations to deliver technical assistance and training to develop promising new ways to eliminate hunger. When programs prove successful, we stimulate the coalition and bring in new partners to enable the expansion of the programs to more communities. Our goal is *to identify, develop, and expand innovative, cost-effective programs that empower poor women to help themselves, their families, and their communities become free from hunger.*

Credit with Education

Since 1989, Freedom from Hunger has developed Credit with Education in Mali and Ghana, the starting points for a regional network of programs in West Africa. Bolivia is the proving ground for the Andean countries of South America; Honduras for Central America; and Thailand for tropical Asia.

Women interested in receiving loans come together to form "credit associations," composed of about 20 to 30 members, the great majority of whom are very poor women. The members guarantee repayment of each other's loans, so they must agree that each woman is capable of making a sufficient profit from her proposed income-earning activity. After training the new members to manage their own association within specified rules, Freedom from Hunger makes a four- to six-month loan to the credit association. The members then break the large loan into small loans averaging $64 per individual.

> *"Aid is only a short-term solution to breaking the cycle of hunger if it does not change the conditions that prompted the need for the assistance."*

Women invest in activities in which they are already skilled and need no technical assistance, such as food processing and selling, raising chickens, operating a small shop, and making or buying and selling clothing. It is crucial that each borrower earn enough cash to pay back her loan with interest, deposit some personal savings, and have enough money left to acquire food and other necessities for the family.

Learning sessions led initially by a facilitator from the local staff address three areas critical to improving household health and nutrition: (1) use of existing health services such as immunizations and family planning, (2) household diets and feeding methods (especially for infants, children, and pregnant and breastfeeding women), and (3) assuring an adequate food supply, particularly during the "hungry season" when food is scarce and expensive before the next harvest.

This education component, in addition to fostering learning about credit association management and the basic economics of small enterprise, allows credit association members to identify the hunger-related problems they confront in their daily lives and to discover their own solutions. For example, the mother of an underweight child may not realize that her child is too small, because most babies she sees are also underweight. As soon as she recognizes the problem, she can begin to think of her own solutions.

Both the credit and the education components of this strategy are designed to be self-managed by credit association members, with technical assistance from a national or local organization, and the credit funds are capitalized by a national lending agency at commercial interest rates. This strategy allows the program to become cost-effective, sustainable, and replicable on a large scale. . . .

Encouraging Results

Evaluations of the first few years of program development are very encouraging. In 1991, field studies compared randomly selected members of credit associations with randomly selected residents of villages that were not yet participating in Credit with Education. The study in Mali showed:

- 86% of the credit association members reported increased income, compared to 27% of the controls.
- 90% of the members reported more savings (that can be used to assure adequate food supplies during the "hungry season"), compared to 27% of the controls.
- 60% of the members felt their families listened to them more (one sign of increased personal empowerment), compared to 19% of the controls.
- 65% of the members knew the proper age for introducing solid food to an infant, compared to 20% of the controls.
- 85% of the members felt that the health and nutrition of their preschool children had improved, compared to 40% of the controls.

Similar evidence was found in a parallel study in Honduras, half a world away.

These self-reported impact data suggest this innovative approach is an effective tool for eliminating chronic hunger and malnutrition. To attract major investments by governments and international organizations, however, larger scale demonstrations are needed to show how well the programs work when implemented on a broad scale for the benefit of thousands and thousands of people in need.

Humanitarian Intervention Can Relieve Famine

by Tony P. Hall

About the author: *Tony P. Hall is a Democratic congressman from Ohio.*

I believe humanitarian intervention needs to be viewed in the context of the right to food. One of the key international provisions of the "Freedom from Want Act," which I introduced in 1991, was a section which called for a Convention on the Right to Food. This section, which later was accepted as an amendment to the Foreign Aid Authorization bill, proposed an international Convention on the Right to Food as a tool to increase global respect for the right to food, especially among governments and armed opposition groups.

A Declaration on the Right to Food

This legislation asked the United States to propose to the United Nations General Assembly that a Declaration and a Convention on the Right to Food be adopted and submitted to the countries of the world for ratification. Such a convention would contain the following elements: (1) the obligations of each country's government to ensure the realization of the right to food by the people of that country; (2) the obligations of the international community to ensure the realization of the right to food by the people of all countries, including the provision of both emergency and nonemergency assistance; (3) the obligations of individual governments, and of armed opposition groups, to ensure the realization of the right to food during times of war or other forms of armed conflict; and (4) sanctions against governments or armed groups that fail to take adequate steps to ensure the realization of the right to food by the people of the country.

In 1991, while leading a congressional delegation to Ethiopia, I urged President Meles Zenawi to convene a Humanitarian Summit for the Horn of Africa. This summit, which took place in May of 1992, was attended by five heads of state from the region, United Nations observers, and representatives of nongovernmental organizations. The summit produced a document outlining hu-

Statement of Tony P. Hall in *International Hunger Crisis: Hearings Before the Subcommittee on Foreign Agriculture and Hunger of the Committee on Agriculture, House of Representatives*, 103rd Cong., 1st sess., June 9, 1993, ser. no. 103-19.

manitarian guidelines to be used in the region.

This Summit, plus the World Declaration and Plan of Action for Nutrition arising from 1992's International Conference on Nutrition, helped to raise the right to food as a matter of global concern. But a Convention on the Right to Food would provide the required clear set of principles to support future acts of humanitarian intervention.

Universal Guidelines Are Needed

The humanitarian interventions with which I am most directly familiar—to help the Iraqi Kurds and the people of Somalia—seemed to be handled on a piecemeal basis. Individual United Nations resolutions provided the authority for the interventions, and the operations were fashioned as events unfolded. I believe we need to have universally acknowledged guidelines in place. A Convention on the Right to Food would set the overall framework, but specific operating procedures also would enable future humanitarian interventions to run more smoothly.

In the Kurdish situation, it seemed there were problems within the United Nations system in determining which U.N. entity was in charge. In Somalia, the crisis worsened month by month, and many of us criticized the United Nations for not intervening sooner and more effectively. When I visited Somalia in January 1993, everyone I talked to—from the relief workers to the military leaders—had complaints about the performance of the United Nations.

The United Nations and the world community seemed to have to make up the rules for each situation as they went along. As we face future humanitarian crises that will require international action, we shouldn't have to reinvent the wheel for each response.

While it is true that each crisis will have its own special challenges, our general approach should be clarified. The first step, which I have mentioned, is to have in place international authority through a Convention on the Right to Food for humanitarian intervention. That way, we wouldn't lose time debating new U.N. resolutions to approve action while lives are on the line.

The next step would be to increase the authority of the U.N. Under Secretary General for Humanitarian Affairs. This position was called for by the Select Committee on Hunger in the "Freedom from Want Act" and in

> *"As we face future humanitarian crises that will require international action, we shouldn't have to reinvent the wheel for each response."*

subsequent select committee initiatives. While this office is ably led, I would like to see it have more power to coordinate and supervise U.N. leadership in humanitarian crises. This office can play a lifesaving role in achieving the earliest possible mobilization of world response to a humanitarian disaster.

Given the serious logistical and military obstacles that often arise in a humanitarian crisis, a U.N.–coordinated, ready-to-respond "humanitarian strike force" should be created. We have seen the critical role played by United States air and sea power in the Kurdish and Somali situations. As the world's remaining superpower, we are in a position to offer certain logistical and deployment capabilities that other nations cannot. We should stand ready to contribute these elements to an international response force. The tragic loss of multinational soldiers in Somalia must not be allowed to discourage other nations from stepping forward to offer their military in humanitarian service to the world community.

> *"The world community needs to agree that using food as a weapon or blocking food is a human rights crime."*

This international humanitarian force would provide the logistical and security assistance necessary to allow relief to be distributed. Relief itself should continue to be provided by private voluntary organizations. They also are in the best position to help those they serve move from the process of relief to rehabilitation. However, as we have learned in Iraq, Somalia, Liberia, Angola, and Sudan, these organizations cannot do their job when they are under attack, when their hands are tied by those in control, or when their own safety is untenable. That's why it is important to resolve the security concerns.

I am deeply frustrated by the delays we have seen in aiding the Kurds, Somalia, and Sudan. Relief groups on the ground in these places have sought to provide early warning, but the response was slow—with many lives lost as a result.

Much of the reason for this is political. Humanitarian disasters tend to get put on the back burner because of competing issues and "famine fatigue." We in Congress need to fight to make such human suffering a priority and press for the earliest diplomatic intervention to address it.

Most of these crises are manmade. They arise because of civil or ethnic conflict or because of war between neighboring countries. In our diplomatic efforts, we need to place a special emphasis on negotiating skills to address combatants whose actions deny food to innocent civilians. I also firmly believe that it will help greatly if we start thinking of the suffering they cause as violations of human rights. The world community needs to agree that using food as a weapon or blocking food is a human rights crime, and that those who engage in such conduct are criminals. I recommend that we elevate the right to food and expand our concept of human rights in the post–Cold War era.

Poor Countries Should Implement Famine-Prevention Systems

by Alex de Waal

About the author: *Alex de Waal is the associate director of the London-based Africa Watch, which is a division of Human Rights Watch, an organization that monitors and protests human rights violations worldwide.*

Reports of mass starvation in Somalia in 1992 and the threat of widespread hunger across much of southern Africa prompted by-now-familiar appeals for emergency food shipments. Unfortunately, the complicated logistics of procuring and delivering large-scale aid mean that food can never arrive in time to stave off a crisis once it is imminent. What's more, the urgent need to deal with the immediate problem obscures lessons that the West has repeatedly failed to learn: No country has moved from being famine-stricken to famine-free by receiving food aid. And no government is so poor that it cannot afford a famine-prevention system. Only by making emergency food shipments as well as development aid conditional on fundamental changes in recipient countries can the world eliminate famine and avoid institutionalizing an ineffective international dole.

Successful Famine-Prevention Systems

The basic measures needed to head off famine were enumerated more than a century ago by the Indian Famine Commission of 1883, whose findings still form the foundation of the successful Indian famine-prevention system. The centerpiece of that system is jobs: during an emergency, invoked when unemployment reaches a certain level, the government guarantees paid employment to all able-bodied people without an income. The government also releases stockpiled food to ensure that grain is readily available at a reasonable price.

A crucial spur to this commitment is public pressure: citizens use the press to

Alex de Waal, "Preventing Famine at Its Source," *Technology Review*, November/December 1992. Reprinted with permission from *Technology Review*, copyright 1992.

complain of shortages and pressure their representatives to act. Because few members of parliament could expect votes from an electorate dying of hunger, the government takes action well in advance of a food emergency. The result is that no food need be imported from abroad, and food handouts are kept to a minimum.

Although India is the finest example of a large-scale, efficient famine-prevention system, Africa has also seen its share of successes. In Botswana, the government immediately begins to buy food on the international market whenever there is a domestic shortfall. Year after year, the country has managed to cut rates of child undernutrition despite repeated droughts and production shortfalls that dwarf those in Sudan and Ethiopia, sites of recent large-scale famine. Any Western food aid to Botswana—and the country *has* received generous amounts—is regarded as a luxury that is used to replenish stocks, not as a necessary precondition for starting a relief program.

Cape Verde and Kenya have also coped with major food shortages because elected representatives have pressured the government for deliveries of cheap or free food purchased on the world market. And Sudan in the 1970s and Zimbabwe in the 1980s relied on long-term grain-storage plans to meet short-term crises. Famine occurred when Sudan exported its reserves in 1984 and 1990, and when Zimbabwe ran down its stockpiles in 1990.

Sustaining Corrupt Governments

Under such conditions, donors often deliver aid with no questions asked because they wish to maintain good commercial or strategic relations with recipients. But while Western aid has a marginal effect once famine is underway, it does play a vital role in sustaining corrupt governments. Food aid sold to urban citizens who can afford to pay provides the single greatest source of revenue for Africa's poorest countries.

Meanwhile, rural populations become pawns in the domestic conflicts common to Africa, further undermining their chances of survival. Battles and raids destroy crops and livestock, and people driven from their homes are forced to become refugees. Governments fighting guerrilla movements stop people from migrating in search of jobs and more productive land, and armed conflict prevents the flow of food from surplus to deficit areas. During the great Ethiopian famine of 1983–85, the government bombed markets in rebel

> *"No government is so poor that it cannot afford a famine-prevention system."*

hands and prevented traders from transporting food to those who needed it. In Somalia, clan-based militias took advantage of their ready access to cheap modern firearms to fight over land, water, cattle, trade routes, and international aid, again preventing food from reaching intended recipients.

Aid donors rarely consider the conduct of such internal wars and are indifferent to the extent that governments spend funds on weapons. And Westerners too often equate democracy with multiple parties while ignoring other pillars of a strong civilian society such as the press, judiciary, trade unions, and professional associations. Although donor governments have recently begun to cite progress on human rights as a criterion for allocating aid, the thinking on such issues remains depressingly superficial.

Most important, donors devote little thought to making assistance programs accountable to the supposed beneficiaries—citizens—relying instead on government-to-government contracts. Recipient countries should be required to enshrine in domestic law a clear obligation to provide famine relief, and award an independent watchdog agency legal powers to prosecute negligent parties. For their part, donors must guarantee advance food allocations to famine-prone countries rather than waiting for urgent appeals. Donors, too, should conduct public inquiries into the performance of relief programs to learn from past mistakes and discipline, dismiss, and even prosecute negligent officials. Finally, if development programs are to help consign famine to history, they should be subject to the same public scrutiny.

Democracy Prevents Famine

by Sylvia Nasar

About the author: *Sylvia Nasar is a writer for the* New York Times.

The world still thinks of famine the way that Thomas Malthus did, as Mother Nature's revenge on hapless humanity. In fact, famine is anything but what the dour English economist called "nature's last most dreadful resource." As in Somalia in the early 1990s, it is often a man-made disaster, an avoidable economic and political catastrophe.

The kind of famine that struck there—created by clan warfare, not by crop shortages or endemic poverty—is the rule, not the exception, according to economists who have studied famines in Africa, Asia and Europe.

Enough to Go Around

World food production has kept well ahead of population growth. Drought or flood does often precede famines. But declines in food production rarely account for them, says Amartya Sen, a Harvard economist whose 1981 book, *Poverty and Famines*, changed the way many scholars analyze hunger. Typically, as thousands die, there's enough food in the country to go around or enough money to import it.

Disaster strikes because the poorest, most downtrodden members of society suddenly can no longer afford to buy food, usually because of sudden unemployment or a surge in food prices. And, particularly since World War II, whether or not a country starves depends more on whether it has a free press and democratic government than on whether it has enough grain, trucks or foreign aid.

In eastern and sub-Saharan Africa, for example, there has been, on average, twice as much food available per person as in other flood- or drought-prone countries that managed to avoid mass deaths.

One of the worst recent famines—Bangladesh's in 1974—took place in a year

Sylvia Nasar, "It's Never Fair to Just Blame the Weather," *The New York Times*, January 17, 1993.

of unusually high rice production. As Martin Ravallion, a World Bank economist who specializes in poverty in Asia, described it: Severe flooding disrupted rice planting and threw landless rural laborers out of work. Then false fears of shortages doubled rice prices in a few weeks. For the poor, who spend more than three-quarters of their wages on food, the blow was catastrophic.

But the famine, which was largely over even before the rice crop was harvested, was hardly inevitable.

"Almost everything the government did made things worse," said Mr. Ravallion. Bangladesh's authoritarian rulers sent the army out to "bash hoarders," convincing people that it had lost control and fueling the price surge. The United States contributed by announcing that it would withhold food aid to punish Bangladesh for, of all things, selling jute to Cuba.

Politics and Starvation

But poor countries need not starve. Famine relief has almost as long a history as famines. In the 4th century B.C., a Sanskrit book on statecraft advises: "During famine, the king should make a store of foodstuffs and show favor to the subjects or institute the building of forts or water works."

France and England suffered through dozens of famines in the Middle Ages.

> *"Whether or not a country starves depends more on whether it has a free press and democratic government than on whether it has enough grain."*

But since 1500, when they began growing enough to feed the population, their poor never starved because granaries were bare, as Malthus thought, but because they couldn't afford the grain.

Robert Fogel, a University of Chicago economic historian and an author of *Time on the Cross*, a book that challenged the conventional wisdom about the economics of slavery, has analyzed 500 years of food consumption, health and productivity in Britain and France. Even during the worst harvests, he concluded, inventories never fell below three months' worth of grain. But even a 5 percent drop in production sent prices zooming.

Kings James I and Charles I largely succeeded in averting famines between 1600 and 1640 by forcing merchants, bakers and brewers to sell their food stocks cheaply. Alas, the English civil war ended such benign intervention for the next 100 years.

In 1846–1851, Ireland starved in the potato famine largely because Parliament would not raise English taxes enough to save it, though it raised $60 million for the Crimean War.

Democracy Prevents Famine

Modern transportation has made it easier to move relief supplies. But far more important are the incentives governments have to save their own people.

It's no accident that the familiar horror stories of the 19th and early 20th centuries occurred in one-party states, dictatorships or colonies: China, British India, Stalin's Russia.

"There has never been a famine in any country that's been a democracy with a relatively free press," said Professor Sen. "I know of no exception. It applies to very poor countries with democratic systems as well as to rich ones."

India, for example, has had no episodes of mass starvation since independence in 1947, despite food shortages in 1967, 1973, 1979 and 1987.

In western India, droughts led to surges in unemployment in 1972 and 1973. The average amount of food per capita in the area was half that in sub-Saharan Africa, but public works projects kept people from starving.

Meanwhile, Somalia, Ethiopia and the Sudan paid heavily for the absence of democracy. Wars, corruption and government reluctance to admit problems let droughts grow into starvation.

"There are countries that are not democratic and don't have famines—Latin America, for example," said Professor Sen. "My point really is that if famine is about to develop, democracy can guarantee that it won't. When newspapers are controlled, it's amazing how ignorant and immune from pressure the government can be."

Mao Tse-Tung's Delusions

In Mao's China, up to 30 million may have starved during the Great Leap Forward. The government confiscated millions of villagers' family plots to gather them into collective farms, assuming the owners would keep working out of loyalty to socialist ideals. Output plummeted.

But Beijing did nothing, partially because it did not realize the program had failed; it actually increased the amounts that rural areas were required to send to cities. By 1960, as the famine was coming to a peak, the authorities thought they had 100 million more metric tons of grain than they did.

"In the process of deluding the world," said Professor Sen, "you delude yourself."

But even with the world alerted, handing out foreign grain isn't the best solution.

"It's just as important what happens to domestic markets and relative incomes as how effectively the army can deliver food to people," said Mr. Ravallion. "The indigenous institutions can do it much better."

Giving out make-work jobs, as India has often done, can help the poor buy grain and rebuild the roads and bridges for food trucks. Getting them back to their farms can help them grow it. Even announcing that shipments are on the way can drive the price down so they can afford it.

History suggests that America's mercy mission of 1992–93 won't solve Somalia's starvation problem. Stable governments let farmers grow and democracy helps protect the poor.

Satellite Technology Can Help Prevent Famine

by Fabrizio del Piero

About the author: *Fabrizio del Piero is an Italian journalist specializing in international affairs.*

For decades, Western nations have been putting surveying satellites in orbit to observe the earth but, inevitably, thinking mainly of their own national interests. For example, better weather forecasts are obtained thanks to geostationary spacecraft placed at the equator, over the very center of Africa. Much other data, acquired at the same time, would have been precious for the developing countries, but remained unutilized.

This information is now being put to good use. The Rome-based Food and Agriculture Organization (FAO) of the United Nations has brought together European and American space agencies and research institutions willing to put their generosity and advanced technological skills into a complex but worthwhile endeavor to promote food security in the Third World.

The challenge is to create a special system designed to collect, process, analyze, and distribute to developing countries—starting with Africa and the Near East—valuable satellite information and imagery concerning their agricultural production prospects.

Two Components

The system is made up of two components, called ARTEMIS and DIANA. Neither name has anything to do with the Greek-Roman goddess of the hunt. In fact, they are easy-to-remember acronyms standing for complicated technical jargon. ARTEMIS means "Africa Real-Time Environmental Monitoring using Imaging Satellites"; DIANA stands for "Data and Information Available Now in Africa."

ARTEMIS has been in operation at the FAO Remote Sensing Center in Rome since August 1988. It constitutes the receiving and processing component of the system. It was designed by the National Aerospace Laboratory (NLR) of the Netherlands according to FAO specifications and built by the NLR in cooperation with the U.S. space agency NASA and the University of Reading in the United Kingdom. Funding—some $3.5 million—was ensured by a special trust fund from the government of the Netherlands, a generous donor to many FAO projects concerned with rural poverty.

"Through satellite observation, it becomes possible to identify areas where severe crop failures may be expected."

Through an unobtrusive antenna dish installed on a terrace on FAO premises in Rome, ARTEMIS receives directly every hour the data relayed to earth by the European meteorological satellite METEOSAT, in an equatorial orbit over Africa. Daily data from another satellite, the American NOAA-11 orbiting around the poles, is also received on magnetic tape from the U.S. National Oceanic and Atmospheric Administration.

Quick Detail

This wealth of observations relayed to Rome from space and across the continents is stored in a computer and then all combined and processed at lightning speed on special software programs also developed by the NLR and NASA.

"We can very quickly obtain detailed data on location and duration of rain-bearing clouds and estimate associated amounts of rainfall," says Jelle Hielkema, a Dutch expert who is the coordinator of the Environmental Monitoring Group at FAO's Remote Sensing Center. "We can detect abnormal weather patterns, or determine the number of rainfall days and the level of vegetation cover for most locations. This information is available in digital form or, in a matter of minutes, can be produced as color-coded photographs."

These fascinating continental maps may look like a single picture, but are in fact a composite of hundreds of thousands of little pixels (picture elements) observed by the satellites one after the other. Definition (as photographic accuracy in recording ground features is termed) is as high as 5 kilometers.

All this is precious information indeed. In many Third World countries, news from vast regions outside the capital is often scarce, belated, or haphazard. Threats such as pest infestation, persistent drought, or excessive rain should be identified as early as possible for prompt action, but often rely on mouth-to-mouth reports from nomads or occasional travelers. Such scanty, localized reporting prevents authorities from drawing an overall picture that might correctly assess the magnitude of troubles ahead. Through satellite observation, it becomes possible to identify areas where severe crop failures may be expected due to adverse weather conditions, and where timely food aid is needed to avert shortages and even loss of life. It can help pinpoint locations where moisture and vegetation growth may favor infestations of locusts and grasshoppers. It can provide data to help keep a watchful eye on the state of forest resources. On a more positive note, it can anticipate favorable conditions for bumper crops and help national governments be prepared to cope with the surpluses.

In the longer term, the accumulated data bases generated by ARTEMIS can become an additional tool in the task of reconciling development with environmental protection. It can help in rational planning and in assessing changes in the agricultural environment as, for example, caused by global climatic changes.

At the moment, this wealth of information is immediately used by several units at FAO headquarters, such as the "Global Information and Early Warning System" and the Emergency Center for Locust Operations of the Plant Protection Service. But how can we make this data quickly available to the most interested parties—the developing countries?

DIANA

For this purpose FAO has joined forces with the European Space Agency to create DIANA, the second component of the project. DIANA is a special satellite communications system which will enable the direct transmission of the high-volume ARTEMIS data to users at regional and national levels. Funds—some $8 million—have been provided by the governments of Italy, Belgium, Spain, the United Kingdom, Ireland, Norway, and Finland.

From FAO's headquarters in Rome, the centrally processed data will be sent through the Italian space

> *"We should make full use of all that is available in support of our task—to be the sentinels of mankind against hunger."*

telecommunication agency TELESPAZIO to the INTELSAT commercial satellites. From there, it will be beamed back to earth to be received by interested recipients in other continents on inexpensive personal computers linked to low-cost user terminals. . . .

"It is just the beginning, on a demonstration basis. We are confident that soon many more users will be keen to join the system throughout Africa," says Zdenek Kalenksy, a Canadian heading FAO's Remote Sensing Center. "The usefulness of ARTEMIS-DIANA is so evident that in a further phase it is planned to extend part of its services to Asia and Latin America. Our satellite data also cover these regions. And we should make full use of *all* that is available in support of our task—to be the sentinels of mankind against hunger."

Bibliography

Books

Dennis T. Avery — *Saving the Planet with Pesticides and Plastic: The Environmental Triumph of High-Yield Farming*. Indianapolis: Hudson Institute, 1995.

Bread for the World — *Hunger 1994: Transforming the Politics of Hunger*. Silver Spring, MD: Bread for the World, 1993.

Lester R. Brown and Hal Kane — *Full House: Reassessing the Earth's Population Carrying Capacity*. New York: Norton, 1994.

Francis M. Deng and Larry Minear — *The Challenges of Famine Relief: Emergency Operations in the Sudan*. Washington: Brookings Institution, 1992.

Jean Drèze and Amartya Sen — *Hunger and Public Action*. New York: Oxford University Press, 1990.

Jean Drèze and Amartya Sen, eds. — *The Political Economy of Hunger*. 3 vols. New York: Oxford University Press, 1991.

John Osgood Field, ed. — *The Challenge of Famine: Recent Experience, Lessons Learned*. West Hartford, CT: Kumarian Press, 1993.

David Heiden — *Dust to Dust: A Doctor's View of Famine in Africa*. Philadelphia: Temple University Press, 1992.

Bill Rau — *From Feast to Famine: Official Cures and Grassroots Remedies to Africa's Food Crisis*. London: Zed Books, 1991.

Robert Rodale — *Save Three Lives: A Plan for Famine Prevention*. San Francisco: Sierra Club Books, 1991.

Katie Smith and Tetsunao Yamamori, eds. — *Growing Our Future: Food Security and the Environment*. West Hartford, CT: Kumarian Press, 1992.

Carol B. Thompson — *Harvests Under Fire: Regional Cooperation for Food Security in Southern Africa*. London: Zed Books, 1991.

Nan Unklesbay — *World Food and You*. New York: Food Products Press, 1992.

Periodicals

Ronald Bailey — "Thwarting the Grim Reaper," *Forbes*, November 8, 1993.

Felicity Barringer — "Whether It's Hunger or 'Misnourishment,' It's a National Problem," *The New York Times*, December 27, 1992.

Bibliography

Sharon Begley	"The Population Debate," *Newsweek*, September 12, 1994.
Richard E. Bissell	"The Natural Resource Wars: Let Them Eat Trees," *The Washington Quarterly*, Winter 1994. Available from MIT Press Journals, 55 Hayward St., Cambridge, MA 02142.
Harold Brookfield and Christine Padoch	"Appreciating Agrodiversity: A Look at the Dynamism and Diversity of Indigenous Farming Practices," *Environment*, June 1994.
Lester R. Brown	"Earth Is Running Out of Room," *USA Today*, January 1995.
Stephen Budiansky	"10 Billion for Dinner, Please," *U.S. News & World Report*, September 12, 1994.
Kevin Clarke	"Who's Hungry Now?" *Salt*, March 1993. Available from 205 W. Monroe St., Chicago, IL 60606.
Priscilla Enriquez	"An Un-American Tragedy: Hunger and Economic Policy in the Reagan-Bush Era," *Food First Action Alert*, Summer 1992. Available from 398 60th St., Oakland, CA 94618.
Leonard Fein	"Mending the World: A Jewish Approach to Social Justice," *Commonweal*, January 14, 1994.
Forum for Applied Research and Public Policy	Fall 1991. Special section on plant genetics. Available from Executive Sciences Institute, 1005 Mississippi Ave., Davenport, IA 52803.
Forum for Applied Research and Public Policy	Winter 1993. Special section on hunger.
Jeffrey L. Fox	"Do Transgenic Crops Pose Ecological Risks?" *Bio/Technology*, February 1994. Available from Reprints Department, 65 Bleecker St., New York, NY 10012-2467.
Glamour	"Going to Bed Without Supper," October 1991.
George C. Graham	"Starvation in the Modern World," *The New England Journal of Medicine*, April 8, 1993. Available from Dr. Graham, PO Box 205, Gibson Island, MD 21056.
Garrett Hardin	"Limits to Growth Are Nature's Own," *Insight*, December 20, 1993. Available from 3600 New York Ave. NE, Washington, DC 20002.
Paul Harrison	"Sex and the Single Planet: Need, Greed, and Earthly Limits," *The Amicus Journal*, Winter 1994. Available from 40 W. 20th St., New York, NY 10011.
Hal Kane	"Growing Fish in Fields," *World Watch*, September/October 1993. Available from 1776 Massachusetts Ave. NW, Washington, DC 20036-1904.
Carolyn Lochhead	"Hunger Hype," *Insight*, June 27, 1988.
Michael Mortimore and Mary Tiffen	"Population Growth and a Sustainable Environment," *Environment*, October 1994.

Andrew S. Natsios	"Food Through Force: Humanitarian Intervention and U.S. Policy," *The Washington Quarterly*, Winter 1994.
The New Internationalist	"Raw Food: People, Plants, and Politics," November 1991.
The New Internationalist	"Sex, Lies, and Global Survival," September 1992.
David Norse	"A New Strategy for Feeding a Crowded Planet," *Environment*, June 1992.
David Osterfeld	"Overpopulation: The Perennial Myth," *The Freeman*, September 1993. Available from the Foundation for Economic Education, Irvington-on-Hudson, NY 10533.
Robert Rector	"Hunger and Malnutrition Among American Children," *The Heritage Foundation Backgrounder*, August 2, 1991. Available from the Heritage Foundation, 214 Massachusetts Ave. NE, Washington, DC 20002-4999.
Peter Rosset et al.	"Myths and Root Causes: Hunger, Population, and Development," *Backgrounder*, Fall 1994. Available form Food First, 398 60th St., Oakland, CA 94618.
Nevin S. Scrimshaw	"The Consequences of Hidden Hunger: The Effect on Individuals and Societies," *Vital Speeches of the Day*, December 15, 1991.
Jane E. Stevens	"Growing Rice the Old-Fashioned Way, with Computer Assist," *Technology Review*, January 1994.
Joachim von Braun	"A Policy Agenda for Famine Prevention in Africa," *Food Policy Report*, October 1991. Available from the International Food Policy Research Institute, 1776 Massachusetts Ave. NW, Washington, DC 20036.

Organizations to Contact

The editors have compiled the following list of organizations concerned with the issues debated in this book. The descriptions are derived from materials provided by the organizations. All have publications or information available for interested readers. The list was compiled on the date of publication of the present volume; names, addresses, and phone numbers may change. Be aware that many organizations take several weeks or longer to respond to inquiries, so allow as much time as possible.

Bread for the World (BFW)
1100 Wayne Ave., Suite 1000
Silver Spring, MD 20910
(301) 608-2400
fax: (301) 608-2401

BFW is a Christian organization devoted to eliminating hunger and poverty. It maintains the Bread for the World Institute on Hunger and Development, an institute that researches and attempts to influence government policies related to hunger. BFW publications include background papers, the monthly *Bread for the World Newsletter*, and an annual report, recent titles of which include *Transforming the Politics of Hunger: Hunger 1994* and *Causes of Hunger: Hunger 1995*.

Carrying Capacity Network (CCN)
1325 G St. NW, Suite 1003
Washington, DC 20005
(202) 879-3044

CCN is concerned about world population issues and disseminates information to other organizations working on issues related to the earth's carrying capacity. It publishes the *Immigration Briefing Book*; the bimonthly *Clearinghouse Bulletin*, which includes environmental legislation updates; and the quarterly *Focus*, which provides in-depth coverage of current environmental issues.

Food for the Hungry
7729 E. Greenway Rd.
PO Box E
Scottsdale, AZ 85260
(800) 248-6437
fax: (602) 998-4806

Food for the Hungry is a Christian organization that works to end world hunger through self-development assistance. It sponsors emergency disaster relief and rehabilitation, health education, and agricultural development programs. Its publications include the monthly newsletter *Feeding the Hungry*.

Food Research and Action Center (FRAC)
1875 Connecticut Ave. NW, Suite 540
Washington, DC 20009
(202) 986-2200
fax: (202) 986-2525

FRAC seeks to increase public awareness of the problems of hunger and poverty in the United States. The center provides legal assistance, conducts research, and offers strategies for local and statewide antihunger policies. FRAC publishes the bimonthly newsletter *Foodlines,* as well as analyses of food programs, annual poverty updates, informational pamphlets, and studies on hunger and poverty.

Freedom from Hunger
1644 DaVinci Court
Davis, CA 95617
(916) 758-6200
fax: (916) 758-6241

Freedom from Hunger works to eliminate chronic hunger by providing needy families and communities with resources and information. The organization emphasizes leadership development and self-help programs. Its publications include the quarterly *Newsbriefs* and *A Geography of American Poverty.*

The Heritage Foundation
214 Massachusetts Ave. NE
Washington, DC 20002
(202) 546-4400
fax: (202) 544-6979

The foundation is a conservative public policy research institute. It publishes position papers on a wide variety of topics through its publications the weekly *Backgrounder*, the quarterly *Policy Review*, and the periodic Heritage Lectures series. *Backgrounder* titles related to hunger include "How the Really Poor Live: Lessons for Welfare Reform," "Hunger and Malnutrition Among America's Children," and "Combatting Family Disintegration, Crime, and Dependence: Welfare Reform and Beyond."

Institute for Food and Development Policy (Food First)
398 60th St.
Oakland, CA 94618
(510) 654-4400
fax: (510) 654-4551

Food First is a nonprofit research and educational center that focuses on issues of hunger and democracy worldwide. The institute asserts that antidemocratic institutions promote hunger and environmental deterioration. Food First publishes development reports, the quarterly newsletter *Food First News and Views*, and the books *Food First: Beyond the Myth of Scarcity* and *Needless Hunger: Voices from a Bangladesh Village.*

International Food Policy Research Institute (IFPRI)
1200 17th St. NW
Washington, DC 20036
(202) 862-5600
fax: (202) 467-4439

The institute works to reduce hunger and malnutrition by researching alternative strategies and policies for food production and consumption in developing countries. IFPRI publishes policy papers, research reports, and the quarterly newsletter *IFPRI Report*.

Negative Population Growth (NPG)
210 The Plaza
PO Box 1206
Teaneck, NJ 07666-1206
(201) 837-3555
fax: (201) 837-0288

NPG advocates negative population growth for the United States and the world. It believes the world will face universal poverty and pollution unless population control programs are enforced. NPG publishes numerous policy and forum papers, including *Zero Net Migration, Why We Need a Smaller U.S. Population and How We Can Achieve It*, and *Sustainable Immigration*.

Results
236 Massachusetts Ave. NE, Suite 300
Washington, DC 20002
(202) 543-9340
fax: (202) 546-3228

Results advocates the notion that world hunger can be overcome by individual contributions of effort and money. The organization believes influencing legislation is the key to abolishing hunger and conducts its own citizens' lobby. Results publishes the quarterly newsletter *Entry Point* and the monthly action sheet *Idea Letter*.

World Hunger Year (WHY)
505 8th Ave., 21st Fl.
New York, NY 10018
(212) 629-8850
fax: (212) 465-9274

WHY is concerned with the issues of hunger and poverty. The organization seeks to inform the public of the causes of hunger and to develop programs and policies to combat hunger and poverty worldwide. WHY conducts research, compiles statistics, and offers educational programs. It publishes pamphlets and educational materials on hunger and poverty and the quarterly *WHY Magazine*.

Worldwatch Institute
1776 Massachusetts Ave. NW
Washington, DC 20036-1904
(202) 452-1999
fax: (202) 296-7365

Worldwatch Institute is an interdisciplinary research organization that works to inform policymakers and the public about global and environmental issues. It publishes the bimonthly *World Watch* magazine, periodic *Worldwatch Papers*, and the annual *State of the World* report.

Index